I0100064

ISBN 978-0-615-93485-3

Table of Contents

Preface

America's space program has a long history of achievement, honor, greatness and celebration. The ability to fly above the atmosphere less than sixty-years after we learned how to fly above the ground is incredible.

I have been following the space program since I was a kid. I remember when Project Mercury, the first manned space project was introduced to the public in 1958. I remember listening to the flight progress on the radio, uninterrupted coverage from launch to splashdown.

Flying in space is never routine. The mission of putting American astronauts on the moon and safely returning them to the Earth required launching the largest vehicle ever built into earth orbit, precisely guiding them towards the moon, docking the command and lunar modules, orbiting the moon, landing on the moon and reversing the process to fly back to earth. Each step required technology and skills that had only been developed in a relatively short amount of time.

That's not to say there has not been disappointment, setbacks and failures in NASA's attempt to conquer what President John F. Kennedy called the new frontier. There have been many. In the beginning there were more failures than successes just to put an American in space. Step-by-step NASA overcame the barriers of the great unknown and went on to make what seemed impossible look easy. Each success would feed the next, and "Go fever" would one day come back to bite NASA.

Unfortunately, the public and the media will always focus on the disasters and failures more than NASA's achievements. The tragedy of the Apollo 1 fire, the shuttles Challenger and Columbia accidents, and the near disaster of Apollo 13 will always be a reminder that we all are only human.

As the thrill of going to the moon waned in the public eye, NASA was mandated to do much more with less, which is always dangerous.

Risks had to be taken that at times called for the astronauts to put their faith in science and their lives on the line.

To me, the effort this country made to put a man on the moon in less than 10 years was one of the greatest engineering feats in the history of mankind. As former astronaut Jim Lovell said, "It's not a miracle, we just decided to go."

Losing human life in the pursuit of science and space exploration is never easy to accept. Although we have learned what not to do from these accidents, there is always a hidden stone left unturned or ignored that has come back to haunt us at some time.

The Columbia disaster inspired me to write this book. Watching the news media spin their interpretation and an inept investigation board put on a smoke and mirror show for the public has made my job easy to tell Columbia's version of this catastrophe. I know that many people are going to label me a conspiracy theorist, and that is fine. If I were a journalist, I would probably have to agree with them. I am an engineer at heart. I read the data. The story that the Space Shuttle Columbia told of the accident is quite different than that of the news media.

Many thanks go out to my wife Elizabeth, who had to endure countless hours hearing my reasoning and watching me research and compose this book. Others family and friends who helped, either directly or indirectly, are my cousin Larry, my brother in-law Ted, and my good friend Roland (a.k.a. Butch).

Let's Get This Straight

Who truly believes that the cause of the space shuttle Columbia disaster was caused by a huge hole in the leading edge of the left wing? Because of the television and published news media there are some pretty big numbers of people that believe that story. Unfortunately, with only the news media as a source of information to the general public those numbers are justified.

And what percentage of the news media truly believes that the cause of the space shuttle Columbia disaster was caused by a huge hole in the leading edge of the left wing? Wow, almost 100 percent! That is truly amazing, but not surprising; since most journalists who covered the Columbia accident probably do not know why the pointy end of an airplane goes forward.

Well, you are wrong. There was no hole in the leading edge of the left wing that brought down the Shuttle Columbia. How do I know this? The answer really is simple. Figuratively speaking, the Columbia told us exactly what was happening onboard the Orbiter during the last seven-and-a-half minutes of flight before breaking up over the skies of Texas.

The general public and most members of the news media do not understand the onboard data a space shuttle sends back to flight controllers in Houston. They may be able to read the information, but unless you have knowledge of how highly technical aircraft fly I am sure a very small percentage of people can understand what all that information really means. Most people watched the videos and look at pictures, and listen to whatever information they hear from the media. They will pick out the parts they understand, ignore what does not make sense and come to some kind of a conclusion they can understand. Whether their answer is right or wrong is not an issue to them. Most will reason that the news media will always tell them the truth.

Although I am not a graduate engineer, I am educated in mechanical and electronic engineering. I was a field service technical representative on high tech F-15 aircraft most of my adult life. As a federal employee for over thirty years, I also understand the government bureaucracy. While reading Columbia's flight data from the NASA website and using my experience from the F-15, I was able to figure out what really happened to Columbia. I am sure that most engineers at NASA and the aviation industry that have looked at the data and have run the numbers have figured out what really happened by now, too. Aside from the political reasons and job preservation within the government, I just do not understand why the truth of this accident has taken so long to be told.

Seven astronauts were killed when the space shuttle Columbia broke apart and burned up while reentering Earth's atmosphere on February 1, 2003. Crew members were left to right, front row: Rick Husband, Kalpana Chawla, William McCool; second row: David Brown, Laurel Clark, Michael Anderson, Ilan Ramon.

I am not one to voice my opinion unless I feel that it is absolutely necessary, and this is one of those moments. For anyone to contrive the investigation in a manner that is inconsistent with the data is an injustice to the astronauts who lost their lives, their families, friends and the

2

reputation of NASA. The fact is that we lost the space shuttle Columbia, and a crew of seven astronauts who were some of America's most valuable scientific assets. Even though most people do not appreciate the benefits we enjoy from America's space program, the caliber of these people and the invaluable sacrifices they made to realize their dreams of working in space.

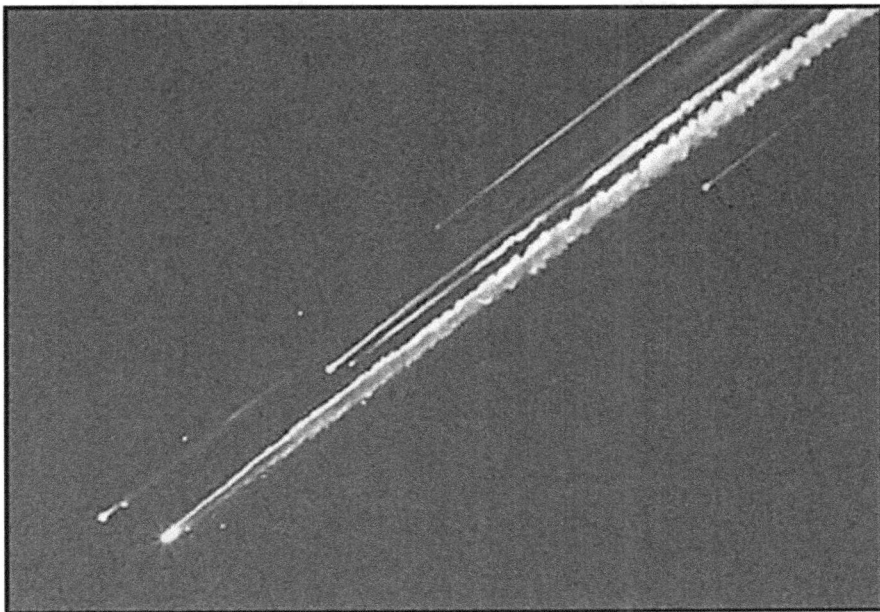

Watching the video of Columbia breaking up while falling through the Earth's atmosphere and watching seven people perish together was one of the most tragic scenes we have ever witnessed in our lifetime. The horror of this event was no less painful than watching as the space shuttle Challenger explodes during launch before our eyes that fateful day in January 1986.

On January 28, 1986, just 73 seconds after liftoff from the Kennedy Space Center in Florida, the space shuttle *Challenger* exploded. All seven passengers perished, including Christa McAuliffe, a civilian teacher chosen for the flight. Scientists believe a leak in one of the seals on a solid rocket booster caused the explosion. The tragedy had serious repercussions for the United States space program, precipitating a comprehensive review of the goals and procedures of the program.

During that tragedy, the decisions of NASA manager Lawrence Malloy outweighed the lives of the Challenger crew. Mr. Malloy chose to launch the shuttle Challenger over the vehement objections from the very people who designed and built the solid rocket boosters. Hours before the launch, managers at Morton-Thiokol stated their concerns that the O-ring seals between the rocket segments could fail from the extreme cold that morning. The investigation confirmed that the cold temperatures caused the O-ring material to contract, reducing the ability to contain the pressures of the hot gases inside the rocket motor. I believe that Lawrence Malloy should have been prosecuted for jeopardizing the safety of the crew and taking those lives, but that is another story.

What is just as aggravating about the Columbia investigation is watching the news media coerce the outcome of an accident investigation, by insisting that what appears to be the obvious truth was the sole cause of Columbia's demise. Cameras and microphones are very powerful tools, used by the news media to shape views and opinions of the general public. Unfortunately, the media will only tell you what they believe or want you to know.

The ultimate fallacy was seeing NASA acquiesce to the news media, and spending millions of dollars creating an illusion to validate the media. I find that to be absolutely absurd.

I have read the telemetry (information the shuttle transmits to ground controllers while in flight), the way an engineers and flight controllers would look at the information. When analyzing the data in a logical and chronological order, step-by-step, you can discern what happened to the shuttle in the last seven-and-a-half minutes of the flight to a much higher degree of accuracy.

As a tech rep on F-15 aircraft, my job was to investigate and correct problems that occurred during training and combat missions. I learned how to retrieve and interpret recorded flight data, to understand system events and unexpected problems during flight. The avionics system of the F-15 is similar to that of the shuttle fleet, in that the Central Computer (CC) and Flight Control Computer (FCC) monitors nearly every component of the avionics and flight control systems of the vehicle several times a second. The system was designed to monitor and control flight conditions, and detect any system anomalies. The information allows the aircrew and aircraft systems to manage the flight dynamics of the vehicle. Also, every time there is an event or a system changes state the CC records the time-of-flight and the aircraft dynamic flight characteristics into memory, for technical or engineering analysis after flight.

High tech aircraft share another common similarity with the shuttle in that computers are necessary to fly the vehicle. Because of extremely high external forces on the aircraft during flight, computers are used to manage the flight controls systems by combining pilot control inputs, sensor information, hydraulic actuators and mechanical assemblies. The space shuttle, the most sophisticated and highly technical vehicle ever built, has a quadruple redundant avionics system. What that means is that there are multiple computer systems, working simultaneously and in synchronization to control the vehicle, and constantly monitoring the other computer systems. If one system fails, there are multiple backup systems to take over the control of the vehicle. Visual and audible alarms will occur if this should happen, but the vehicle will **always** be in control.

The aircraft and Central Computer are highly technical electronic machines that have no reason to lie, pretend, cover-up or deceive the information recorded during flight. The computer will tell you exactly what happened, at what time, to which aircraft (spacecraft) system and the flight dynamics of the vehicle at that exact moment in time, in chronological order. This is a commonly used post-flight procedure in aviation for troubleshooting avionics, flight control and propulsion systems. All you have to do is look at the data.

The space shuttle flies in an environment that is beyond the realm of conventional aircraft, from sea level to beyond the atmosphere in space. The shuttle is the only vehicle that can withstand the temperature extremes of near absolute zero temperature of space to the searing heat of nearly 4000 degrees Fahrenheit during re-entry. Therefore, the shuttles have additional monitoring systems within the vehicle. There is a network of temperature and pressure sensors throughout the spacecraft to measure the structural integrity and monitor the flight control systems. The sensors are electrically connected to the computers with wire harnesses, much like the human nerve system to the brain. The harnesses are routed through the airframe at very strategic locations so as not to interfere with the flight dynamic system assemblies of the vehicle. One of the least susceptible locations to route aircraft wiring is in and around the main landing gear wheel wells. A wheel well is basically a box within the airframe to stow the landing gear assemblies during flight. Normally, the only time during flight the wiring in a wheel well is exposed to the environment outside the airframe is just prior to landing. The doors are opened during final approach, allowing the wheels to extend to the down-and-locked position.

With all the basic information in place, let's take a closer look at mission STS-107 from the beginning. We will analyze the launch, what happened while Columbia was in orbit, and take you through the re-entry phases of the flight.

The Launch

While sitting on the launch pad prior to liftoff, a layer of ice will form on the outer surface of the external tank. Liquid oxygen and other propellants are stored in two huge tanks inside the outer skin of the orange external tank. During the launch, the propellants are combined in the combustion chambers of the Orbiter engines. The visual flame is actually a controlled chemical reaction, or explosion, that creates the thrust to lift the vehicle off the launch pad. Because of the extreme cold temperatures necessary to keep these gases liquefied, any humidity in the immediate area of the launch will condense and freeze on the surface of the external tank. Since the Kennedy Space Center at Cape Canaveral is located next to the Atlantic Ocean, there is always an abundance of humidity in the air; and because of the extremely cold temperatures inside the external fuel tank ice will form on the surface. That is just basic science.

What makes this environment significant to the investigation is that dry foam alone has a very low density. In contrast, ice has a very high density. The structure of ice is nothing more than crystallized water. Ice will shatter into tiny particles along the lines separating the crystals when subject to vibration or colliding with a solid object, similar in the way that dry foam will fragment into tiny particles on impact. The object that appeared to strike the Orbiter could have been a chunk of ice, or could have been frozen foam. If that is true, the density of frozen foam will be somewhere between that of dry foam and solid ice. To accurately calculate the density of frozen foam at that moment is nearly impossible without specifically knowing the amount of ice embedded in the foam.

We do know that approximately eighty-two seconds after the launch of STS-107, the Orbiter was beginning to fly through the highest flight dynamic pressure of the launch while soaring through the atmosphere. An object appeared to tear away from either the external fuel tank, or possibly the nose of the Orbiter. No one can say with a high degree of certainty what the object was or where the object came from. Through analysis of the high-speed film used during launch, the most commonly accept belief is that a piece of insulating foam appeared to depart the outer skin of the external tank and struck the Orbiter somewhere near the left wing. However, several engineers within the NASA agency questioned if the object could have been a piece of foam, ice, or a frozen piece of foam.

There are many variables involved in determining what happened when the object struck the Orbiter. Most people (especially the news media) only visualize in two dimensions, much like the page you are reading. You can easily understand the length of the page and the width of the page you are reading, two dimensions. You can sense the same two dimensions looking at a street map. For example, the direction of North and South are the length, while East and West are the width. Now, let's say you are standing on the street with your map; you now introduce a third dimension, your height.

When you look at a point on the ground some distance away from you, your line of sight forms an angle relative to the ground. The farther away from you the point is, the smaller the angle your line of sight is to the ground. I make this point to illustrate that the relative angle that the object struck the surface of the shuttle is relevant to determining how much damage was caused to the Orbiter. Simply, the more shallow the angle of impact, the less damage was done to the Orbiter.

Now, we will add a fourth dimension to the analysis of the object, which is speed. The element of relative speed is as important as any other variable in the investigation. The speed, the angle and density of that object approaching the outer skin of the shuttle will determine the amount of energy released when the object collided with the shuttle, which will determine how much damage was caused during impact.

High Speed cameras captured the impact of an object glancing off the left wing. Although inconclusive, much of the debris appears to be on the underside of the wing, indicating a low angle of impact to the wing. Some of the debris may have struck the leading edge head-on. No one can say with 100% certainty.

During the flight in orbit

While Columbia was in orbit, there was a lot of activity throughout the NASA community. Administrators called upon NASA and corporate engineers to determine the amount of damage Columbia may have incurred during launch. A lot of time and effort was expended to make an assessment. But, without knowing precisely what struck the Orbiter, the density of the object, the angle of impact or the relative velocity of the object compared to the Orbiter, their conclusions were merely educated guesses.

Many NASA engineers at several research centers throughout the country analyzed the video footage of the launch. Many computer models were run clear up to the day before re-entry to determine if the Orbiter's could survive re-entry into the Earth's atmosphere. Some of the scenarios considered ranged from complete violation of the Thermal Protective System (TPS) tiles, to varying degrees of gouging into the tiles. Some gouging is considered as normal pockmarks of damage as seen on previous flights.

As you will see in the email correspondence, many engineers were less concerned about damage to the leading edge of the wing as they were of the protective tiles covering the left main landing gear wheel well. Many engineers studied the possibility that tiles under the Orbiter could have been damaged or lost from ice dislodging from the external tank vent pipe. All shuttles had shown this kind of damage on previous flights. Aside from aerodynamic drag, many engineers had questioned why the vent pipe had not been moved to the opposite side of the tank away from the Orbiter some time ago.

These engineers were concerned about launch debris striking and damaging the thermal protective tiles, particularly the left main landing gear door. They questioned if the intense heat of re-entry would blow one or both tires on the left main landing gear. They wondered if the shuttle could land with a broken foot, so to speak. They questioned if the crew should try to land on blown tires, or should they attempt to

11

land with the gear up, something that had never been actually done or even tried in a simulator. They did not know what to expect. However, the thought of the Orbiter not reaching the Kennedy Space Center was never a consideration to anyone within NASA community, everyone from administrators to Mission Control.

What does all this mean? To know what happened with any degree of accuracy, you have to know the size, density, velocity and the angle the object struck the orbiter to be able to precisely understand the amount of damage that could have been caused by the impact. The best approach NASA engineers could devise was to look at both ends of the spectrum and come up with the best and worst case scenarios of re-entry for the amount of damage to the Orbiter.

While in orbit, the following briefings and correspondences were taking place between NASA engineers and administrators to decide what the dangers were to the shuttle during re-entry. The first briefing presented to NASA administrators took place on January 21, 2003, five days after launch. The second briefing was presented on January 23, 2003, seven days after launch. All briefing slides from NASA are unedited…

Preliminary Debris Transport Assessment of Debris Impacting Orbiter Lower Surface in STS-107 Mission

January 21, 2003

Carlos Ortiz (281) 226-5775
Arturo Green (281) 226-5540
Jack McClymonds (714) 372-6753
Jeff Stone (714) 934-1773
Abdi Khodadoust (714) 235-7746

BOEING

Subcontract 1970483303

W.B.S. 1.2.2.1 / 20037

PDRD SC004

STS-107 Debris Impacting Orbiter Wing

13

Debris Impacts Orbiter Lower Surface

- **Issue** – At about 82 seconds into the flight, a large piece of debris was seen emanating from the ET bipod area and later seen impacting the Orbiter lower surface tiles

- **Background**
  - Preliminary assessment of debris impact conditions predicted an impact to the Orbiter lower surface at location XO1049, YO185 (results provided on January 17, 2003)
    - Impact Velocity estimated to be 750 ft/sec.
    - Impact Angle estimated to be less than 20 degrees
  - Refinement of the results show reduction of impact angle and impact velocity
  - Analysis methodology and results were presented to the Aero Panel on January 21, 2003
    - Aero Panel concurrence was obtained
    - Aero Panel recommended sending results to Orbiter Program for damage assessment

BOEING

14

Debris Impact Conditions to Be Evaluated for Area on Orbiter Lower Surface

- **Actions Taken**
  - Defined impacts area based on film observations and debris trajectory modeling
    - Large uncertainty in trajectory computation does not allow a good prediction of the impact area
  - Performed debris trajectory computations to define impact conditions inside impact area.
    - Debris particle emanates from bipod ramp area (XO 389, YO 50)
    - Two debris sizes analyzed:
      - 20" x 10" x 6" (representing flange foam)
      - 20" x 16" x 6" (representing bipod ramp)
    - Debris material considered to be foam (density = 2.4 lb/ft3)
    - Particle subjected to initial lateral motion to simulate lateral loading of bipod ramp
  - Impact conditions inside predicted impact area was derived as follows:
    - Actual Impacts: Particle impact information as computed by the debris trajectory program
    - Near Impacts: Particle velocity obtained for specific points in particle trajectory
    - Debris Database: to define particle impact angles at locations in the landing gear wheel well

BOEING

15

Results Show Low Impact Angles on the Orbiter Lower Surface

- **Results -**
  - Completed evaluating results for trajectory analysis of foam debris of size = 20"x10"x6"
    - Impact velocity inside predicted impact area range between 650 and 730 ft/sec.
      - Impact velocity at wing RCC may vary between 700 and 720 ft/sec.
      - Impact velocity at Landing wheel well varies between 650 and 730 ft/sec.
    - Impact angles can be expected to be larger near wing leading edges because of wing curvature
      - RCC impacts can be as high as 22 degrees in some regions
    - Impact angles at the landing wheel well are expected to be less than 10 degrees
  - Results for trajectory analysis of foam debris of size = 20"x16"x6" are currently under evaluation

BOEING

16

Predicted Impact Area Derived from Film Observations and Trajectory Analysis

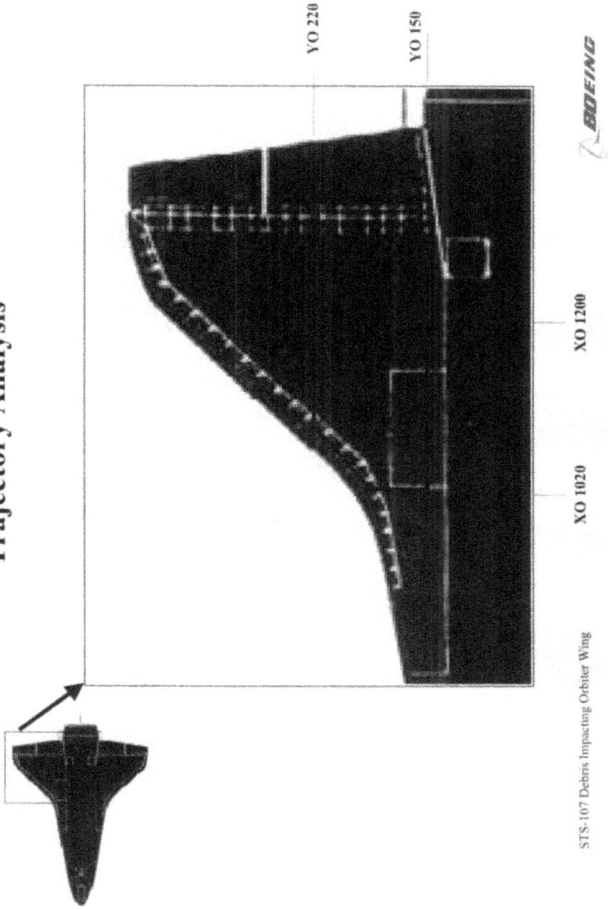

YO 220

YO 150

XO 1200

XO 1020

STS-107 Debris Impacting Orbiter Wing

BOEING

Velocity and Impact Angle Distribution Inside Impact Area
(Debris Size = 20" x 10" x 6", Density = 2.4 lb/ft3)

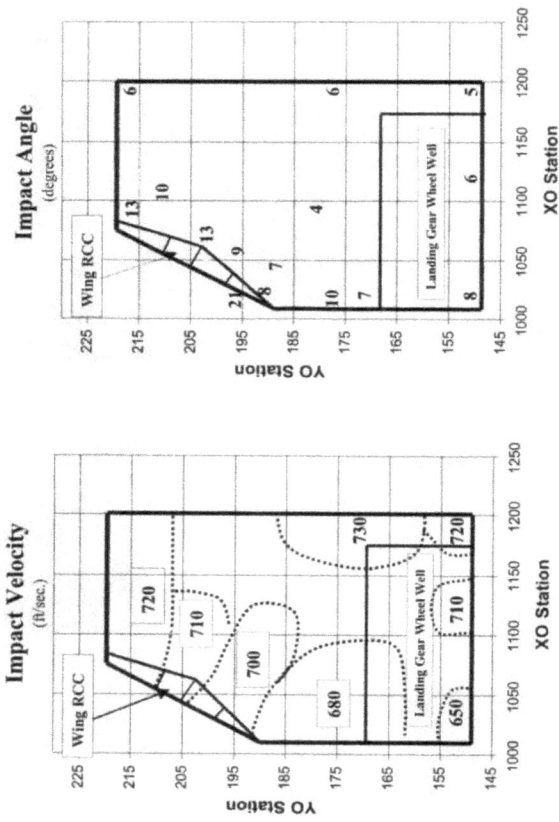

Impact Angle (degrees)

Impact Velocity (ft/sec.)

STS-107 Debris Impacting Orbiter Wing

18

More Results Underway

- **Conclusions -**
  - Impact conditions were presented for a debris of size = 20"x10"x6"
    - Impact velocity inside predicted impact area range between 650 and 730 ft/sec.
    - Impact angles can be expected to be larger near wing leading edges because of wing curvature
    - Impact angles at the landing wheel well are expected to be less than 10 degrees
  - Results for trajectory analysis of foam debris of size = 20"x16"x6" are currently under evaluation
    - Preliminary assessment of the data shows impact velocity range between 558 and 700 ft/sec.
    - Impact angles generally low (in same order as those presented for particle size = 20"x10"x6")
    - Expected completion of task is 1/22/03.

BOEING

Back-Up

STS-107 Debris Impacting Orbiter Wing

BOEING

Results of Impact Analysis for particle size = 20" x 10" x 6"

XT	YT	ZT	VMAX (ft/sec.)	VX (ft/sec.)	VY (ft/sec.)	VZ (ft/sec.)	IMPANG (degrees)
1755	193	625	660	682	104	20	9.0
1759	194	630	696	680	107	25	9.4
1744	190	637	693	680	107	36	8.7
1755	191	641	698	688	107	41	7.8
1800	197	648	702	693	105	46	8.8
1747	190	628	696	677	104	21	7.0
1759	192	629	682	674	105	23	7.1
1751	188	637	695	676	106	36	10.4
1754	198	641	690	681	104	40	7.8
1754	187	644	694	684	103	44	6.6
1755	197	627	693	684	104	23	11.8
1748	195	630	691	682	107	27	13.3
1756	194	638	699	689	109	37	8.9
1805	203	646	712	703	109	42	11.3
1788	199	647	711	751	109	46	10.4
1782	200	627	700	691	109	24	21.5
1803	211	633	707	698	110	28	9.6
1802	204	641	713	703	110	36	12.8
1790	202	644	711	702	110	42	11.3
1781	200	647	712	702	108	46	11.1
1744	186	625	683	675	102	18	6.5
1718	181	637	675	665	101	22	6.0
1742	184	636	653	646	86	30	2.8
1652	199	638	635	627	86	32	10.4
1583	199	634	611	603	82	34	2.0
1786	198	621	705	697	104	16	7.5
1796	201	624	702	694	105	18	7.7
1798	194	617	681	682	104	20	9.1
1830	210	620	723	715	106	12	5.4
1799	205	620	710	702	106	15	7.9
1790	202	623	707	699	106	17	8.1
1762	198	628	694	686	107	21	11.8
1788	196	620	705	697	102	14	7.0
1798	198	623	696	691	103	17	7.2
1750	191	615	687	676	103	19	6.6
2023	238	615	767	758	103	7	1.1
1830	210	617	723	715	106	12	5.4

STS-107 Debris Impacting Orbiter Wing

NASA was making an attempt to answer why foam had separated from the vehicle and collide with the Orbitor. The briefing on January 21, had a lot of preliminary information. More data was analyzed and NASA gave another briefing on January 23…

Orbiter Assessment of STS-107 ET Bipod Insulation Ramp Impact

P. Parker

D. Chao

I. Norman

M. Dunham

January 23, 2003

BOEING

Order of Analysis

- Orbiter assessment of ascent debris damage includes
  - Evaluation of potential for debris to damage tile and RCC
    - Program "Crater" is official evaluation tool
      - Available test data for SOFI on tile was reviewed
      - No SOFI on RCC test data available
    - Even for worst case, SIP and densified tile layer will remain when SOFI is impactor
  - Thermal analysis of areas with damaged tiles
    - Thermal analysis will predict potential tile erosion and temperatures on structure
  - Structural assessment based on thermal environment defined above
    - Basis is previous Micrometeriod and Orbital Debris (M/OD) study performed in 1996

24

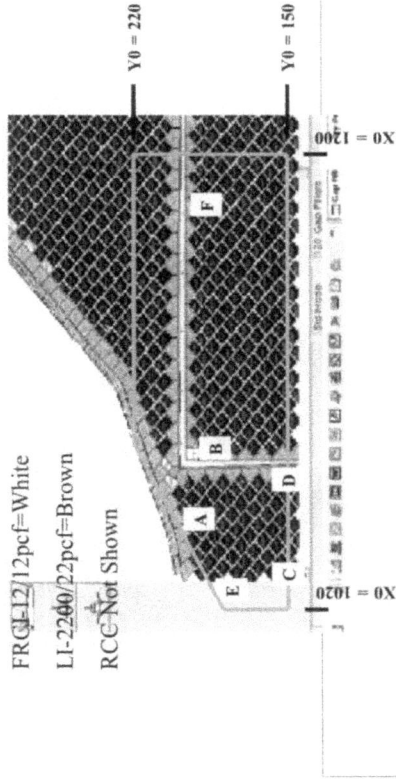

System Integration Inputs Were Matched Against Orbiter Tile/RCC to Determine Critical Locations

LI-900/9pcf=Black

FRCI-12/12pcf=White

LI-2200/22pcf=Brown

RCC=Not Shown

Y0 = 220

Y0 = 150

X0 = 1200

X0 = 1020

BOEING   2/21/03   3

25

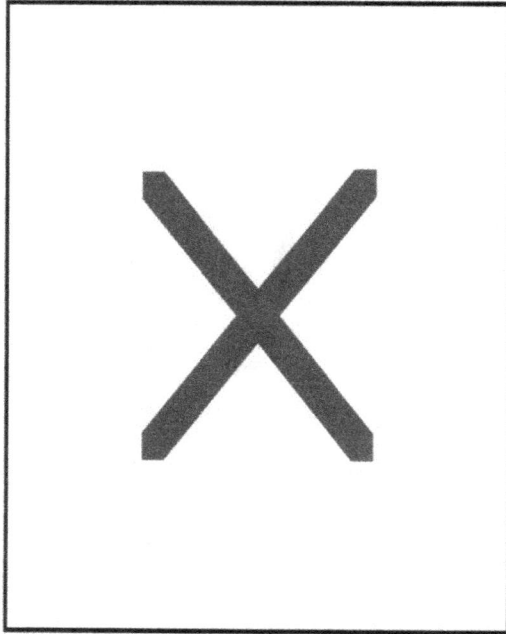

Damage Results From "Crater" Equations Show Significant Tile Damage

- "Crater" indicates that multiple tiles would be taken down to densified layer
  - However, program was designed to be conservative due to large number of unknowns
  - Crater reports damage for test conditions that show no damage

Tile Information		Letter	Location		Impactor		Calculated Damage		
Type	Thickness		X	Y	Angle	Velocity	Depth	Length	Width
9 lb	2.6 - 2.8	A	1060	190	13	720	4.7	25.8	7.2
22 lb	2.6 - 2.8	A	1060	190	13	720	3.2	25.8	7.2
9 lb	2.3 - 2.4	B	1090	180	6	700	2.8	31.9	7.2
9 lb	2.0 - 2.4	C	1036	150	8	680	3.3	29.8	7.2
22 lb	2.0 - 2.4	C	1036	150	8	680	2.3	28.6	7.2
9 lb	1.9 - 2.0	D	1075	150	8	710	3.4	32.2	7.2
12 lb	2.8 - 3.1	E	1029	177	10	680	2.9	19.0	2.4
22 lb	2.8 - 3.1	E	1029	177	10	680	2.6	19.0	2.4
9 lb	1.7	F	1184	182	6	730	2.8	32.8	2.4

Damage data and tile thickness are given in inches.

Debris Size = 20" x 16" x 6"

(Density = 2.4 lb/ft³)

27

Review of Test Data Indicates Conservatism for Tile Penetration

● **The existing SOFI on tile test data used to create Crater was reviewed along with STS-87 Southwest Research data**

  – Crater overpredicted penetration of tile coating significantly

    ◆ **Initial penetration to described by normal velocity**

      • Varies with volume/mass of projectile (e.g., 200ft/sec for 3cu. In)

    ◆ **Significant energy is required for the softer SOFI particle to penetrate the relatively hard tile coating**

      • Test results do show that it is possible at sufficient mass and velocity

    ◆ **Conversely, once tile is penetrated SOFI can cause significant damage**

      • Minor variations in total energy (above penetration level) can cause significant tile damage

  – **Flight condition is significantly outside of test database**

    ◆ **Volume of ramp is 1920cu in vs 3 cu in for test**

(Potentially) Similar STS-50 Impact Demonstrates that Damage is Possible

- Damage to aft lower tile (0.5"d x 9"L x 4" W) on wing was found after STS-50 landing; wheel well camera also observed missing ET bipod ramp insulation similar in size
- Small variation in energy input could substantially increase damage
- Incidence angle for STS-107 is predicted higher than STS-50

Volume = 1920in3

L (in)	d (in)	V (ft/sec)	Angle	Vadj (in/sec)	Fit Damage 0.50	damage (depth)	Normal Energy	
20	6	700	3.2	69		0.53	100%	STS-50 (estimated conditions)
20	6	770	3.2	116		0.75	121%	STS-50 plus 10% velocity
20	6	700	5.2	361		1.60	264%	STS-50 plus 2 deg incidence angle
20	6	600	3.2	2		0.05	73%	STS-50 "threshold"
20	6	720	10	1100		3.37	1024%	STS-107
20	6	788	10	1243		3.66	1228%	STS-107 + 10% energy
20	6	914	10	1505		4.16	1650%	STS-107 + 50% energy
20	6	720	10	700		2.49	551%	STS-107 with V = 800

Strength (tile) 53

V*	C	density (SOFI)	density (tile)		
400	0.0195	0.0014	0.0052		219912

Volume	V* (in/sec)	Ratio	power	V* (ft/sec)	
0.11	6500	1.0	3.5	542	test
0.33	4500	0.8		375	test
1.00	3200	0.8		267	test
3.00	2500	1.0		208	test
1920	400	1.0		33	flight

Volume vs V* (velocity to penetrate tile coating)

BOEING

2/21/03

7

RCC Predicted Damage at Incidence Angles Greater than 15 Degrees Based on Ice Database

Impactor		Damage
Angle	Velocity (fps)	Depth (in.)
5	720	0.11
10	720	0.18
15	720	0.23
20	720	0.28
25	720	0.33

Debris Size = 20" x 10" x 6"   45° angle of wing was taken into account

Density = 2.4 lb/ft³   Nominal panel thickness is 0.233 in.

RCC is clearly capable of withstanding impacts of at least 15 degrees; relative softness of SOFI (compared to ice) would indicate greater capability

- Maximum reported angle of 21 degrees is not an problem

•Looking at using Window ice and RTV data as an analog

Thermal Analysis Assessment of Debris Impacted Lower Surface in STS-107 Mission Locations

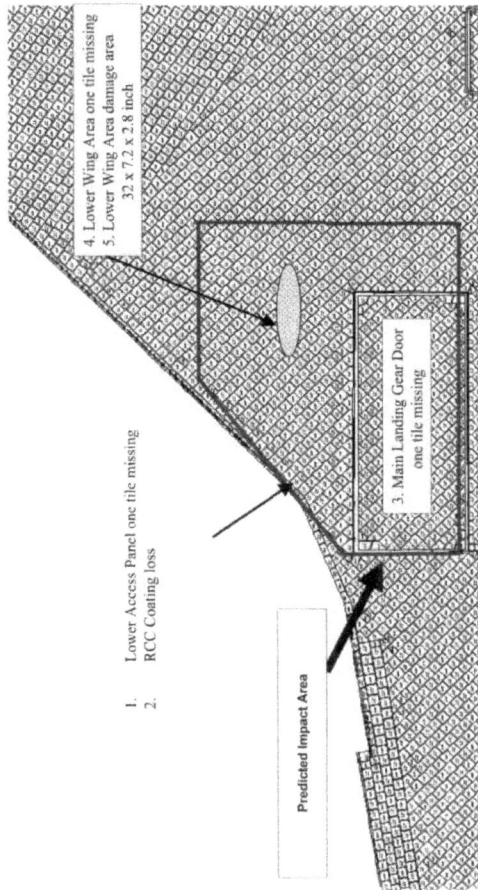

4. Lower Wing Area one tile missing
5. Lower Wing Area damage area
   32 x 7.2 x 2.8 inch

1. Lower Access Panel one tile missing
2. RCC Coating loss

3. Main Landing Gear Door one tile missing

Predicted Impact Area

BOEING

2/21/03

9

Impacted Lower Surface Location Thermal Predictions

Case	Location	Assumptions	Results
1	Access Panel (one tile missing)	Loss to last layer of TMM Densified layer ~.2 inches	Temperature of Al Tube Carrier 790 °F No issue
2	RCC Panel 9 Lower Flange OML (Coating Missing)	Coating loss and Carbon substrate exposed	Substrate thickness: 0.193 inches Loss .09 inches No issue
3	Main Landing Gear Door (one tile missing)	Loss to last 2 layers of TMM Densified layer ~.4 inches	Temperature of Structure 540 °F No issue
4	Lower Wing Area (one tile missing)	Loss to last 2 layers of TMM Densified layer ~.4 inches	Temperature below 350 °F design req. No issue
5	Lower Wing Area (32 x 7.2 x 2.8 inch) Damage	Loss to last layers of TMM Densified layer ~.2 inches	
6	Main Landing Gear Door (several tiles Lost)	Loss to last layers of TMM Densified layer ~.2 inches	

BOEING

10

32

Structural Assessment Provides for Intact Contingency Landing with Damaged Tiles

- Criteria for M/OD study were to assess on-orbit risk that cannot be controlled
- Study allowed for significant degradation beyond design criteria
  - Structural temperatures well beyond 350F design (due to loss of tile)
    - Repair of structure required
  - Small holes in structure, allowing internal plasma flow, were permissible if not in critical area
    - Not expected for STS-107
  - Factor of Safety not maintained for design conditions
  - Critical subsystems were included in evaluation
    - Wing has few subsytems except in landing gear box and elevon cove
      - Wing spars are considered critical structures
- Conditions identified to ensure intact contingency landing

BOEING   2/21/03   12

34

Summary and Conclusion

- Impact analysis ("Crater") indicates potential for large TPS damage
  - Review of test data shows wide variation in impact response
  - RCC damage limited to coating based on soft SOFI
- Thermal analysis of wing with missing tile is in work
  - Single tile missing shows local structural damage is possible, but no burn through
  - Multiple tile missing analysis is on-going
- M/OD criteria used to assess structural impacts of tile loss
  - Allows significant temperature exceedance, even some burn through
    - Impact to vehicle turnaround possible, but maintains safe return capability

Conclusion

- Contingent on multiple tile loss thermal analysis showing no violation of M/OD criteria, safe return indicated even with significant tile damage

2/21/03

13

Did anyone besides me notice that of the thirteen slides in that presentation that only the first slide was dated 1/23/03? Slides 2 through 13 are dated 2/21/03. Things that make you go, hmmm…

The conclusion of these studies was based upon known imagery, analyzing data from previous shuttle flights and applying basic engineering techniques. The decision was that there was no violation of the shuttle Thermal Protection System. Obviously, not all the stones were turned.

From the following email message traffic we can see that some engineers had other concerns about the possible damage to the Orbiter. Their concerns were either ignored or overruled by NASA administrators…

X-Sender: r.h.daugherty@pop.larc.nasa.gov
Date: Tue, 28 Jan 2003 14:15:27 -0500
To: "SHUART, MARK J" M.J.SHUART@larc.nasa.gov
From: "Robert H. Daugherty" r.h.daugherty@larc.nasa.gov
Subject: Foam and Tile
Cc: H.M.ADELMAN@larc.nasa.gov

Mark. . .attached are two files that I've received regarding the concern about ET foam
around the orbiter bipod support coming off and possibly damaging tiles . . . perhaps
around the main gear doors. So far, our involvement has been one of providing the
current model of drag associated with landing with two tires flat prior to touchdown
and some thought exercises of what might happen if the wheel well were burned
into....something that is arguably very unlikely. Interestingly, in the powerpoint pitch,
they talk about a test in which a "crater" caused by an impact test dug out 3 cubic
inches of tile. They say their estimated "flight condition" is 1920 cubic inches of
"crater". Hopefully, I'm reading that wrong, but as they say...that is way outside their
test database. No official request has been made upon us at this time. And there is no
formal simulation going on as far as I know regarding landing with two tires flat prior
to touchdown...its just a coincidence that landing with ONE tire flat is being simulated
right now at the Ames VMS in astronaut training where they are using our newest
load-persistence model so it is a very convenient time to look at two tires flat if they
can squeeze it in. Will keep you informed as I hear more...if I do.
Bob

To: r.m.martin-larc.nasa.gov, d.l.dwoyer

From: "Mark J. Shuart" m.j.shuart@pop.larc.nasa.gov

Subject: Fwd: Foam and Tile

Cc:

Bcc:

X-Attachments:

Ruth, Doug,

I am sending this to both of you since Doug is off-site and I thought the OD ought to know. Also, I am advised that the fact that this incident occurred is not being widely discussed. I'll keep you informed if we get more calls. . . . . .Mark

Date: Tue, 28 Jan 2003 14:15:27 -0500

To: "SHUART, MARK J" M.J.SHUART@larc.nasa.gov

From: "Robert H. Daugherty" r.h.daugherty@larc.nasa.gov

Subject: Foam and Tile

Cc: H.M.ADELMAN@larc.nasa.gov

Mark. . .attached are two files that I've received regarding the concern about ET foam around the orbiter bipod support coming off and possibly damaging tiles . . . perhaps around the main gear doors. So far, our involvement has been one of providing the current model of drag associated with landing with two tires flat prior to touchdown and some thought exercises of what might happen if the wheel well were burned into….something that is arguably very unlikely. Interestingly, in the powerpoint pitch, they talk about a test in which a "crater" caused by an impact test dug out 3 cubic inches of tile. They say their estimated "flight condition" is 1920 cubic inches of "crater". Hopefully, I'm reading that wrong, but as they say...that is way outside their test database. No official request has been made upon us at this time. And there is no formal simulation going on as far as I know regarding landing with two tires flat prior to touchdown…its just a coincidence that landing with ONE tire flat is being simulated right now at the Ames VMS in astronaut training where they are using our newest load-persistence model so it is a very convenient time to look at two tires flat if they can squeeze it in. Will keep you informed as I hear more...if I do.

Bob

To: d.l.dwoyer, r.m.martin
From: "Mark J. Shuart" m.j.shuart@pop.larc.nasa.gov>
Subject: Fwd: Tile Damage Update
   Cc:
   Bcc:
X-Attachments:

Doug, Ruth,

The latest info on the Shuttle is below. It will be interesting to see the extent of the damage after landing on Saturday. . . . . .Mark

Date: Wed, 29 Jan 2003 15:51:28 -0500
To: "SHUART, MARK J" M.J.SHUART@larc.nasa.gov
From: "Robert H. Daugherty" r.h.daugherty@larc.nasa.gov
Subject: Tile Damage Update
Cc: H.M.ADELMAN@larc.nasa.gov

Hi Mark,
Nothing terribly new but a few things talked about today with some folks at the Ames VMS. Apparently the current "official" estimate of damage is 7 inches by 30 inches by half the depth of the tiles down to the densified level. One of the bigger concerns is that the "gouge" may cross the main gear door thermal barrier and permit a breach there. No way to know of course. A JSC colleague and I talked to the sim guys and re urging them to simulate a landing with two tires flat prior to touchdown ... it is as simple as hitting the software button and simply doing it ... but since no Orbiter Program Management is "directing" the sim community to do this it might need to get done "at night". An anecdote they told us is that this was already done by mistake this week and the commander lost control of the vehicle during our load-persistence simulations. It seems that if Mission Operations were to see both tire pressure indicators go to zero during entry, they would sure as hell want to know whether they should land gear up, try to deploy the gear, or go bailout ... we can't imagine why getting information is being treated like the plague. Apparently the thermal folks have used words like they think things are "survivable", but "marginal".
I imagine this is the last we will hear of this.
Take care.
Bob

To: d.l.dwoyer
From: "Mark J. Shuart" <m.j.shuart@pop.larc.nasa.gov>
Subject: Fwd: Main Gear Breech Concerns
Cc:
Bcc:
X-Attachments:

Doug,

Here's the latest from JSC on the damage to the orbiter tiles. Looks like they believe all has been addressed. . . . . .Mark

From: "LECHNER DAVID F. (JSC-DF52) (USA)" <david.f.lechner1@jsc.nasa.gov>
To: "'Robert H. Daugherty'" <r.h.daugherty@larc.nasa.gov>
Cc: M.J.SHUART@larc.nasa.gov, H.M.ADELMAN@larc.nasa.gov,
    "CAMPBELL, CARLISLE C., JR (JSC-ES2) (NASA)"
    <carlisle.c.campbell@nasa.gov>
Subject: RE: Main Gear Breech Concerns
Date: Fri, 31 Jan 2003 12:17:34 -0600

Bob,

I really appreciate the candid remarks. As always your points have generated extremely valuable discussion in our group. Thank you. We have been discussing and continue to discuss the all possible scenarios, signatures and decisions. Your input is beneficial. Like everyone, we hope that the debris impact analysis is correct and all this discussion is mute.

David F-M Lechner
Space Shuttle Mechanical Systems
Mechanical, Maintenance, Arm & Crew Systems (MMACS)
United States Alliance, Johnson Space Center
(381) 483-1685

From: Robert H. Daugherty [mailto:r.h.daugherty@larc.nasa.gov]
Sent: Thursday, January 30,2003 5:23 PM
To: LECHNER, DAVID F. (JSC-DF52) (USA)
Cc: M.J.SHUART@larc.nasa.gov; H.M.ADELMAN@larc.nasa.gov; CAMBELL,
CARLISLE C., JR (JSC-ES2) (USA)
Subject: Main Gear Breech Concerns

Hi David,

I talked to Carlisle a bit ago and he let me know you guys at MOD were getting into
the loop on the tile damage issue. I'm writing this email not really in an official
capacity but since we've worked together so many times I feel I can say pretty much
anything to you. And before I begin I would like to offer that I am admittedly erring
way on the side of absolute worst-case scenarios and I don't really believe things are
as bad as I'm getting ready to make them out. But I certainly believe that to not be
ready for a gut-wrenching decision after seeing instrumentation in the wheel well not
be there after entry is irresponsible. One of my personal theories is that you should
seriously consider the possibility of the gear not deploying at all if there is a substantial
breach of the wheel well. The reason might be that as the temps increase, the wheel
(aluminum) will lose material properties as it heats up and the tire pressure will
increase. At some point the wheel could fail and send debris everywhere. While it is
true there are thermal fuses in the wheel, if the rate of heating is high enough, since the
tire is such a good insulator, the wheel may degrade in strength enough to let go far
below the 1100 psi or so that the tire normally bursts at. It seems to me that with that
much carnage in the wheel well, something could get screwed up enough to prevent
deployment and then you are in a world of hurt. The following are scenarios that might
be possible...and since there are so many of them, these are offered just to make sure
that some things don't slip thru the cracks...I suspect many or all these have been gone
over by you guys already:

1. People talk about landing with two tires...I did too until this came up. If both tires
blew in the wheel well (not talking thermal fuse and venting but explosive decomp due
to tire and/or wheel failure) the overpressure in the wheel well will be in the 40 + psi
range. The resulting loads on the gear door (a quarter million lbs) would almost
certainly blow the door off the hinges or at least send it out into the slip
stream...catastrophic. Even if you could survive the heating, would the gear now
deploy? And/or also, could you even reach the runway with this kind of drag?

2. The explosive bungies...what might be the possibility of these firing due to
excessive heating? If they fired, would they send the gear door and/or gear into the slip
stream?

3. What might excessive heating do to all kinds of other hardware in the wheel well…the hydraulic fluid, uplocks, etc? Are there vulnerable hardware items that might prevent deployment?

4. If the gear didn't deploy (and you would have to consider this before making the commitment to gear deploy on final) what would happen control-wise if the other gear is down and one is up? (I think Howard Law and his community will tell you you're finished)

5. Do you belly land? Without any other planning you will have already committed to KSC. And what will happen during derotation in a gear up landing (trying to stay away from asymmetric gear situation for example) since you will be hitting the aft end body flap and wings and pitching down extremely fast a la the old X-15 landing? My guess is you would have an large vertical decel situation up in the nose for the crew. While directional control would be afforded in some part by the drag chute…do you want to count on that to keep you out of the moat?

6. If a belly landing is unacceptable, ditching/bailout might be next on the list. Not a good day.

7. Assuming you can get to the runway with the gear deployed but with two flat tires, can the commander control the vehicle in pitch and lateral directions? One concern is excessive drag (0.2 g's) during TD throughout the entire saddle region making the derotation uncontrollable due to saturated elevons…resulting in nose gear failure? The addition of crosswinds would make lateral control a tough thing too. Simulating this, because it is so rediculously easy to do (aims going on this very minute at AMES with load-persistence) seems like a no brainer.

Admittedly this os over the top in many ways but this is a pretty bad time to get surprised and have to make decisions in the last 20 minutes. You can count on us to provide any support you think you need.

Best Regards,
Bob

X-Sender: d.l.dwoyer@express.larc.nasa.gov
X-Priority: 1.(Highest)
Date: Fri, 31 Jan 2003 11:00:34 -0500
To: d.c.freeman@larc.nasa,gov
From: Doug Dwoyer <d.l.dwoyer@larc.nasa.gov>

Del,

Should you call Reedy?

Doug

X-Priority: 1 (Highest)
Date: Fri, 31 Jan 2003 07:49:59 -0500
To: d.l.dwoyer@larc.nasa.gov
From: "Mark J. Shuart" <m.j.shuart@larc.nasa.gov>

Doug,

FYI. Bob Daugherty can be the kind of conservative, thorough engineer that NASA needs. I think he is demonstrating that below. I can only hope the folks at JSC are listening…..Mark

Date: Thu, 30 Jan 2003 18:22:41 -0500
To: "LECHNER, DAVID F. (JSC-DF52) (USA)"
<david.f.lechner1@jsc.nasa.gov>
From: "Robert H. Daugherty" <r.h.daugherty@larc.nasa.gov>
Subject: Main Gear Breach Concerns
Zc: M.J.SHUART@larc.nasa.gov, H.M.ADELMAN@larc.nasa.gov,
carlisle .c.campbell1@jsc.nasan.gov

Hi David,
I talked to Carlisle a bit ago and he let me know you guys at MOD were getting into the loop on the tile damage issue. I'm writing this email not really in an official capacity but since we've worked together so many times I feel I can say pretty much anything to you. And before I begin I would like to offer that I am admittedly erring way on the side of absolute worst-case scenarios and I don't really believe things are as bad as I'm getting ready to make them out. But I certainly believe that to not be ready for a gut-wrenching decision after seeing instrumentation in the wheel well not

be there after entry is irresponsible. One of my personal theories is that you should seriously consider the possibility of the gear not deploying at all if there is a substantial breach of the wheel well. The reason might be that as the temps increase, the wheel (aluminum) will lose material properties as it heats up and the tire pressure will increase. At some point the wheel could fail and send debris everywhere. While it is true there are thermal fuses in the wheel, if the rate of heating is high enough, since the tire is such a good insulator, the wheel may degrade in strength enough to let go far below the 1100 psi or so that the tire normally bursts at. It seems to me that with that much carnage in the wheel well, something could get screwed up enough to prevent deployment and then you are in a world of hurt. The following are scenarios that might be possible...and since there are so many of them, these are offered just to make sure that some things don't slip thru the cracks...I suspect many or all these have been gone over by you guys already:

1. People talk about landing with two tires...I did too until this came up. If both tires blew in the wheel well (not talking thermal fuse and venting but explosive decomp due to tire and/or wheel failure) the overpressure in the wheel well will be in the 40 + psi range. The resulting loads on the gear door (a quarter million lbs) would almost certainly blow the door off the hinges or at least send it out into the slip stream...catastrophic. Even if you could survive the heating, would the gear now deploy? And/or also, could you even reach the runway with this kind of drag?

2. The explosive bungies...what might be the possibility of these firing due to excessive heating? If they fired, would they send the gear door and/or gear into the slip stream?

3. What might excessive heating do to all kinds of other hardware in the wheel well...the hydraulic fluid, uplocks, etc? Are there vulnerable hardware items that might prevent deployment?

4. If the gear didn't deploy (and you would have to consider this before making the commitment to gear deploy on final) what would happen control-wise if the other gear is down and one is up? (I think Howard Law and his community will tell you you're finished)

5. Do you belly land? Without any other planning you will have already committed to KSC. And what will happen during derotation in a gear up landing (trying to stay away from asymmetric gear situation for example) since you will be hitting the aft end body flap and wings and pitching down extremely fast a la the old X-15 landing? My guess is you would have an large vertical decel situation up in the nose for the crew. While directional control would be afforded in some part by the drag chute...do you want to count on that to keep you out of the moat?

6. If a belly landing is unacceptable, ditching/bailout might be next on the list. Not a good day.

7. Assuming you can get to the runway with the gear deployed but with two flat tires, can the commander control the vehicle in pitch and lateral directions? One concern is excessive drag (0.2 g's) during TD throughout the entire saddle region making the

44

derotation uncontrollable due to saturated elevons…resulting in nose gear failure? The addition of crosswinds would make lateral control a tough thing too. Simulating this, because it is so rediculously easy to do (aims going on this very minute at AMES with load-persistence) seems like a no brainer.

Admittedly this os over the top in many ways but this is a pretty bad time to get surprised and have to make decisions in the last 20 minutes. You can count on us to provide any support you think you need.

Best Regards,
Bob

--
Doug Dwoyer
  Associate Director for Research and Technology Competencies

Notice that with all the concern about tile loss or damage, there is no documentation in the emails that were made public indicating NASA administrators had asked the Air Force to take high-resolution photographs of the shuttle while in orbit. There are two cameras available to the Air Force, one in Puerto Rico and the other in Hawaii. Although photographing the shuttle in orbit is not the primary intention of these cameras, the cameras have been used on previous shuttle missions to view suspected damage to the Orbiter. The resolution of these cameras is capable of counting rivets on window frames and seeing the expressions on faces of astronauts inside the vehicles. Also, I have never found any correspondence that requested the use of the camera at the end of the shuttle arm to examine the external surface of the Orbiter. Unless there was no camera on the shuttle arm for this mission, the only rational explanations I can think of is that administrators either ignored the very people who manage the shuttle flights, or they knew all along that the object that struck the Orbiter during launch would not have caused enough damage to be concerned. I would hate to think NASA administrators knew the crew was doomed from the beginning, and therefore did nothing. For now, I will give them the benefit of the doubt.

For whatever reason, why NASA administrators and managers sidestepped the use of these valuable tools may never be known or comprehended. Even if the photographs had found missing or damaged tiles, there was no way the crew could have made any repairs while in orbit. However, without knowing precisely what condition the shuttle was in, engineers never got the chance to come up with a solution to the problem.

I remember when NASA was faced with a similar problem during the Apollo 13 mission. Although the Columbia crew was never in the same obvious life-threatening situation as the Apollo crew, the necessity to bring the crew home safely was just as eminent. During that crisis, flight engineers and flight controllers raced the clock and utilized every resource available to them to bring the Apollo crew home. Their effort was one of epic proportions in history. The flights this country made to the moon was one the greatest engineering achievements in the history of mankind. Bringing the crew of Apollo 13 home safely pushed the science of engineering beyond anything that had been done before, or since. I cannot help but wonder what the outcome would have been had the people and engineers behind the shuttle flights been given a viable opportunity to bring Columbia back to the Kennedy Space Center. We will never know.

The Re-entry

From the last seven-and-a-half minutes of data received from the Orbiter, we can piece together a picture of what happened and why. You do not have to be a rocket scientist to understand the data, and as they say a picture is worth a thousand words. The illustrations in this book were downloaded from NASA's own website. The only editing to the slides I have done is show the location of the wing leading edge panel number 8, where the foam from the external tank supposedly struck the left wing.

Also, from the slides I have assembled two tables of information that narrate each event as they occurred. The first table breaks down the sequence of events during the last seven minutes and thirty-two seconds of telemetry from the Orbiter. The second table expands the data to include the location of each sensor within the Orbiter, the computer channel the sensor reports through, the status change of the responding sensor, the relative position of the sensor to panel 8, and whether the wire routing for that sensor is through or near the left main wheel well. In my opinion the information is compelling and irrefutable.

LOS *	Sequence of Events
-7:32	At this point of the re-entry all indications were nominal (normal) onboard the Orbiter.
-7:27	The first indication of off-nominal aero increments indicates that there was a slight amount of aerodynamic drag on some surface of the Orbiter, causing the auto pilot system to make minor correction to the flight control system to make the necessary corrections to keep the Orbiter on the proper trajectory towards the Kennedy Space Center.
-7:15	A thermal couple (temperature sensor, Channel D) indicates a slight rise in temperature in the left main landing gear brake line. The sensor is located inside the wheel well next to the fuselage near the upper surface of the wing.

LOS *	Sequence of Events
-7:00	The Supply Water Dump Nozzle (Channels A and B) and Vacuum Vent ports are opened, causing an expected slight rise in temperature near the cabin area of the Orbiter, nowhere near the suspect damage area of the wing.
-6:51	A thermal couple indicates a slight rise in temperature in the left main landing gear brake line near the brake assembly on the wheels (Channels A). Another thermal couple indicates a slight rise in temperature in the left main landing gear brake line (Channel C) is located inside the wheel well next to the fuselage near the upper surface of the wing.
-6:36	The Left Inboard Elevon lower skin thermal couple located near the trailing edge of the wing shows a significant temperature rise, which leads to speculation of some kind of wire damage between the sensor and computer. The wire harness is routed through the mid-section of the wing towards the fuselage, and then turns toward the nose of the Orbiter next to the left main gear wheel well.
-6:33	The Left Inboard Elevon lower skin thermal couple goes off line, indicating that the computer is no longer receiving data from the sensor.
-6:31	First indication of off-nominal rolling moment increments. The autopilot is sending inputs to the flight control surfaces to correct an un-commanded roll of the Orbiter.
-6:30	The Left Inboard Elevon Actuator Hydraulic System 1 and Left Outboard Elevon Actuator Hydraulic System 3 Return Lines indicate that wire damage may have occurred between the thermal couples and the computer. The wire harness for both sensors is routed through the mid-section of the wing towards the fuselage, and then turns toward the nose of the Orbiter next to the left main gear wheel well.
-6:22	Left Outboard Elevon Actuator Hydraulic System 3 Return Line thermal couple goes off line, indicating that the computer is no longer receiving data from the sensor.

LOS *	Sequence of Events
-6:21	The Left Inboard Elevon Actuator Hydraulic System 1 Return Line thermal couple goes off line, indicating that the computer is no longer receiving data from the sensor.
-5:58	Left Outboard Elevon Actuator Hydraulic System 1 Return Line thermal couple goes off line, indicating that the computer is no longer receiving data from the sensor. The Left Inboard Elevon Actuator Hydraulic System 2 indicates that wire damage may have occurred between the thermal couples and the computer.
-5:57	The Supply Water Dump Nozzle (Channels A and B) and Vacuum Vent ports are closed, the temperature return to nominal rise rates.
-5:56	The Left Inboard Elevon Actuator Hydraulic System 2 goes off line, indicating that the computer is no longer receiving data from the sensor.
-5:46	Debris #1 – 1st report of debris observed leaving Orbiter
-5:44	Debris #2 – 2nd report of debris observed leaving Orbiter
-5:36	Debris #3 – 3rd report of debris observed leaving Orbiter
-5:30	Debris #4 – 4th report of debris observed leaving Orbiter
-5:23	Debris #5 – 5th report of debris observed leaving Orbiter
-5:22	Left Main Gear Brake Line thermal couple (Channel B) located on the main landing gear strut inside the wheel well indicates an unexpected rise in temperature.
-5:12	Start of slow aileron trim change. Reversal of growth trend of derived roll moment coefficient indicates that the autopilot is correcting an un-commanded roll of the Orbiter. Probable cause is additional aerodynamic drag.

LOS *	Sequence of Events
-5:10	Mid Fuselage Left Body Line thermal couple indicates a slight temperature rise behind the wheel well where the wing and fuselage meet. The Left Hand Aft Fuselage Sidewall thermal couple located near the tail section of the Orbiter indicates a slight temperature rise. Neither sensor is near the suspect wing damage, however, the wire harness are routed next to the wheel well.
-5:08	Left Main Gear Strut Actuator thermal couple inside the wheel well indicates a slight temperature rise.
-4:59	Flash #1 – Orbiter envelope suddenly brightened for approximately three-tenths second.
-4:56	Debris #6 – 6th report of debris observed leaving Orbiter
-4:39	Left Main Landing Gear Outboard Wheel thermal couple inside the wheel well indicates a slight temperature rise.
-4:25	Debris #7 – 7th report of debris observed leaving Orbiter
-4:20	Left Hand Forward Brake Switch Valve System Return Line located inside the wheel well near the fuselage indicates a slight temperature rise.
-4:08	Debris #8 – 8th report of debris observed leaving Orbiter
-4:05	Debris #9 – 9th report of debris observed leaving Orbiter
-4:04	Debris #10 – 10th report of debris observed leaving Orbiter
-3:53	Debris #11 – 11th report of debris observed leaving Orbiter
-3:51	Mid Fuselage Port (Left) Sill Longeron located near the fuselage indicates a slight temperature rise. The wire harness to this sensor is routed between the wheel well and fuselage.
-3:45	Debris #12 – 12th report of debris observed leaving Orbiter
-3:35	Debris #13 – 13th report of debris observed leaving Orbiter

LOS *	Sequence of Events
-3:33	Debris #14 – 14th report of debris observed leaving Orbiter
-3:29	Left Lower Wing Skin thermal couple located near the middle of the wing indicates a slight temperature rise. The wire harness to this sensor is routed near the wheel well.
-3:21	Debris #15 – 15th report of debris observed leaving Orbiter
-3:16	Left Main Gear Up-lock Actuator Unlock Line thermal couple located inside the wheel well on the landing gear strut indicates a slight temperature rise.
-3:08	The left Upper Wing Skin thermal couple indicates wire damage may have occurred. Although the sensor is nearly in line with the suspected wing damage, the location is a considerable distance away near the middle of the wing. However, the wire harness to the sensor is routed next to the wheel well.
-2:13	Left Main Landing Gear Outboard Tire Pressure sensor number 1 indicates that the pressure inside the outboard tire is beginning to rise. Basic physics shows that gases try to expand when heated. When there is no room to expand, the pressure rises.
-2:08	Debris #16 – 16th report of debris observed leaving Orbiter. Left Main Landing Gear Outboard Tire Pressure sensor number 2 indicates that the pressure inside the outboard tire is beginning to rise.
-2:04	Left Lower Wing Skin thermal couple goes off line, indicating that the computer is no longer receiving data from the sensor.
-1:49	Left Upper Wing Skin thermal couple goes off line, indicating that the computer is no longer receiving data from the sensor.
-1:38	System 2 Left Hand Aft Brake Switch Valve Return Line thermal couple located near the wing root indicates a slight temperature rise.
-1:37	Flare 1: Asymmetrical brightening of Orbiter shape observed

LOS *	Sequence of Events
-1:32	Flare 2: Asymmetrical brightening of Orbiter shape observed
-1:29	Start of "sharp" aileron trim increase
-1:23	Increase in derived rolling and yawing moment increments
-1:00	Left Main Landing Gear Outboard Tire 1, Left Main Landing Gear Outboard Wheel and Left Main Landing Gear Inboard Tire 1 thermal couples located inside the wheel well indicate wire damage may have occurred.
-0:56	Left Main Landing Gear Inboard Wheel thermal couple located inside the wheel well indicates wire damage may have occurred.
-0:54	Left Main Landing Gear Outboard Tire 1 pressure sensor located inside the wheel well goes off line, indicating that the computer is no longer receiving data from the sensor.
-0:53	Left Main Landing Gear Outboard Wheel thermocouple located inside the wheel well goes offline, indicating that the computer is no longer receiving data from the sensor. Left Main Landing Gear Outboard Tire 2 pressure sensor located inside the wheel well indicates wire damage may have occurred.
-0:52	Left Main Landing Gear Inboard Tire pressure 1 sensor number located inside the wheel well goes off line, indicating that the computer is no longer receiving data from the sensor.
-0:51	Left Main Landing Gear Inboard Tire 2 pressure sensor located inside the wheel well indicates a rise in tire pressure.
-0:49	Left Main Landing Gear Inboard Tire 2 pressure sensor located inside the wheel well indicates wire damage may have occurred.

LOS *	Sequence of Events
-0:44	Left Main Landing Gear Inboard Wheel thermal couple located inside the wheel well goes off line, indicating that the computer is no longer receiving data from the sensor. Left Main Landing Gear Inboard Tire 2 pressure sensor located inside the wheel well goes off line, indicating that the computer is no longer receiving data from the sensor.
-0:38	*Left Main Landing Gear Outboard Tire 2 pressure sensor located inside the wheel well goes off line, indicating that the computer is no longer receiving data from the sensor.*
-0:26	*Left Main Gear Down locked switch located in the wheel well indicates that the left main landing gear may be in the down and locked position.*
-0:10	Left Hand Aft Brake Switch Valve System 2 Return Line thermal couple located inside the wheel well indicates wire damage may have occurred.
-0:01	The ASA 4 Wiring to Left Wing located near the trailing edge wing indicates wire damage may have occurred.
-0:00	Loss of Signal, meaning that all telemetry from the Orbiter has stopped.

* Time to Loss of Signal

The following illustrations are actual slides from an official NASA briefing held March 21, 2003. What is most important is that you watch the sensors as they indicate each problem and note the order that they drop offline. Read the note on each slide. On some of the more complex slides, I have provided a narrative to explain what is being illustrated. Also, the only editing to the NASA slides is to note the location of each sensor and wire harness location relative to panel 8 of the leading edge of the wing (shaded in black).

2D Graphical Event Sequence

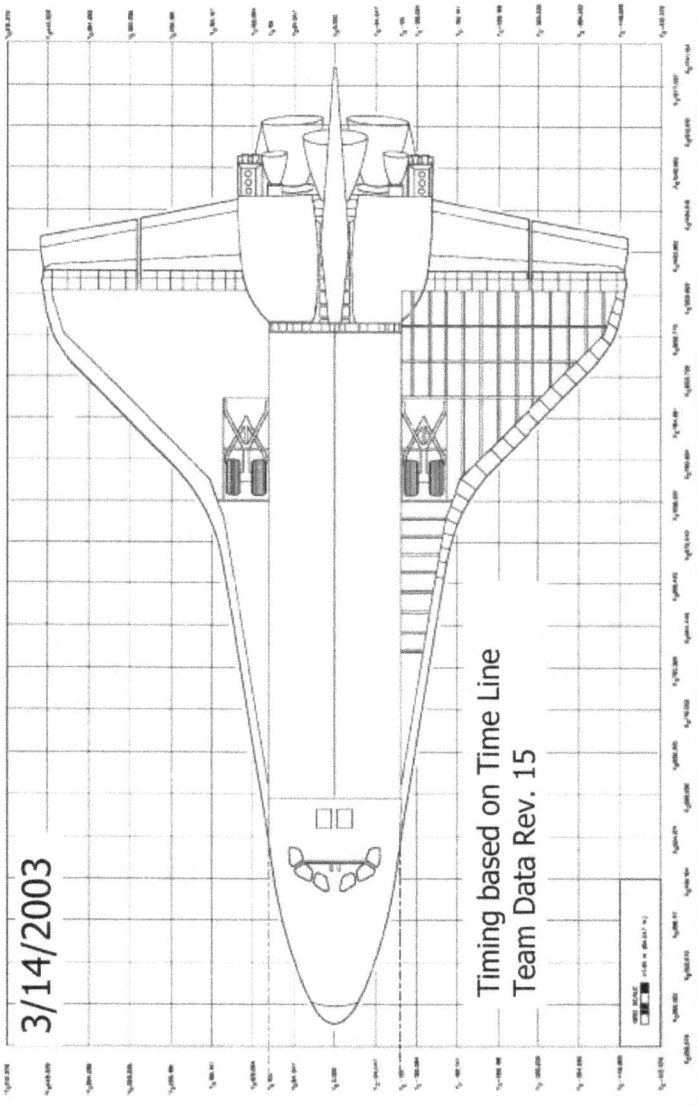

3/14/2003

Timing based on Time Line
Team Data Rev. 15

Introduction

- **The graphical event sequence is a visual time history of relevant sensor information in the left wing and wheel well areas**

  – Covers approximately 8 minute timeframe, from first anomalous sensor reading through last available telemetry

  – Documents known anomalous sensor responses per the latest revision of events timeline from OVEWG Data Review and Timeline team

- **Information contained in the graphical event sequence include :**

  – Sensor location on orbiter and its associated wire bundle in X-Y plane

  – Wire bundle routing

  – Description of each anomalous sensor event

  – Time annotation by (a) GMT, (b) time relative to LOS, (c) time history bar, and (d) ground track

  – Graphical display of temperature rise (based on delta temperature from point it is determined to be anomalous)

Sensor Cabling

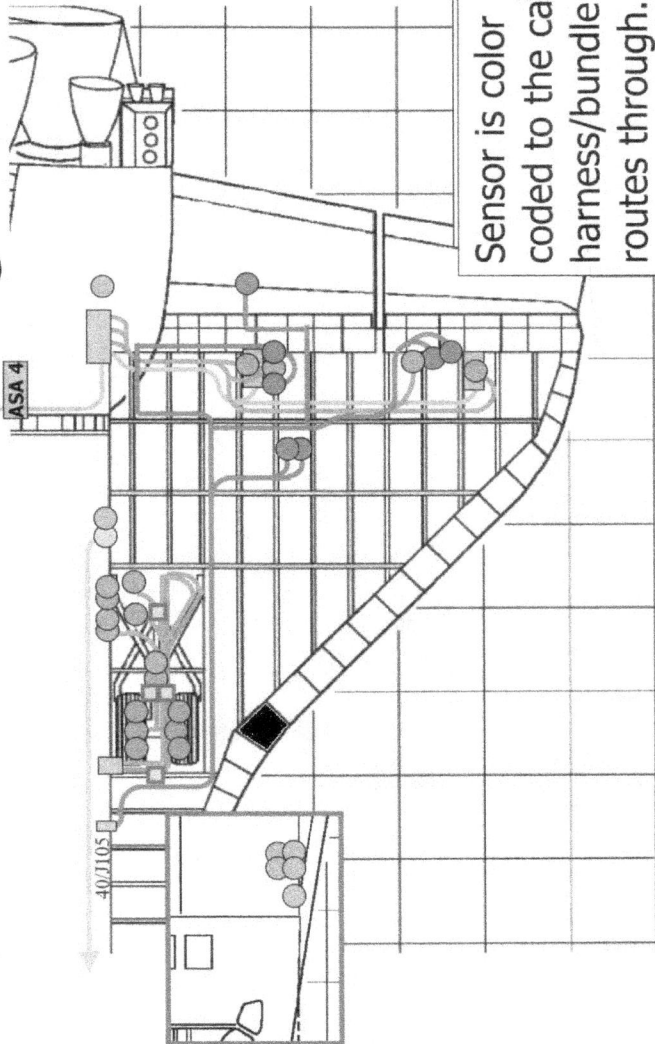

Sensor is color coded to the cable harness/bundle it routes through.

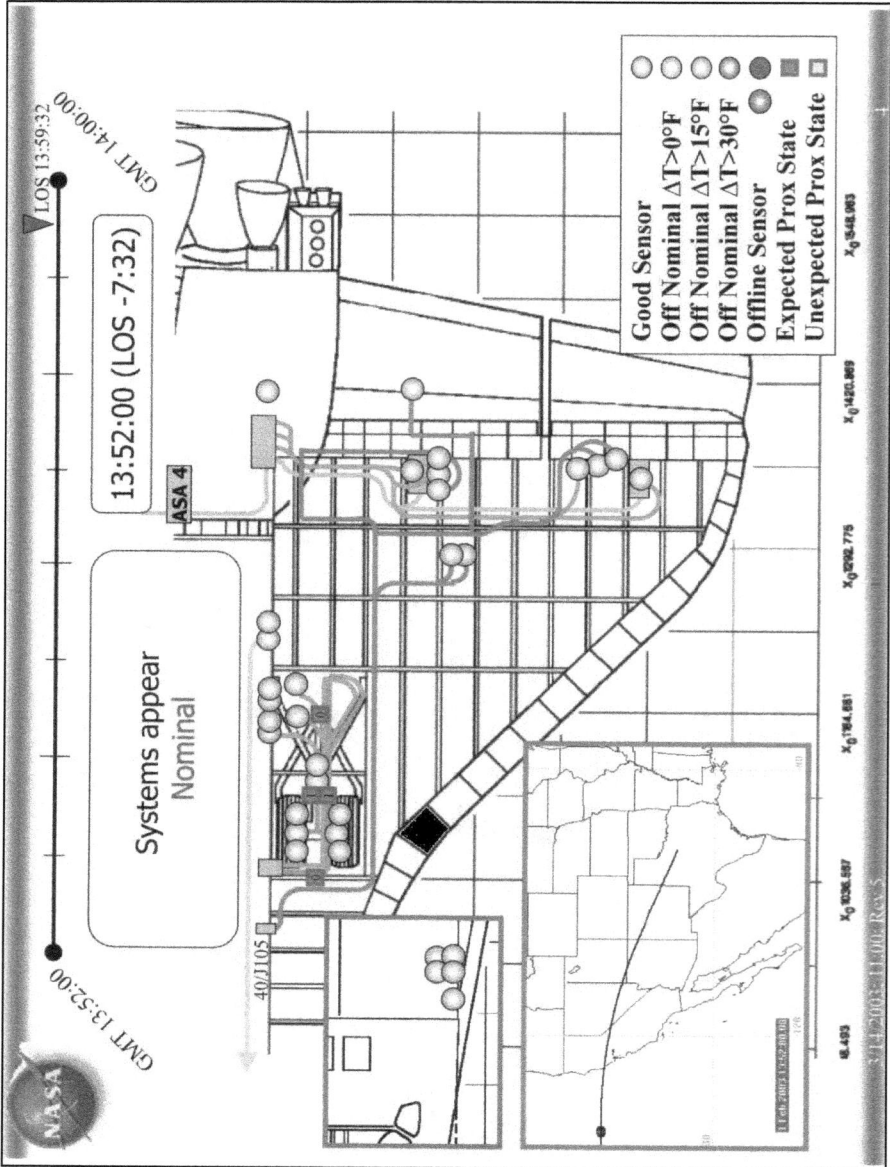

Legend:
- Good Sensor
- Off Nominal ΔT>0°F
- Off Nominal ΔT>15°F
- Off Nominal ΔT>30°F
- Offline Sensor
- Expected Prox State
- Unexpected Prox State

13:52:00 (LOS -7:32)

Systems appear Nominal

ASA 4

40/J105

GMT 14:00:00
LOS 13:59:32
GMT 13:52:00

$X_0$548.993 $X_0$1420.969 $X_0$1292.775 $X_0$1164.581 $X_0$1036.387 $X_0$908.193

1 Feb 2003 13:52:00 UT

3/14/2003 13:00 Rev S

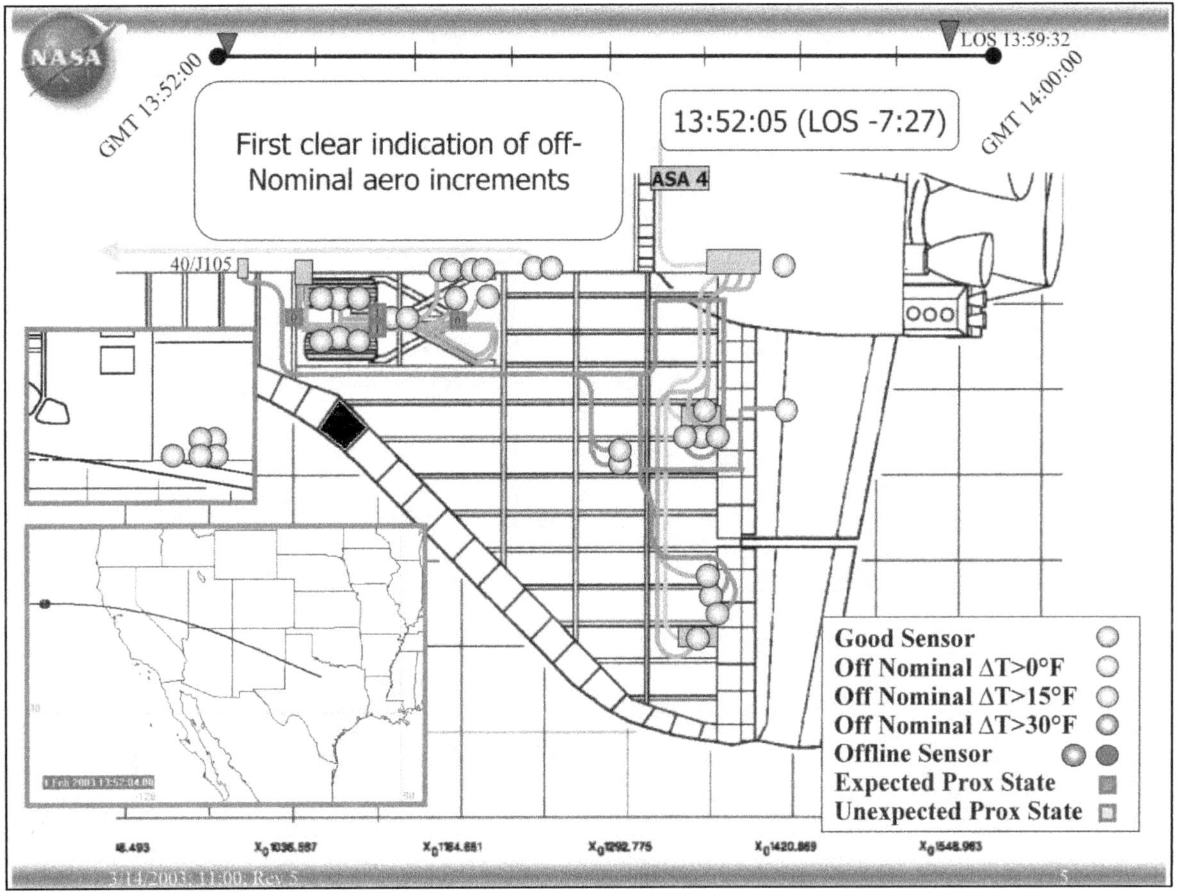

GMT 13:52:00
LOS 13:59:32
GMT 14:00:00
First clear indication of off-Nominal aero increments
13:52:05 (LOS -7:27)
ASA 4
40/J105
Good Sensor
Off Nominal ΔT>0°F
Off Nominal ΔT>15°F
Off Nominal ΔT>30°F
Offline Sensor
Expected Prox State
Unexpected Prox State
X0 1036.587
X0 1164.681
X0 1292.775
X0 1420.869
X0 1548.963
3/14/2003, 11:00, Rev 5
5

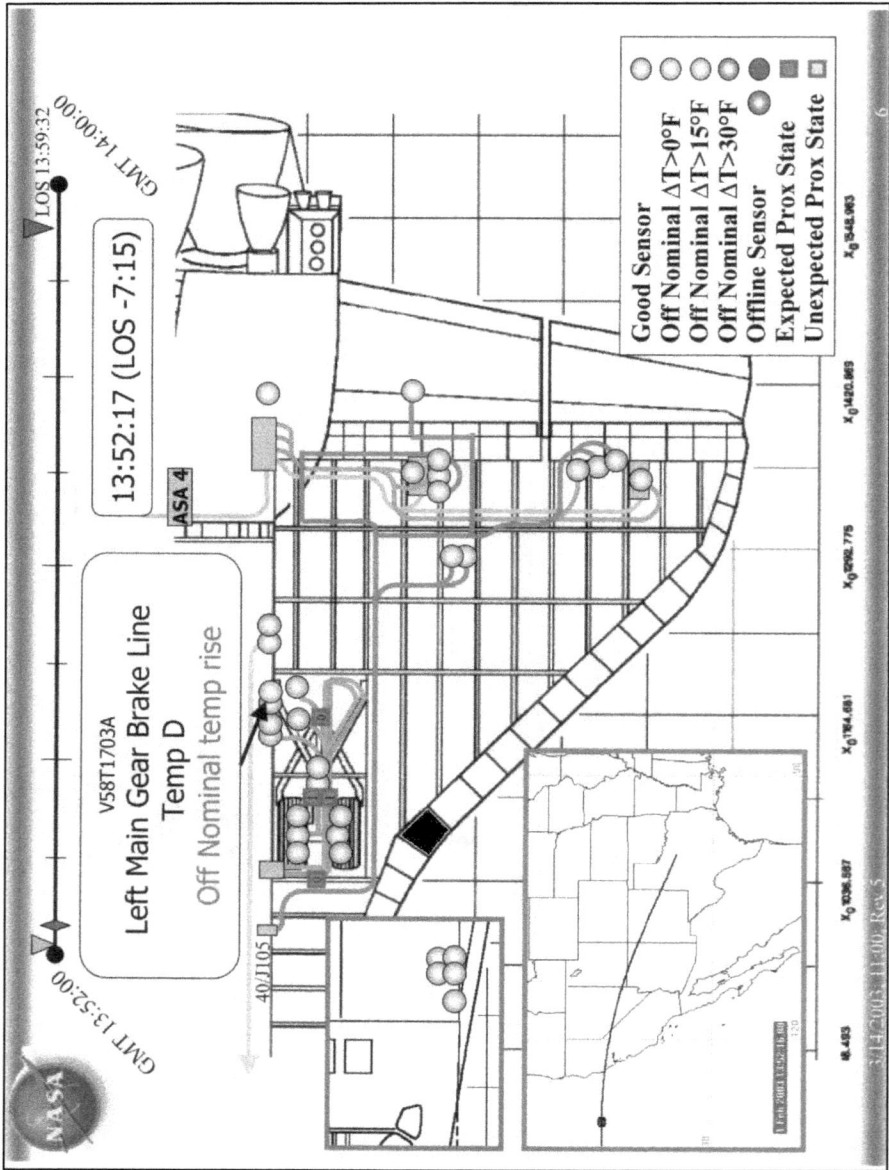

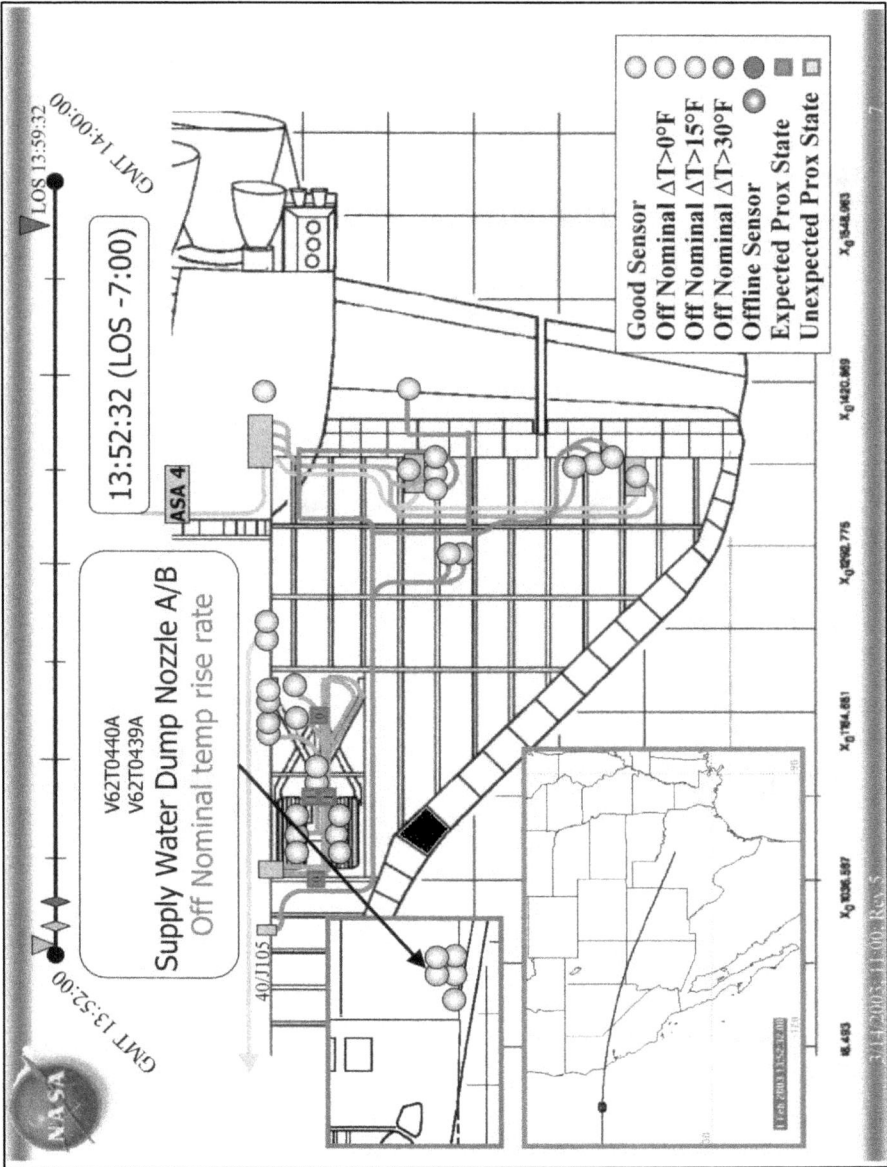

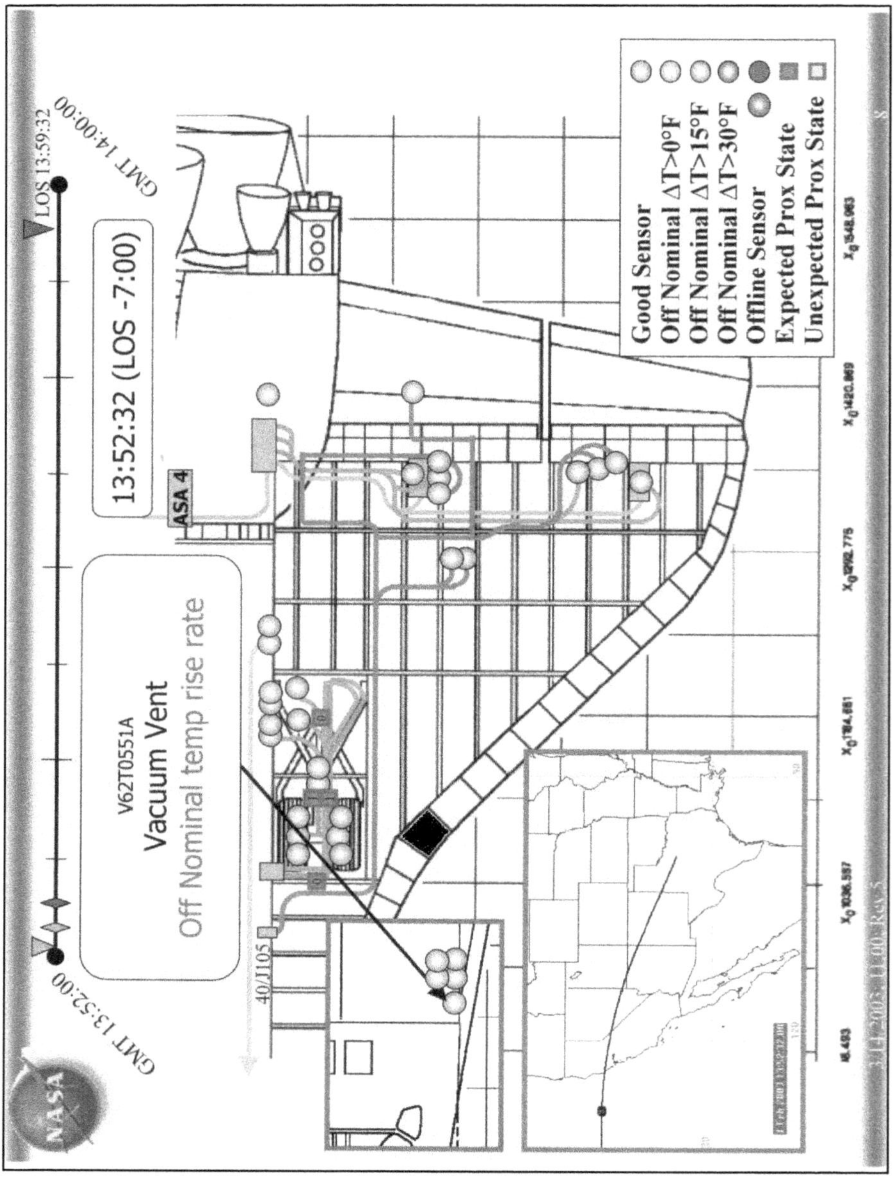

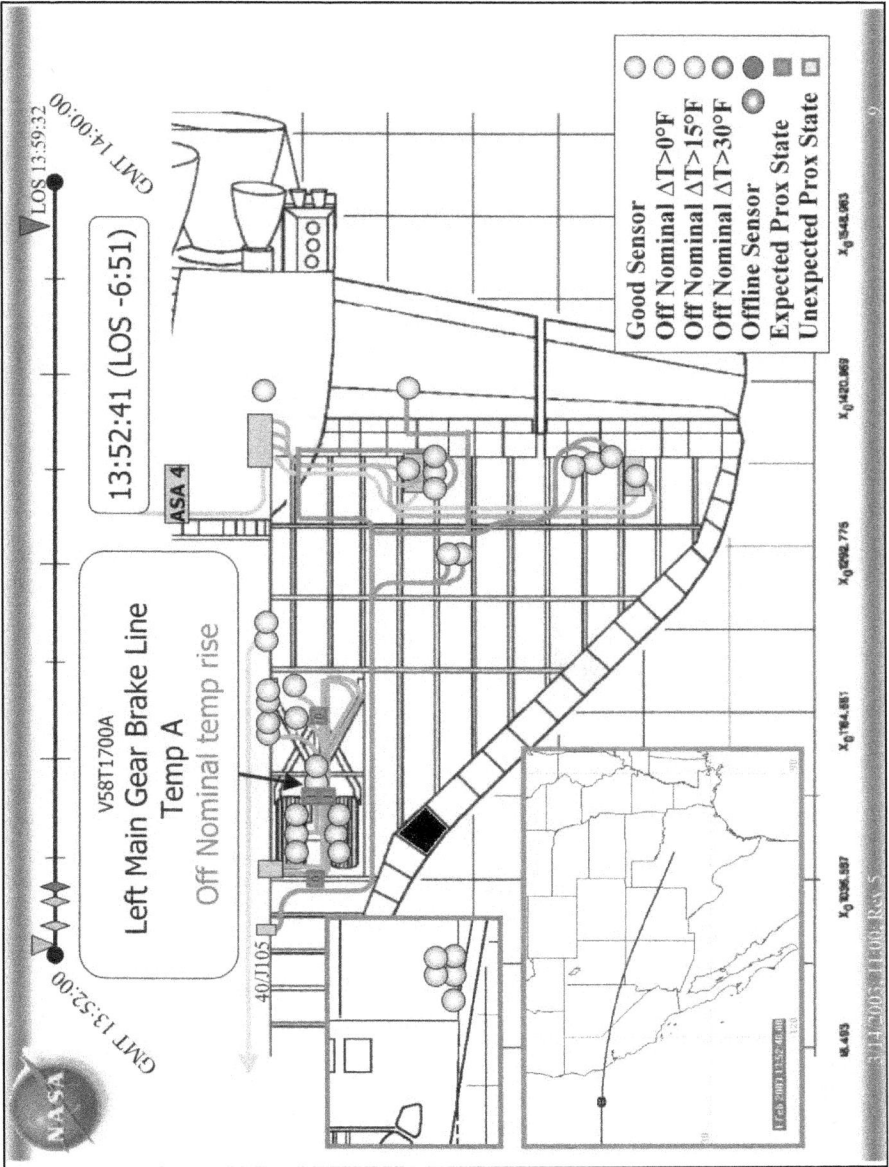

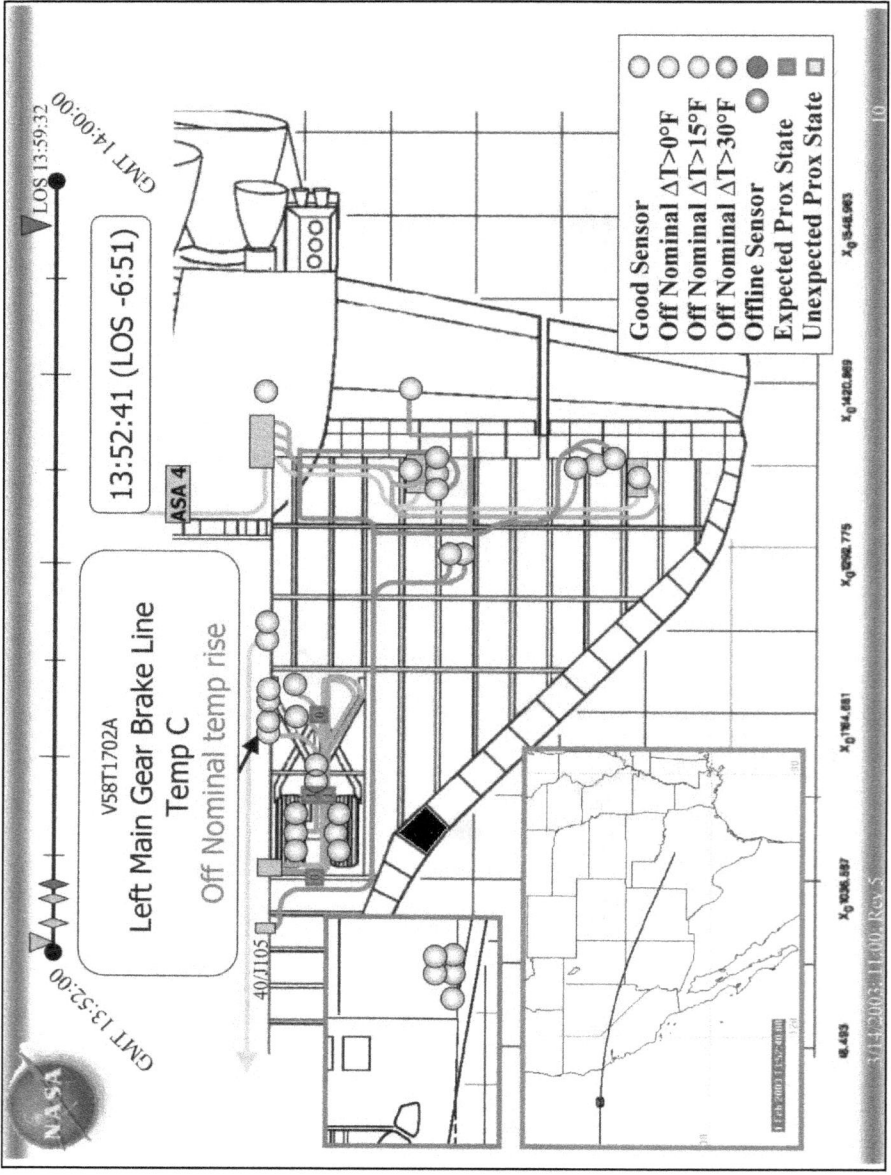

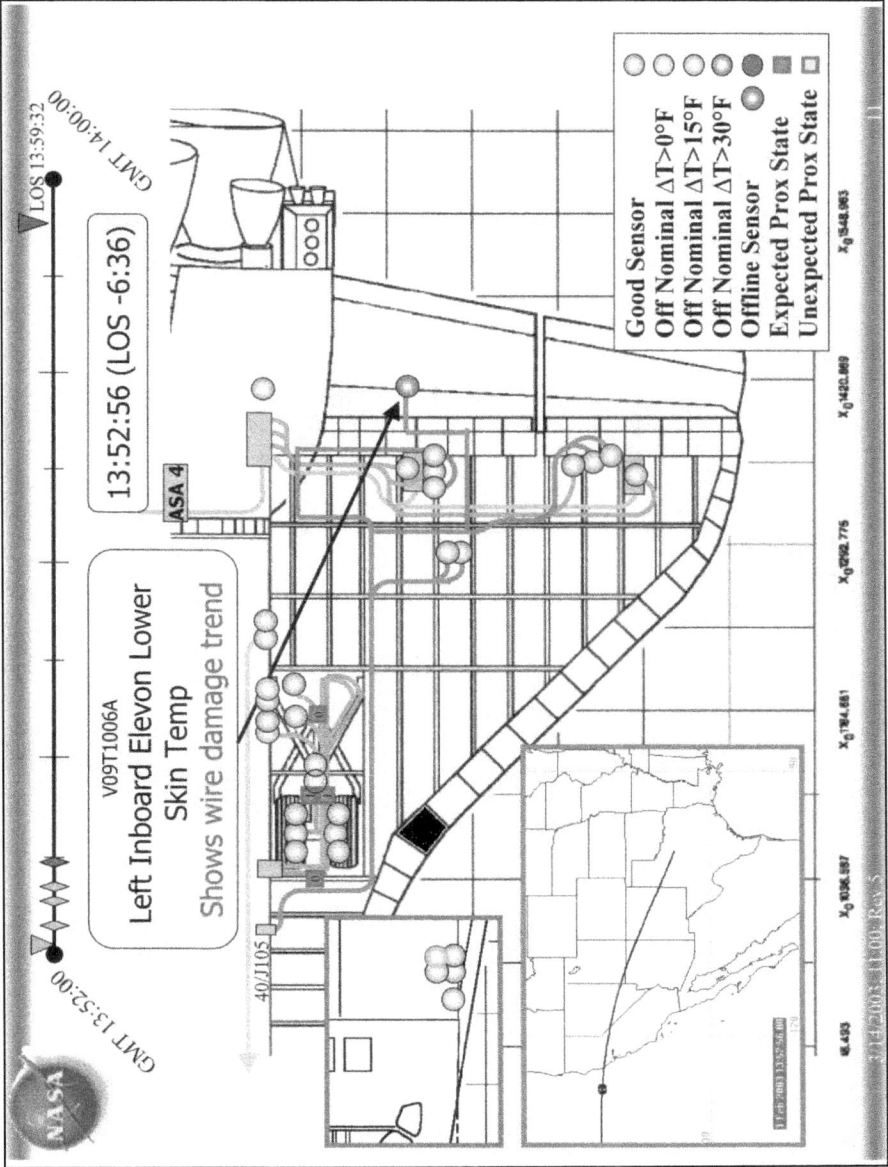

65

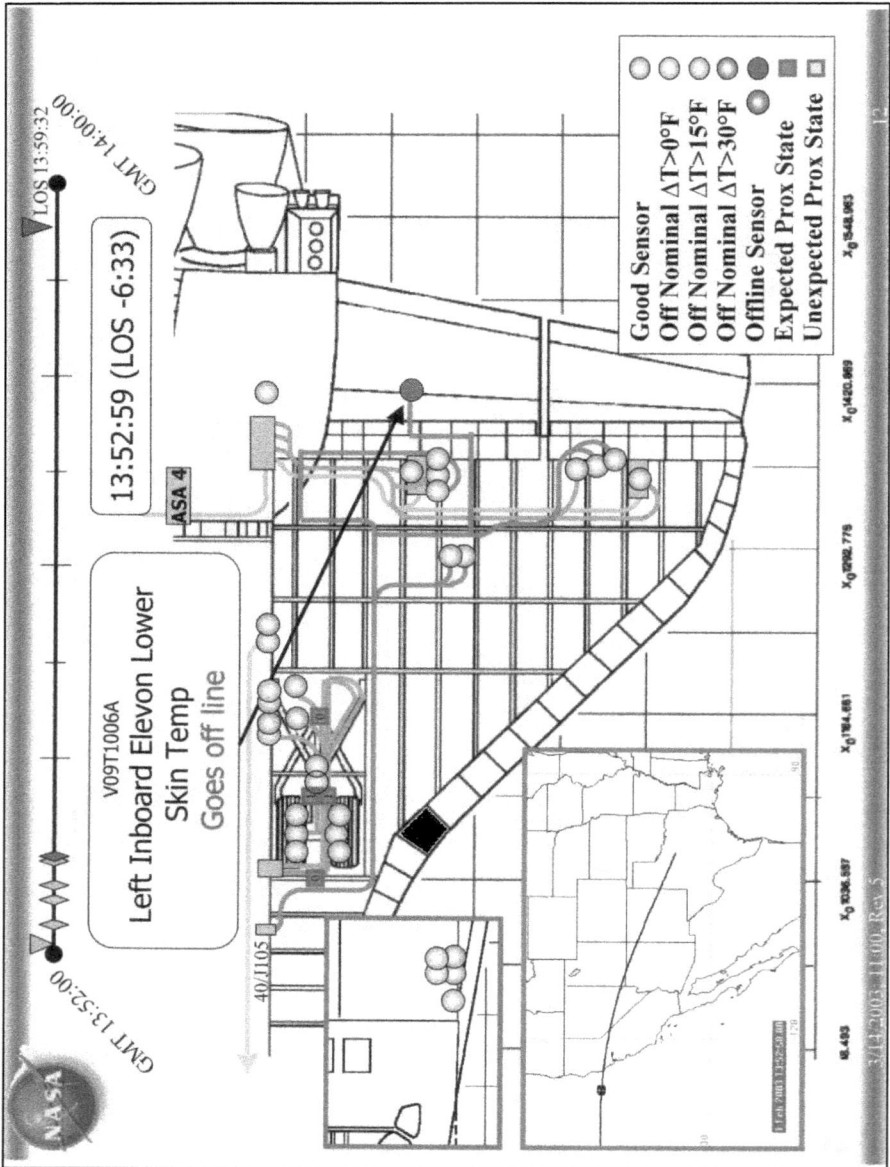

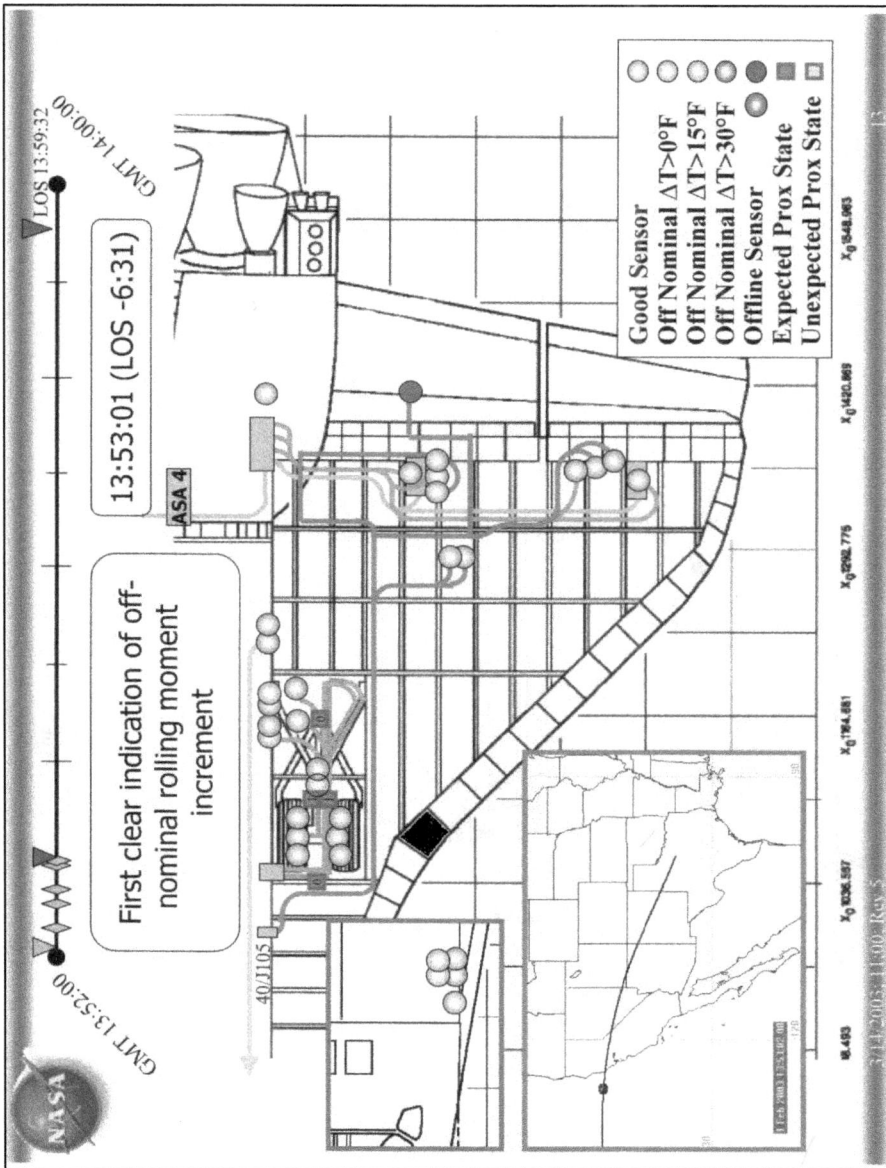

First clear indication of off-nominal rolling moment increment

13:53:01 (LOS -6:31)

ASA 4

40/J105

GMT 13:52:00
GMT 14:00:00
LOS 13:59:32
LOS 13:59:32

Good Sensor
Off Nominal ΔT>0°F
Off Nominal ΔT>15°F
Off Nominal ΔT>30°F
Offline Sensor
Expected Prox State
Unexpected Prox State

$X_0$848.903
$X_0$1420.869
$X_0$2292.775
$X_0$1184.681
$X_0$1036.597

3/Feb/2003 13:00 Rev 5

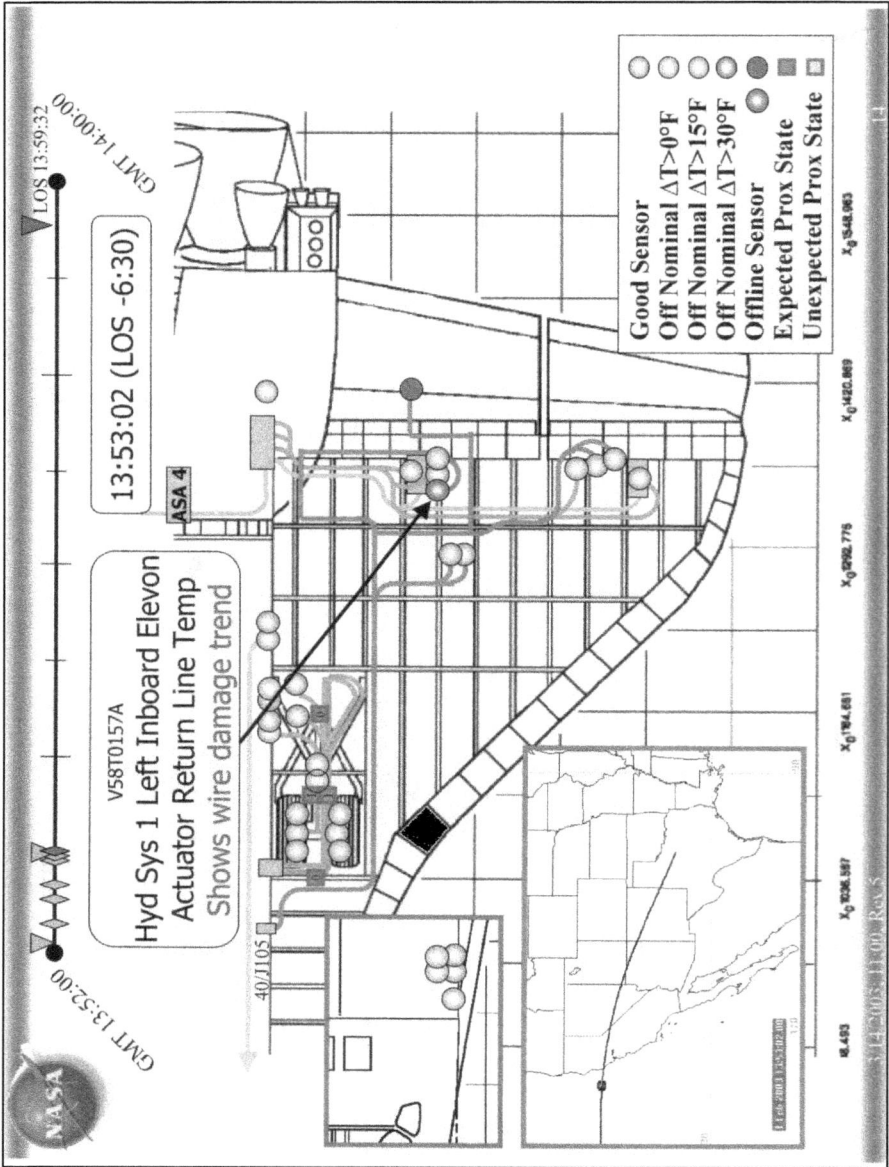

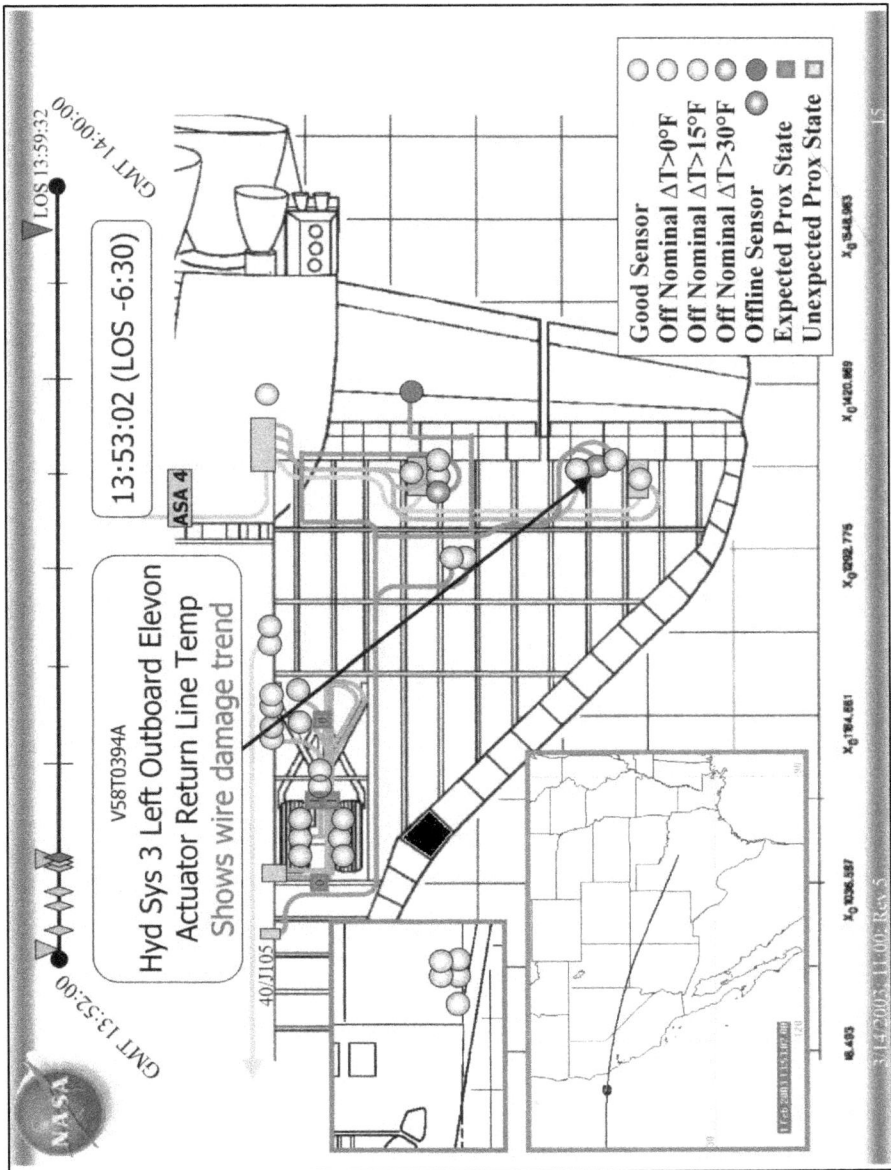

V58T0394A
Hyd Sys 3 Left Outboard Elevon
Actuator Return Line Temp
Shows wire damage trend

13:53:02 (LOS -6:30)

ASA 4

40/J1105

Good Sensor
Off Nominal ΔT>0°F
Off Nominal ΔT>15°F
Off Nominal ΔT>30°F
Offline Sensor
Expected Prox State
Unexpected Prox State

GMT 13:52:00
GMT 14:00:00
LOS 13:59:32

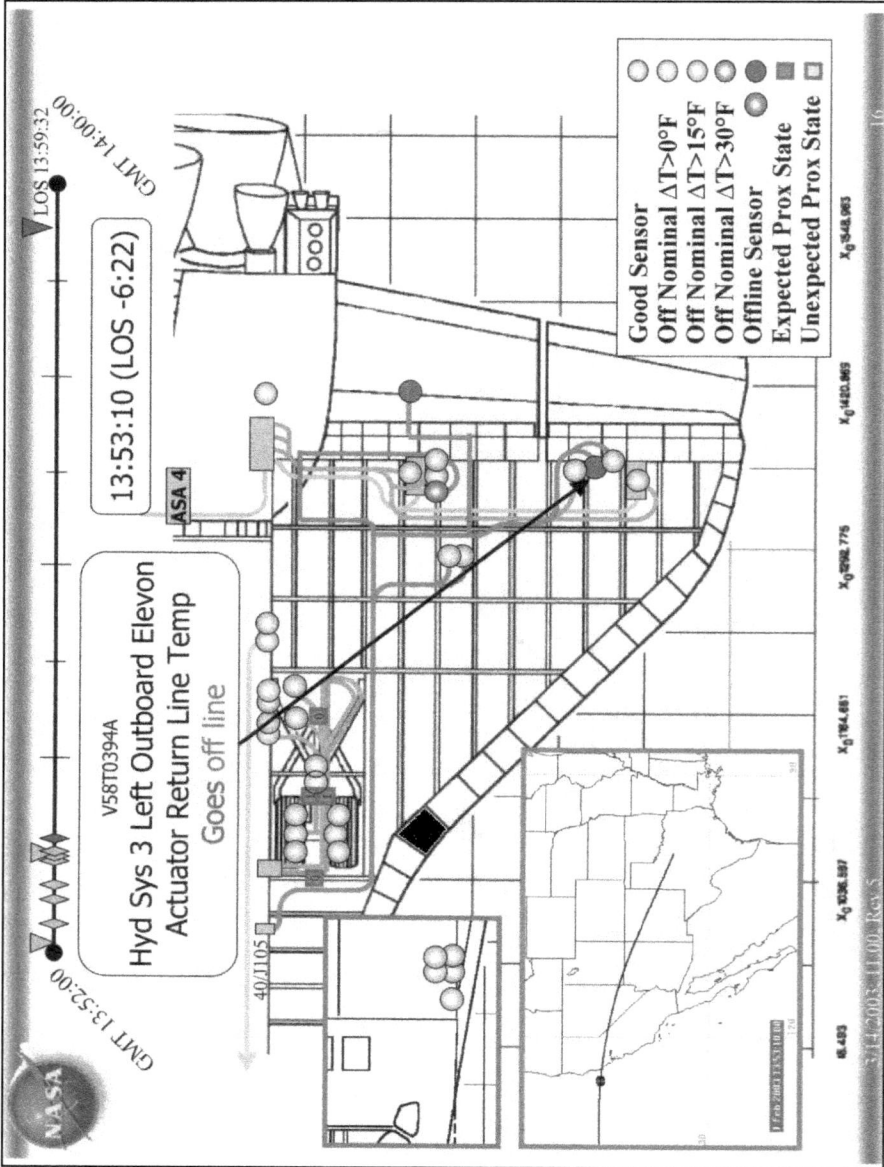

LOS 13:59:32

GMT 14:00:00

13:53:10 (LOS -6:22)

V58T0394A
Hyd Sys 3 Left Outboard Elevon
Actuator Return Line Temp
Goes off line

ASA 4

40/J105

GMT 13:52:00

NASA

Good Sensor
Off Nominal ΔT>0°F
Off Nominal ΔT>15°F
Off Nominal ΔT>30°F
Offline Sensor
Expected Prox State
Unexpected Prox State

X_o548.965
X_o1420.965
X_o1292.775
X_o1164.681
X_o1036.587
68.493

16

3/14/2003, 11:00, Rev 5

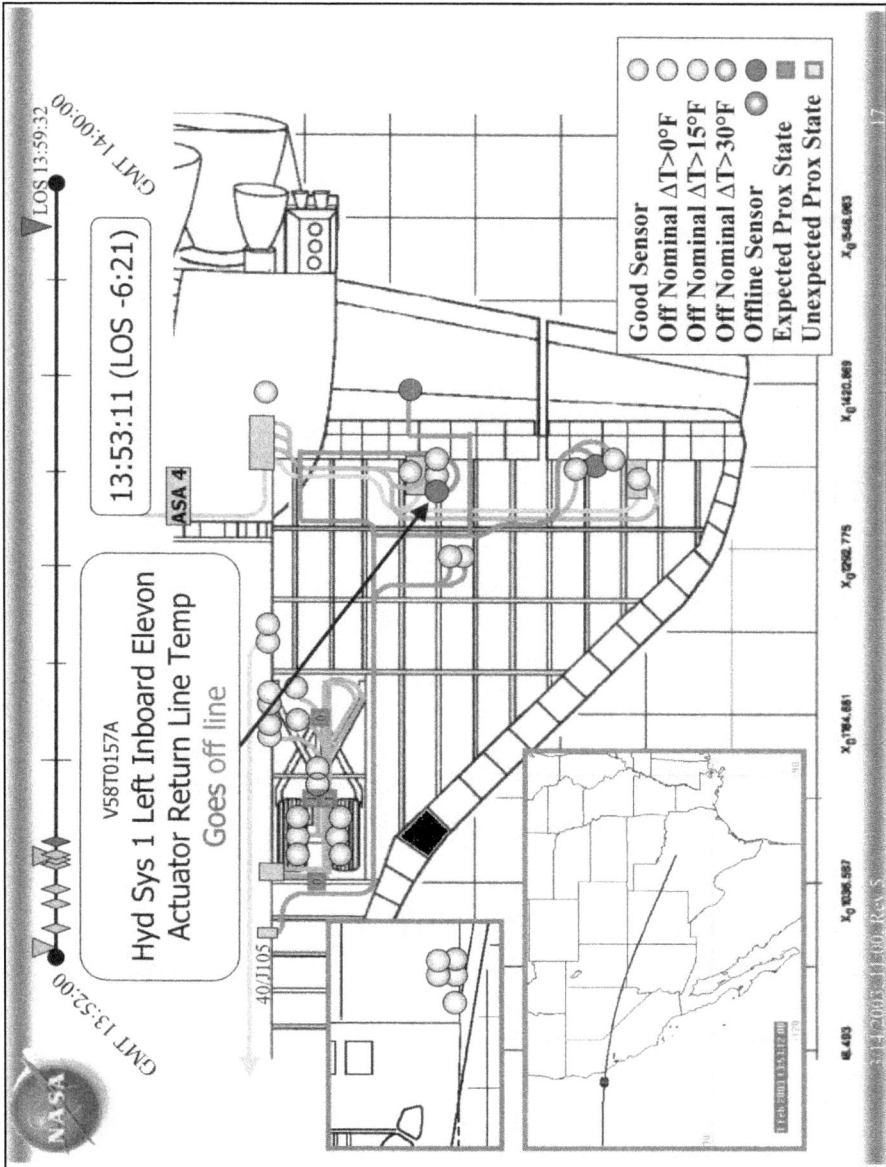

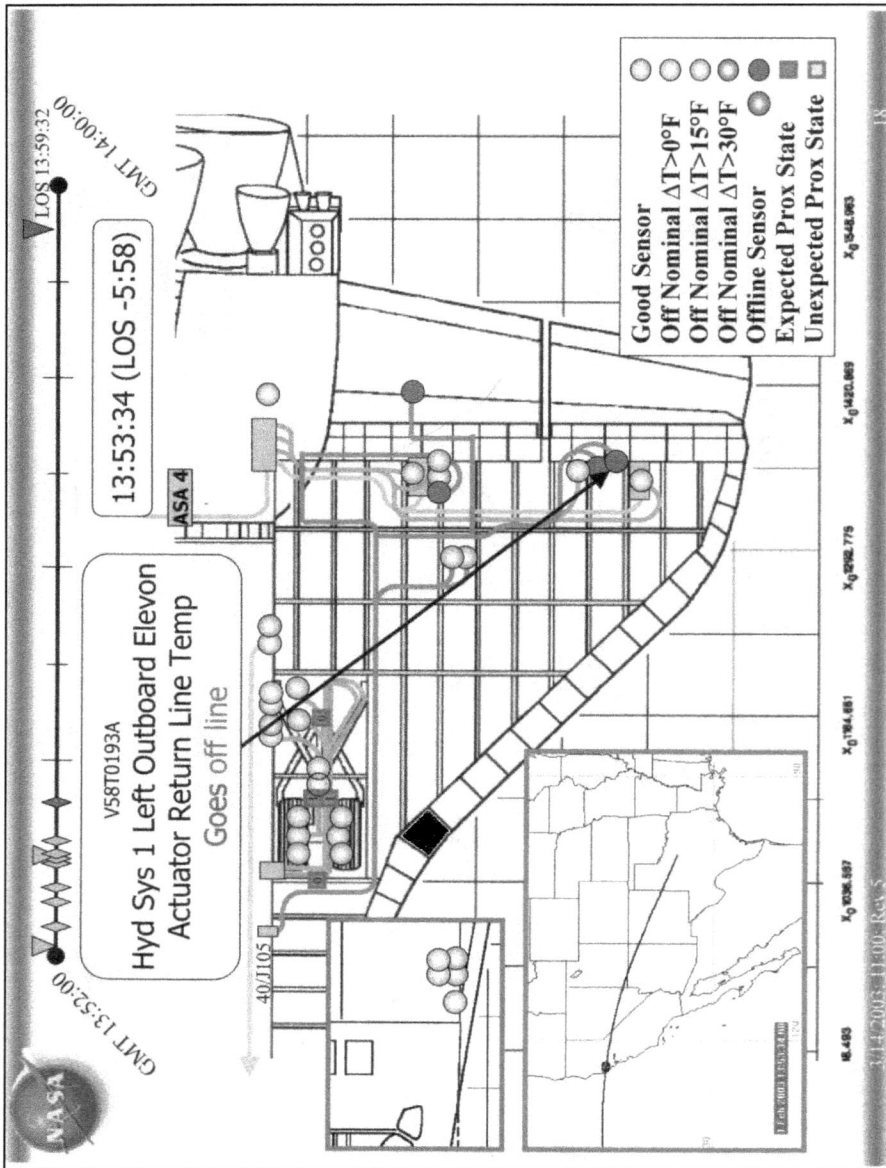

Good Sensor
Off Nominal ΔT>0°F
Off Nominal ΔT>15°F
Off Nominal ΔT>30°F
Offline Sensor
Expected Prox State
Unexpected Prox State

V58T0193A
Hyd Sys 1 Left Outboard Elevon
Actuator Return Line Temp
Goes off line

13:53:34 (LOS -5:58)

LOS 13:59:32
GMT 14:00:00

GMT 13:52:00

NASA

72

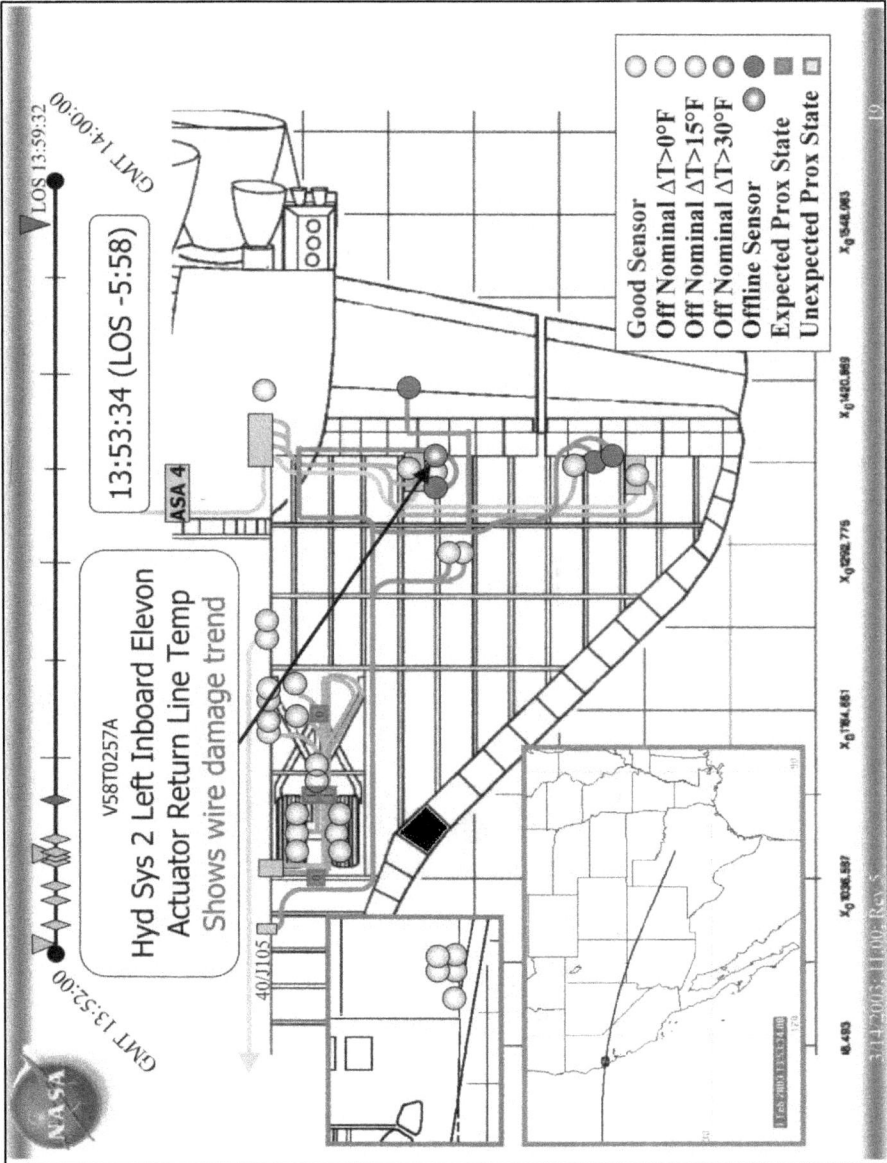

GMT 13:59:32

LOS 14:00:00

13:53:34 (LOS -5:58)

ASA 4

V58T0257A
Hyd Sys 2 Left Inboard Elevon
Actuator Return Line Temp
Shows wire damage trend

40J1105

GMT 13:52:00

Good Sensor
Off Nominal ΔT>0°F
Off Nominal ΔT>15°F
Off Nominal ΔT>30°F
Offline Sensor
Expected Prox State
Unexpected Prox State

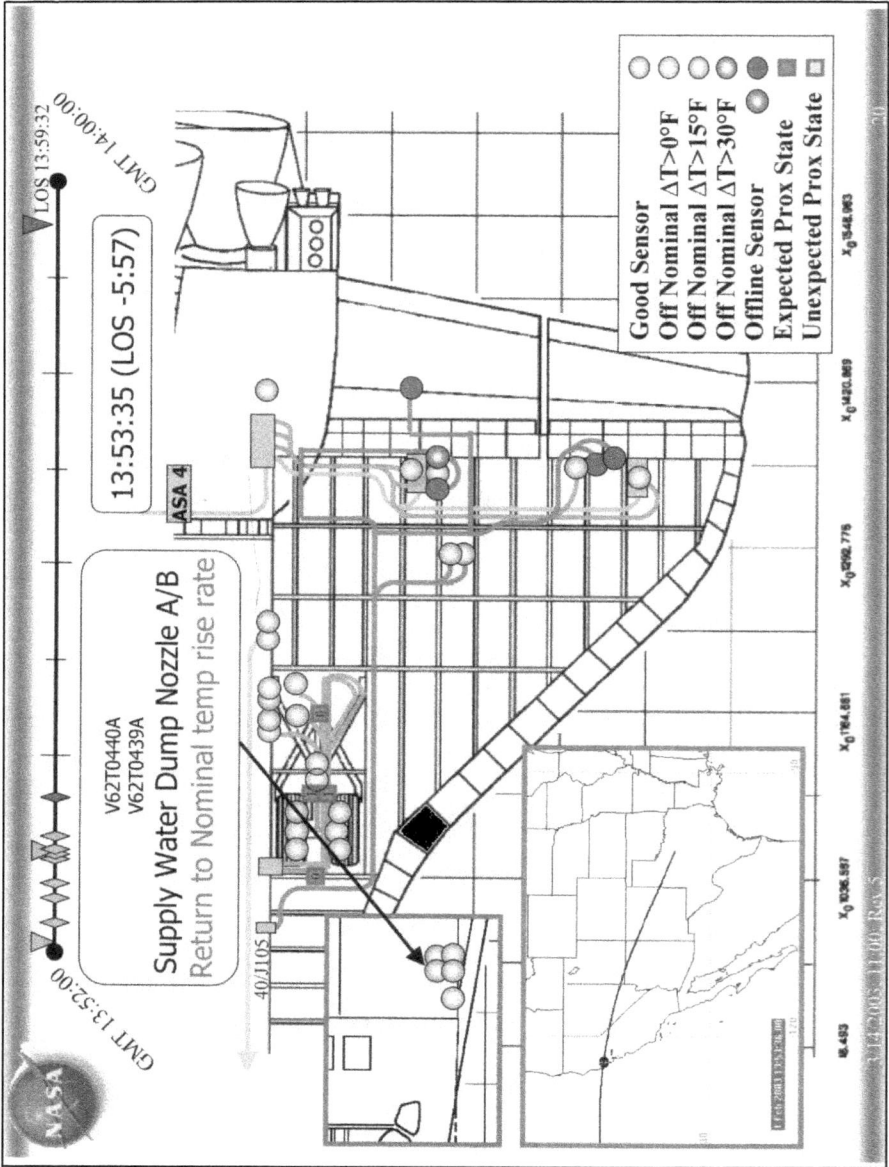

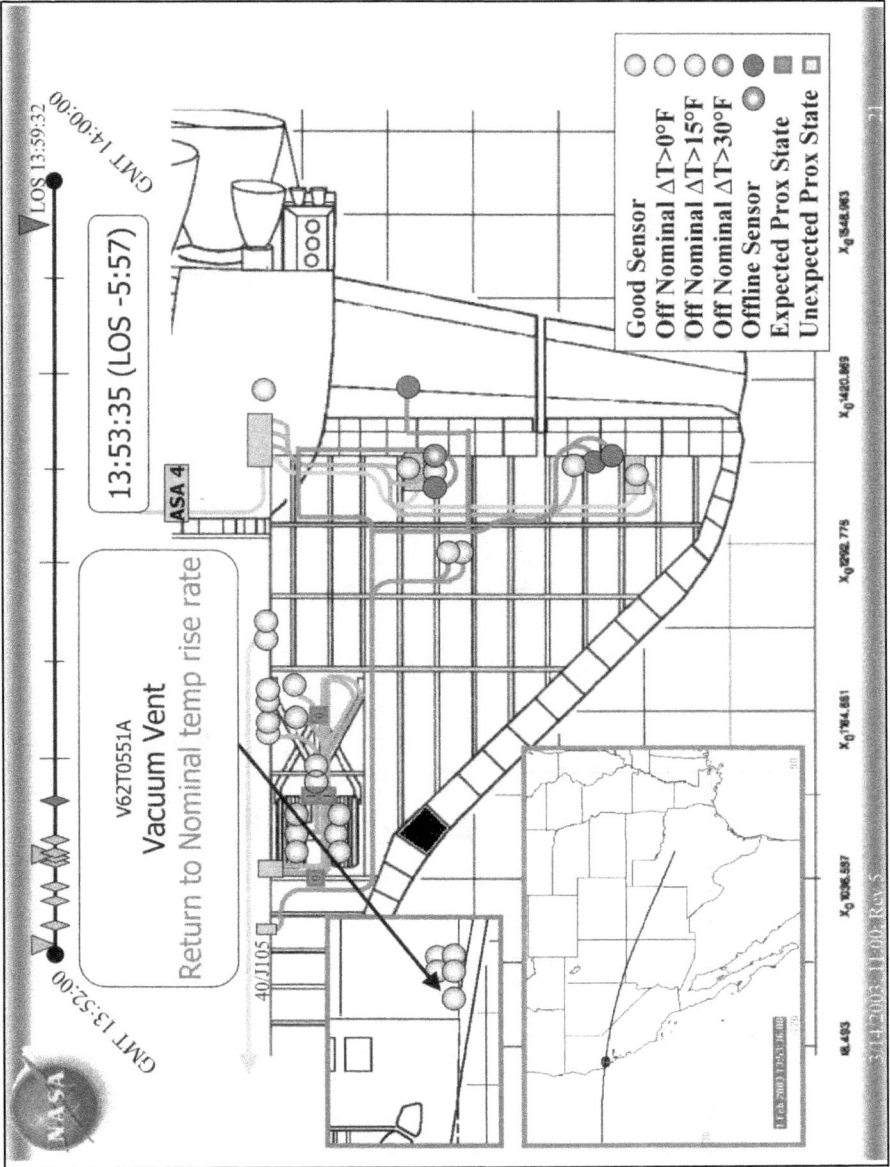

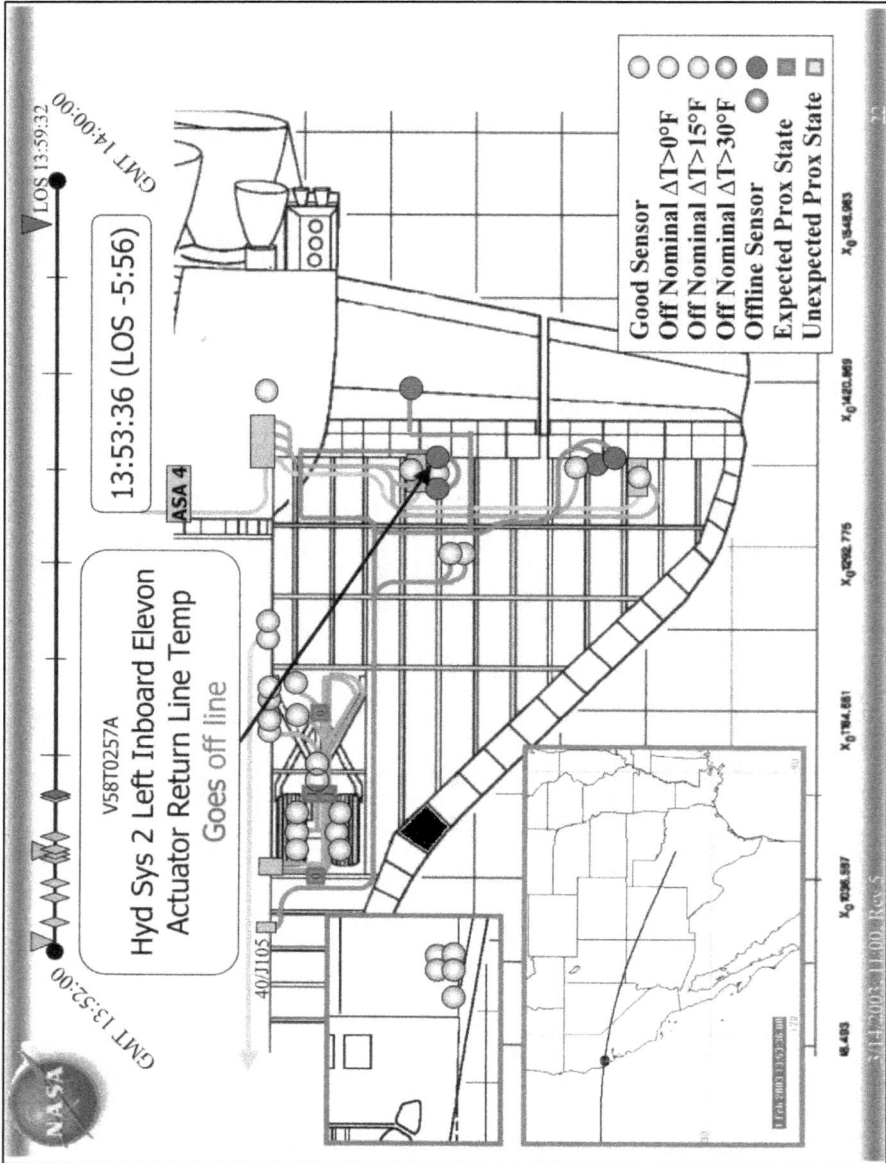

V58T0257A
Hyd Sys 2 Left Inboard Elevon
Actuator Return Line Temp
Goes off line

13:53:36 (LOS -5:56)

GMT 13:52:00
LOS 13:59:32
GMT 14:00:00

ASA 4

40/J1105

Good Sensor
Off Nominal ΔT>0°F
Off Nominal ΔT>15°F
Off Nominal ΔT>30°F
Offline Sensor
Expected Prox State
Unexpected Prox State

76

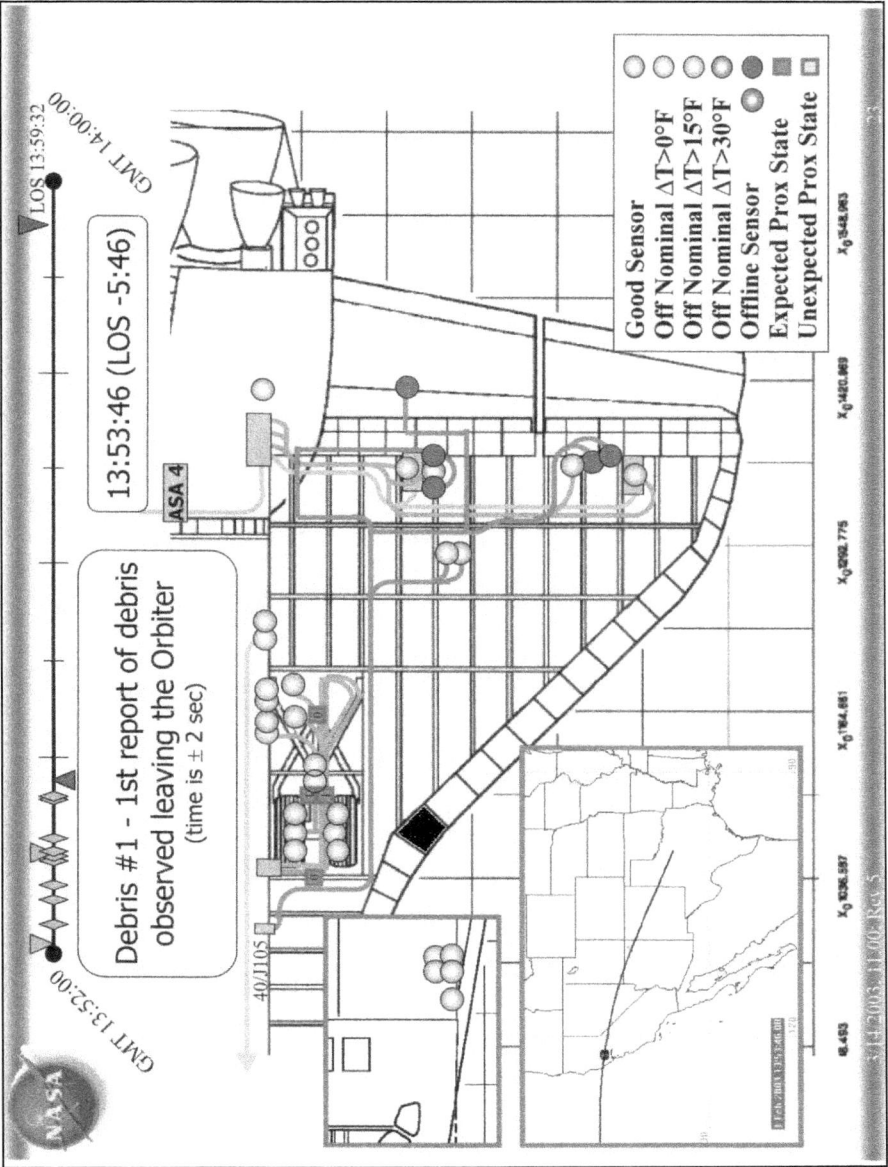

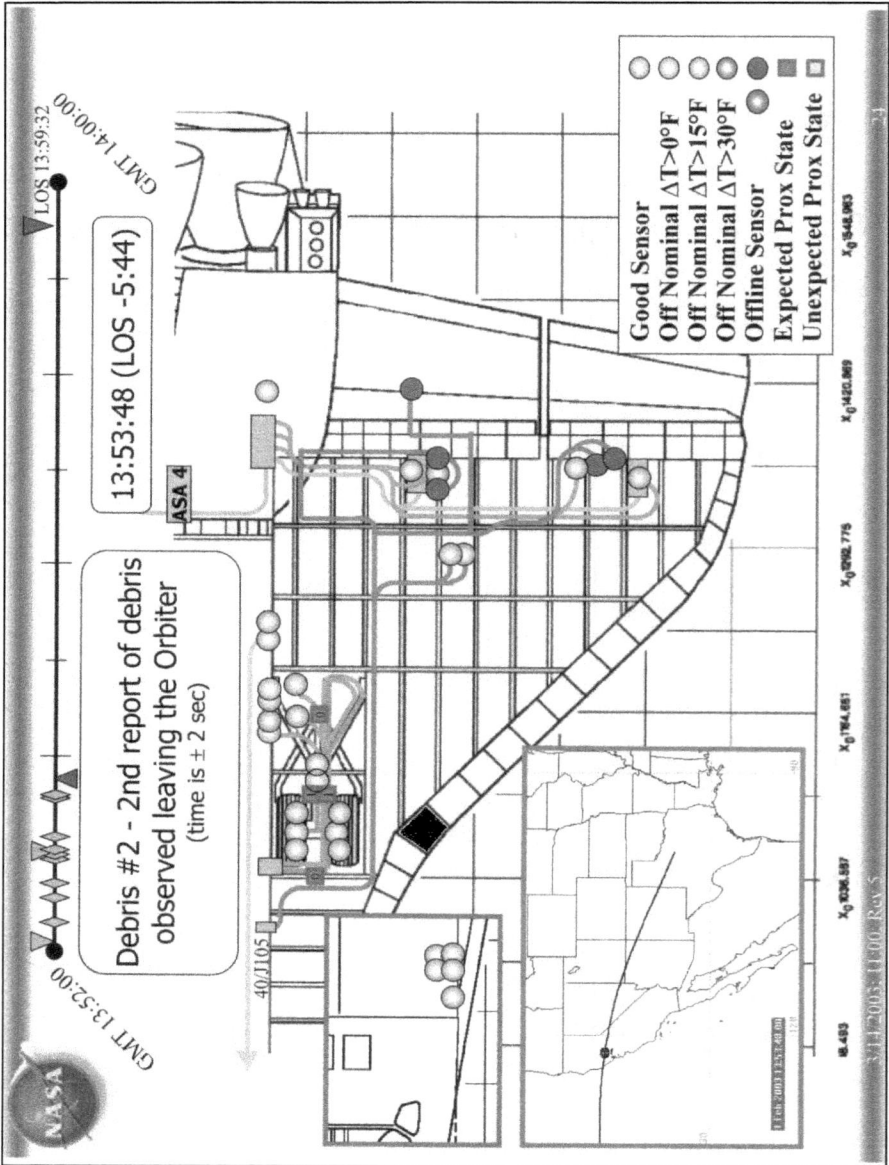

Debris #2 - 2nd report of debris
observed leaving the Orbiter
(time is ± 2 sec)

13:53:48 (LOS -5:44)

ASA 4

40/J105

LOS 13:59:32

GMT 14:00:00

GMT 13:52:00

Good Sensor
Off Nominal ΔT>0°F
Off Nominal ΔT>15°F
Off Nominal ΔT>30°F
Offline Sensor
Expected Prox State
Unexpected Prox State

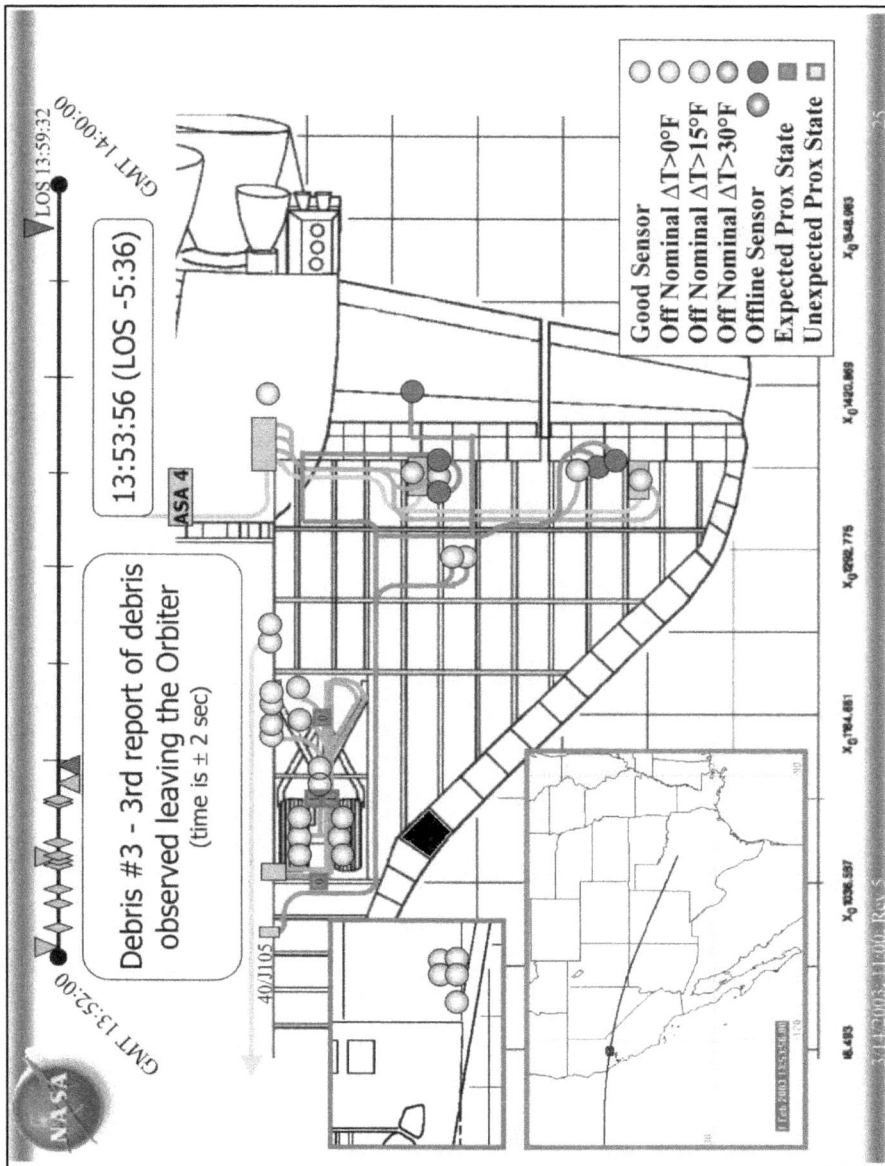

Debris #3 - 3rd report of debris observed leaving the Orbiter
(time is ± 2 sec)

13:53:56 (LOS -5:36)

GMT 13:52:00

GMT 13:59:32 LOS

GMT 14:00:00

ASA 4

40/J105

Good Sensor
Off Nominal ΔT>0°F
Off Nominal ΔT>15°F
Off Nominal ΔT>30°F
Offline Sensor
Expected Prox State
Unexpected Prox State

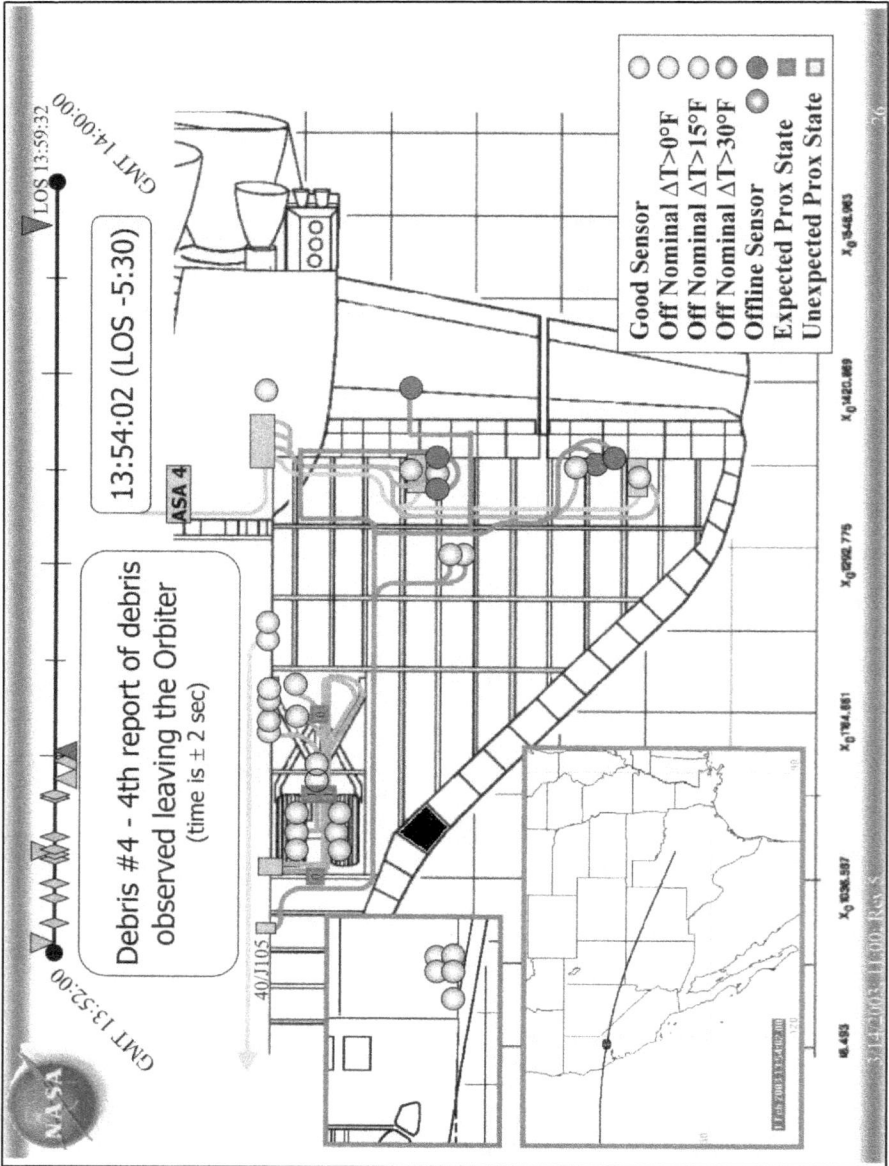

Debris #4 - 4th report of debris observed leaving the Orbiter
(time is ± 2 sec)

13:54:02 (LOS -5:30)

GMT 13:52:00

GMT 14:00:00

LOS 13:59:32

ASA 4

40/1105

Good Sensor
Off Nominal $\Delta T>0°F$
Off Nominal $\Delta T>15°F$
Off Nominal $\Delta T>30°F$
Offline Sensor
Expected Prox State
Unexpected Prox State

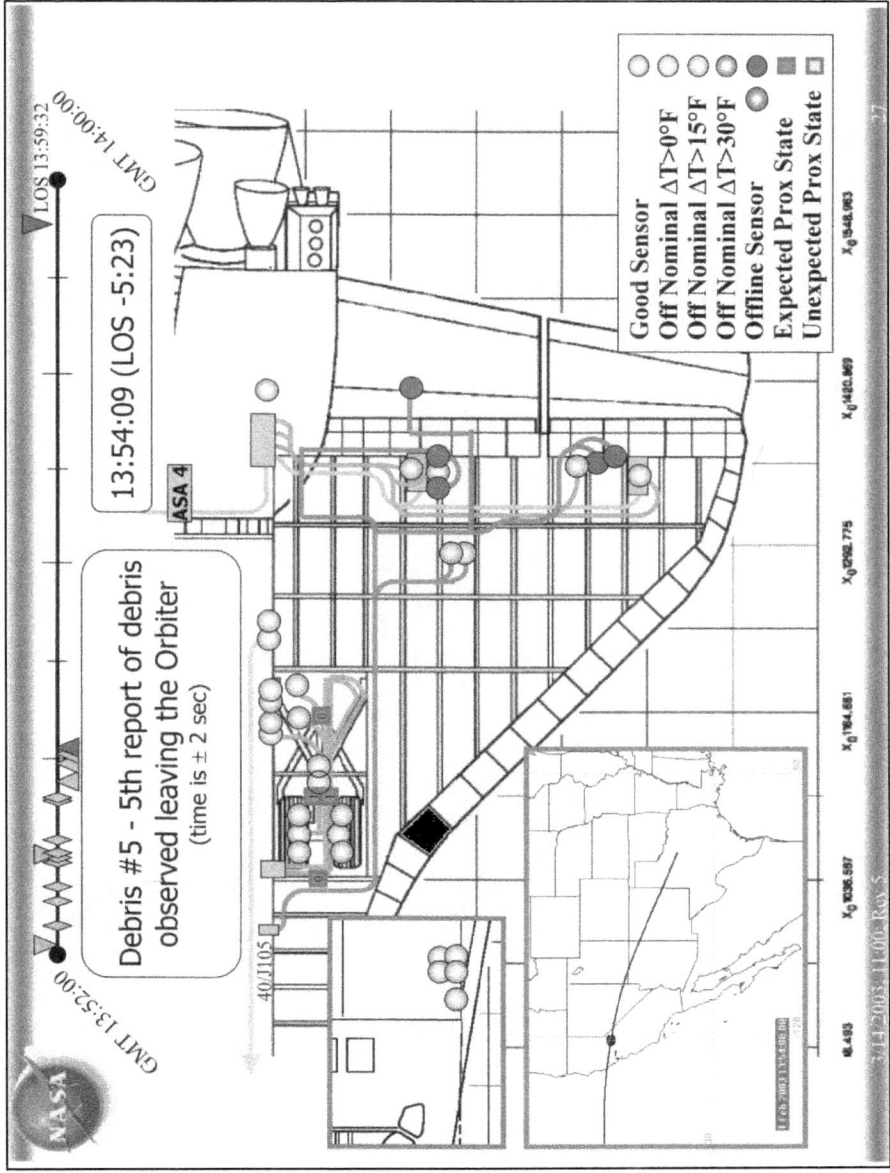

Debris #5 - 5th report of debris observed leaving the Orbiter
(time is ± 2 sec)

13:54:09 (LOS -5:23)

GMT 13:52:00

GMT 14:00:00

LOS 13:59:32

Legend:
- Good Sensor
- Off Nominal $\Delta T > 0°F$
- Off Nominal $\Delta T > 15°F$
- Off Nominal $\Delta T > 30°F$
- Offline Sensor
- Expected Prox State
- Unexpected Prox State

ASA 4

40/J1105

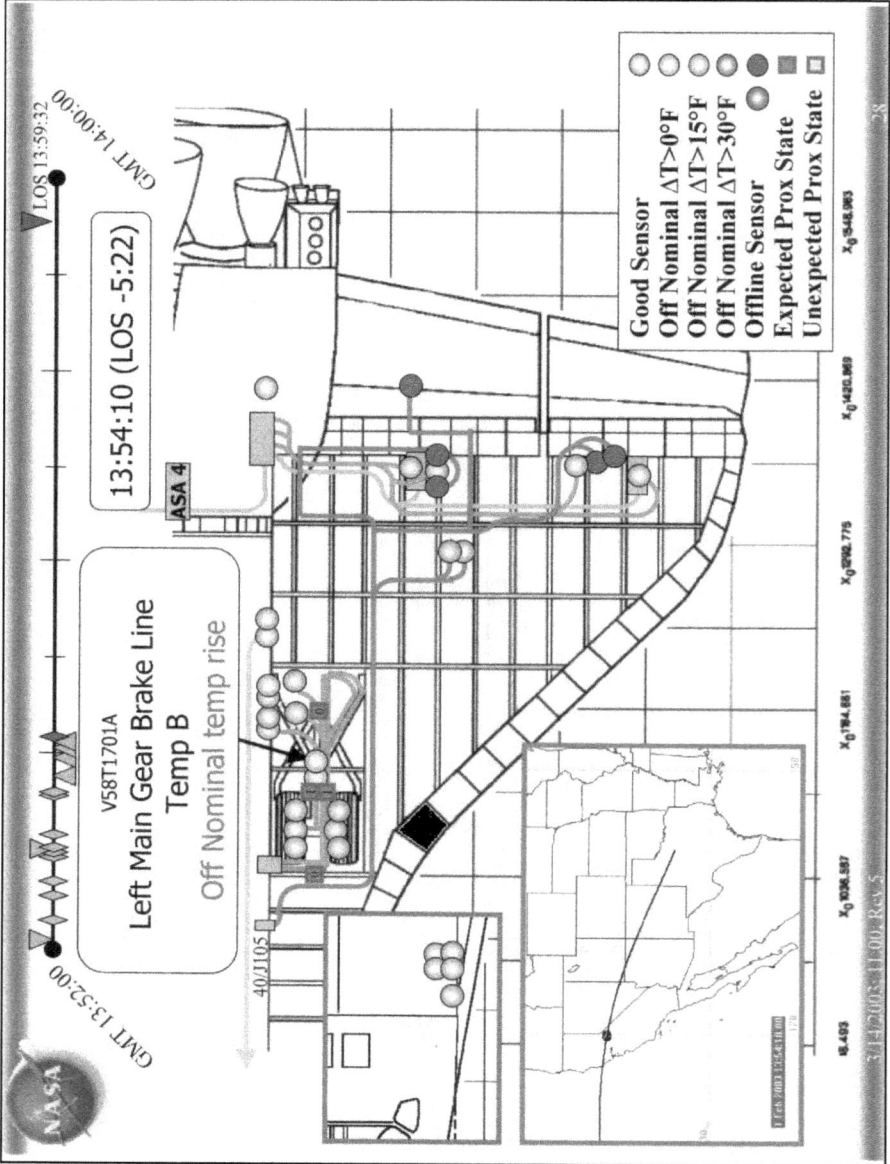

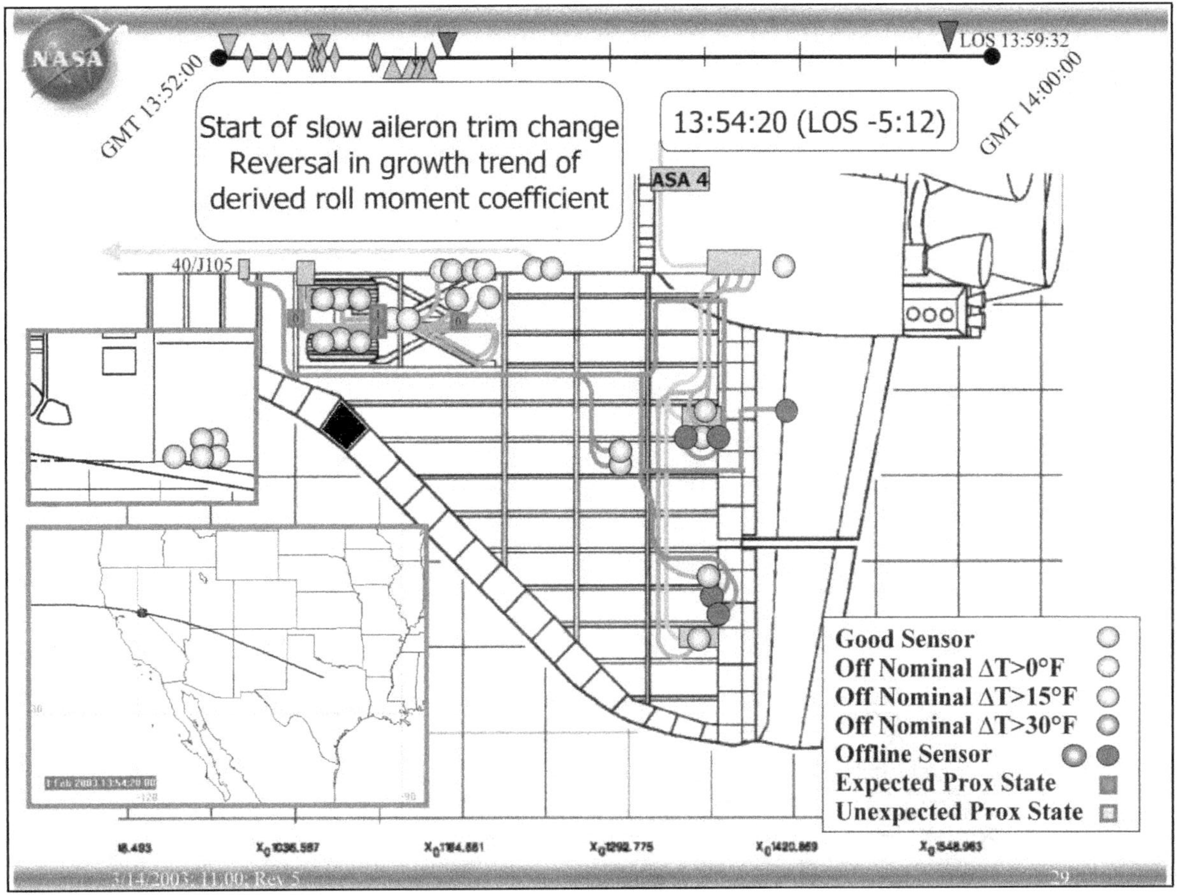
GMT 13:52:00
LOS 13:59:32
GMT 14:00:00
Start of slow aileron trim change
Reversal in growth trend of
derived roll moment coefficient
13:54:20 (LOS -5:12)
ASA 4
40/J105
Good Sensor
Off Nominal ΔT>0°F
Off Nominal ΔT>15°F
Off Nominal ΔT>30°F
Offline Sensor
Expected Prox State
Unexpected Prox State
3/14/2003: 11:00: Rev 5
29

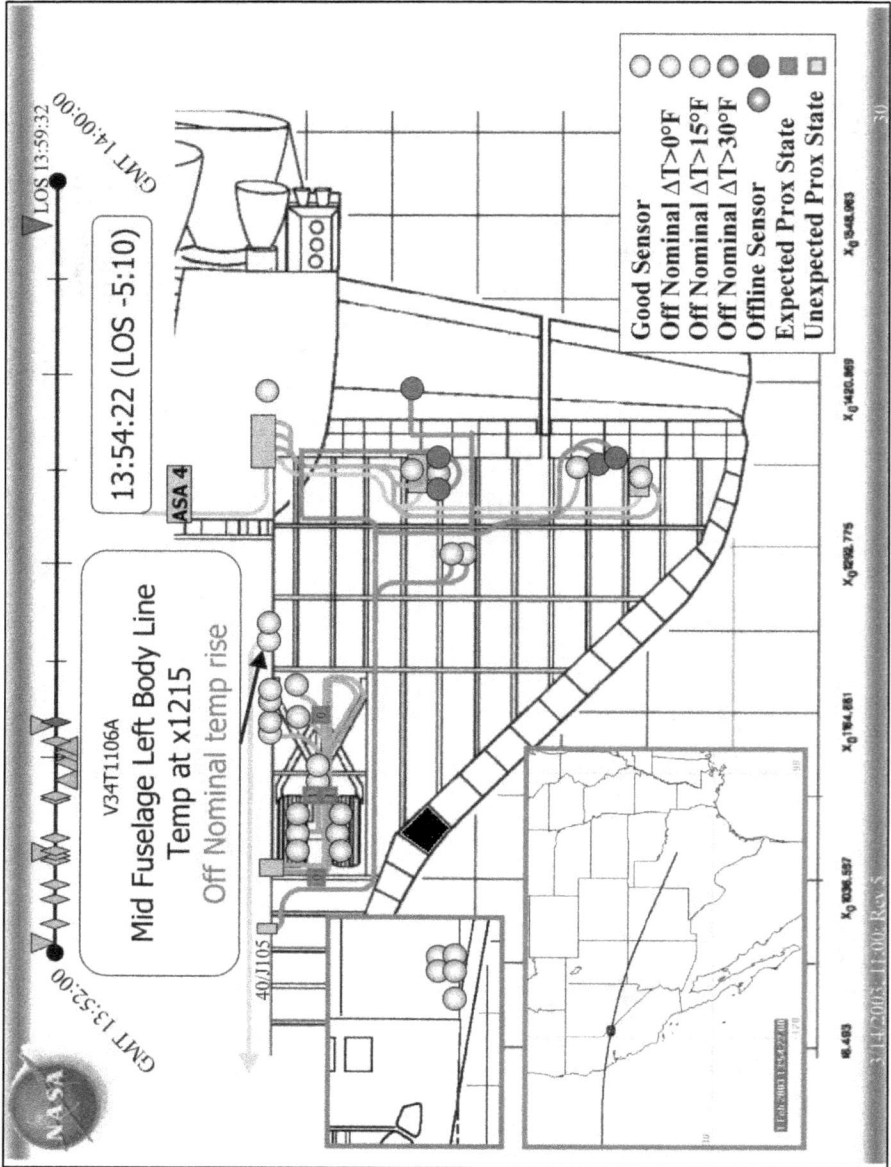

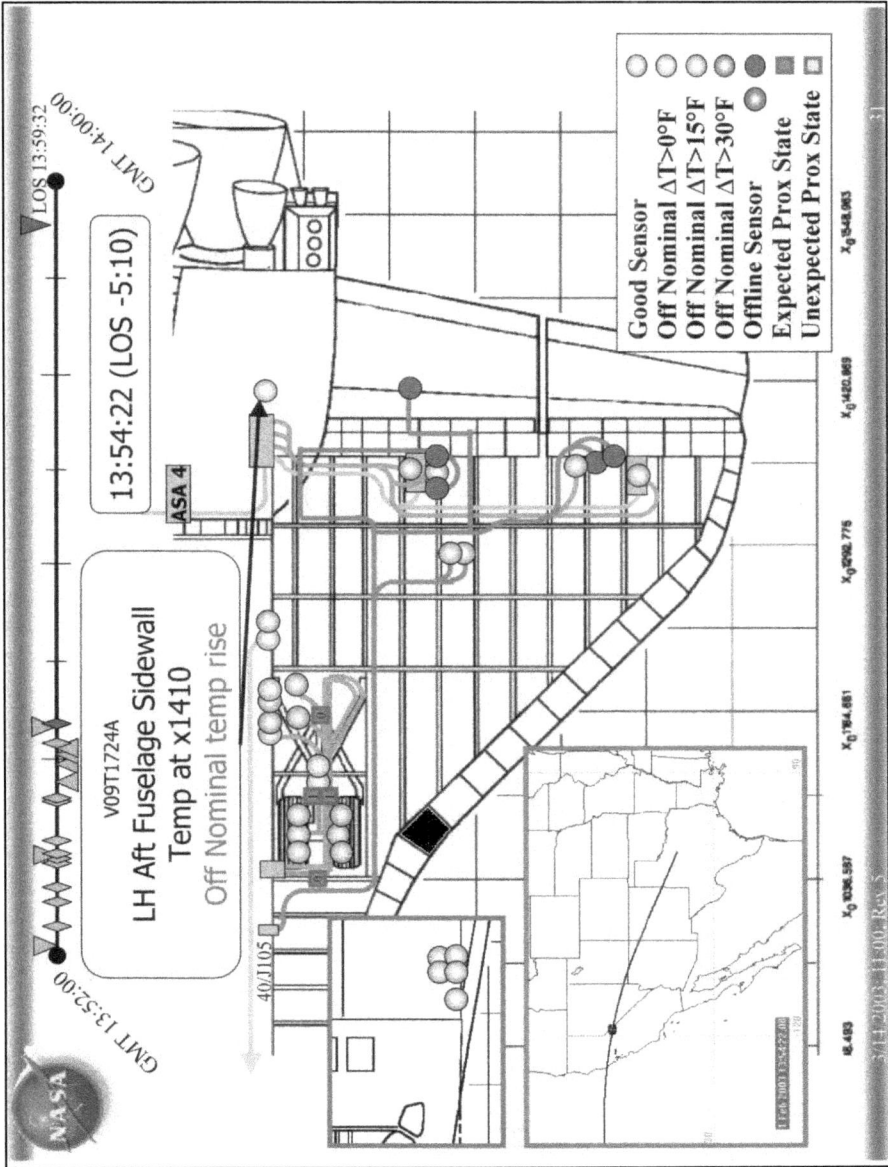

LOS 13:59:32

GMT 14:00:00

13:54:22 (LOS -5:10)

V09T1724A
LH Aft Fuselage Sidewall
Temp at x1410
Off Nominal temp rise

ASA 4

40/J1J05

GMT 13:52:00

Good Sensor
Off Nominal ΔT>0°F
Off Nominal ΔT>15°F
Off Nominal ΔT>30°F
Offline Sensor
Expected Prox State
Unexpected Prox State

NASA

85

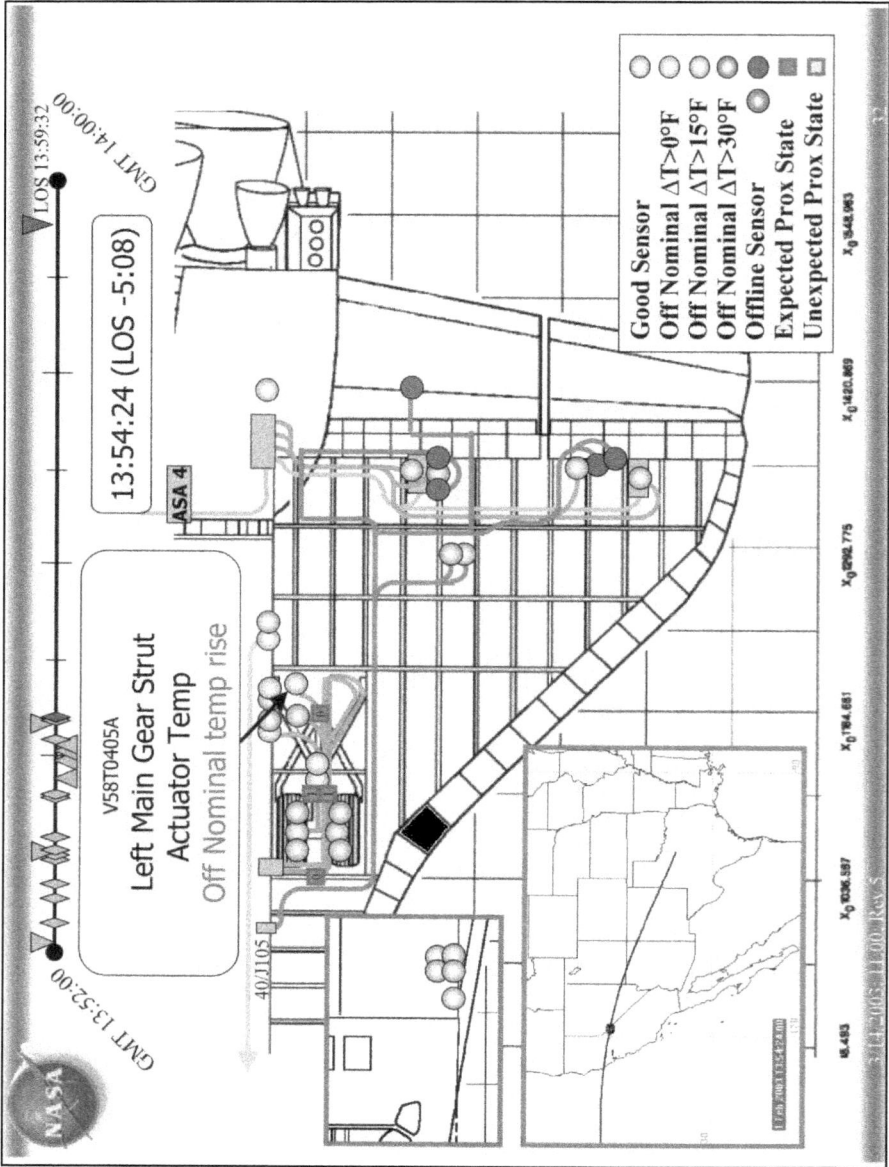

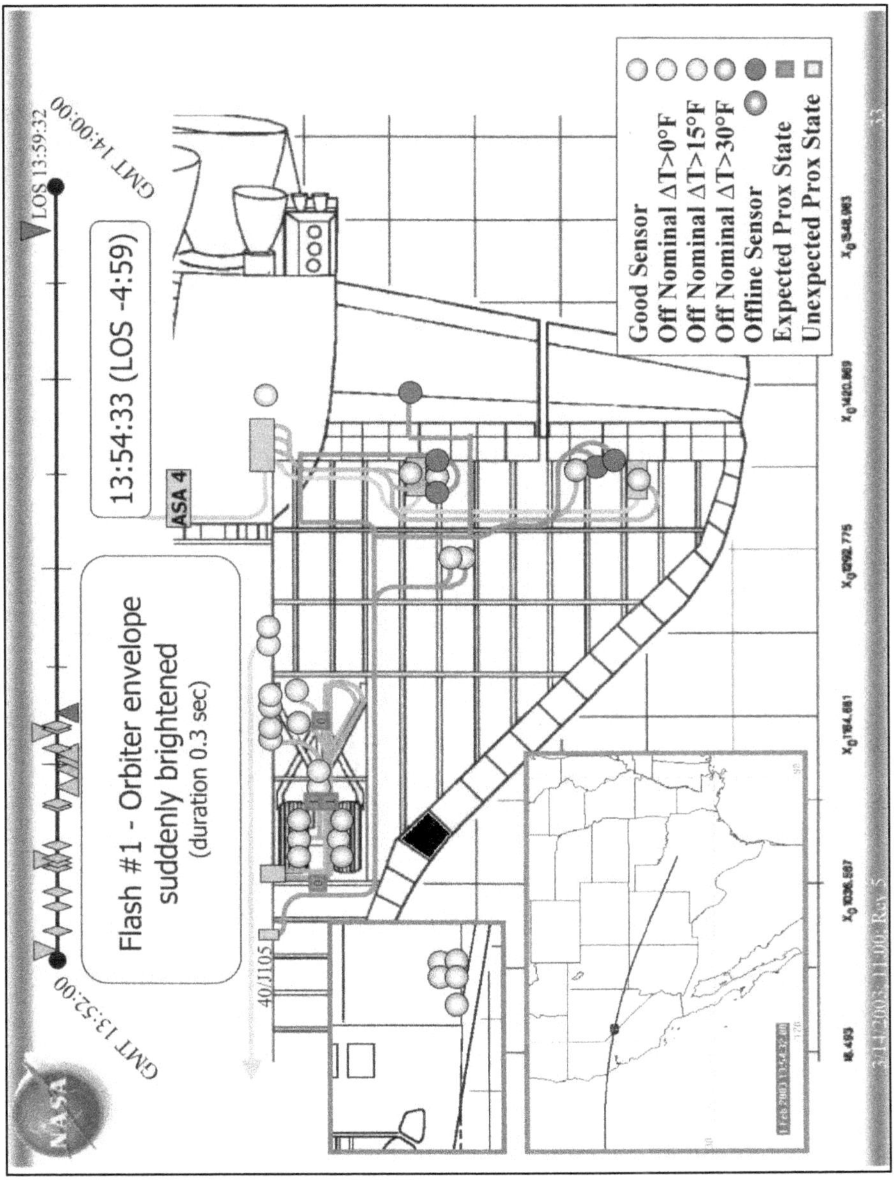

GMT 13:52:00
GMT 14:00:00
LOS 13:59:32
Flash #1 - Orbiter envelope suddenly brightened
(duration 0.3 sec)
13:54:33 (LOS -4:59)
ASA 4
40/J105
Good Sensor
Off Nominal ΔT>0°F
Off Nominal ΔT>15°F
Off Nominal ΔT>30°F
Offline Sensor
Expected Prox State
Unexpected Prox State

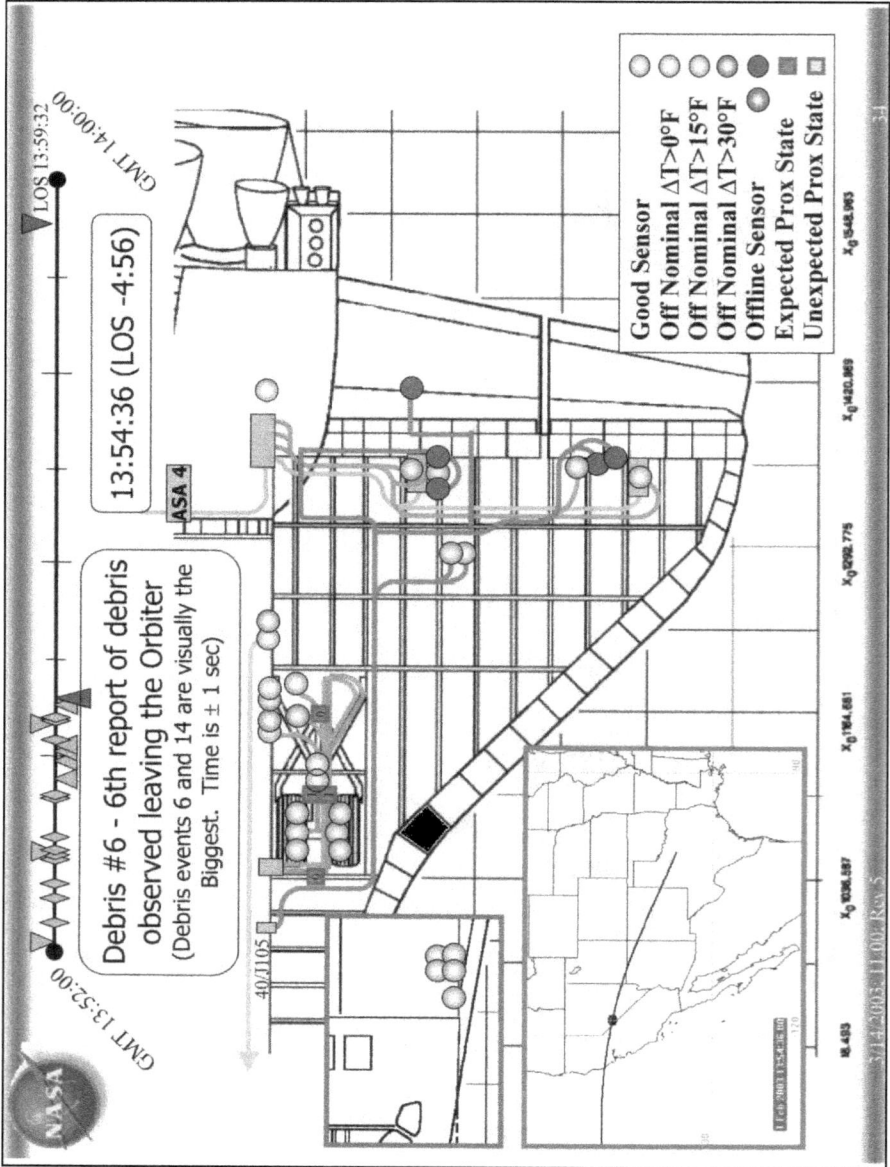

Debris #6 - 6th report of debris observed leaving the Orbiter
(Debris events 6 and 14 are visually the Biggest. Time is ± 1 sec)

13:54:36 (LOS -4:56)

GMT 13:52:00

GMT 14:00:00

LOS 13:59:32

ASA 4

40J1105

Good Sensor
Off Nominal ΔT>0°F
Off Nominal ΔT>15°F
Off Nominal ΔT>30°F
Offline Sensor
Expected Prox State
Unexpected Prox State

X_o548.985

X_o420.969

X_o292.775

X_o164.681

X_o036.587

88

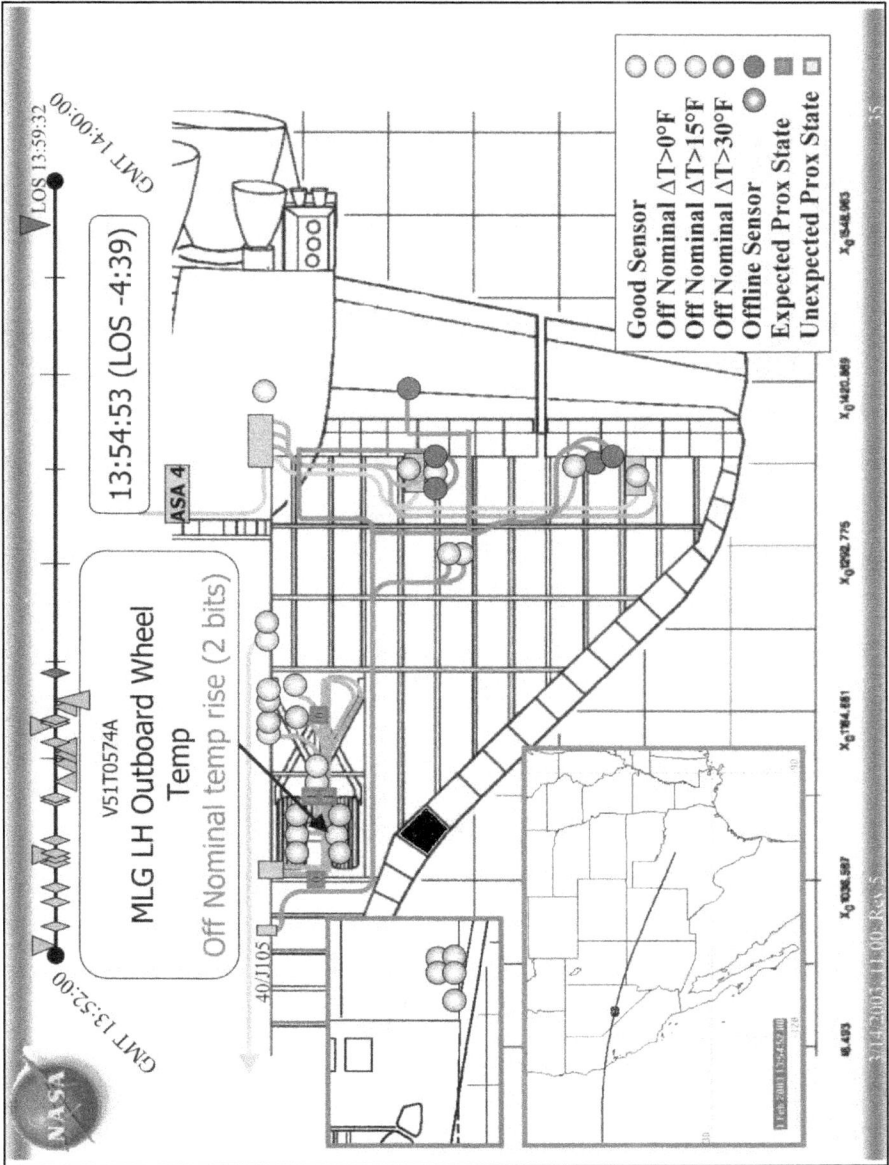

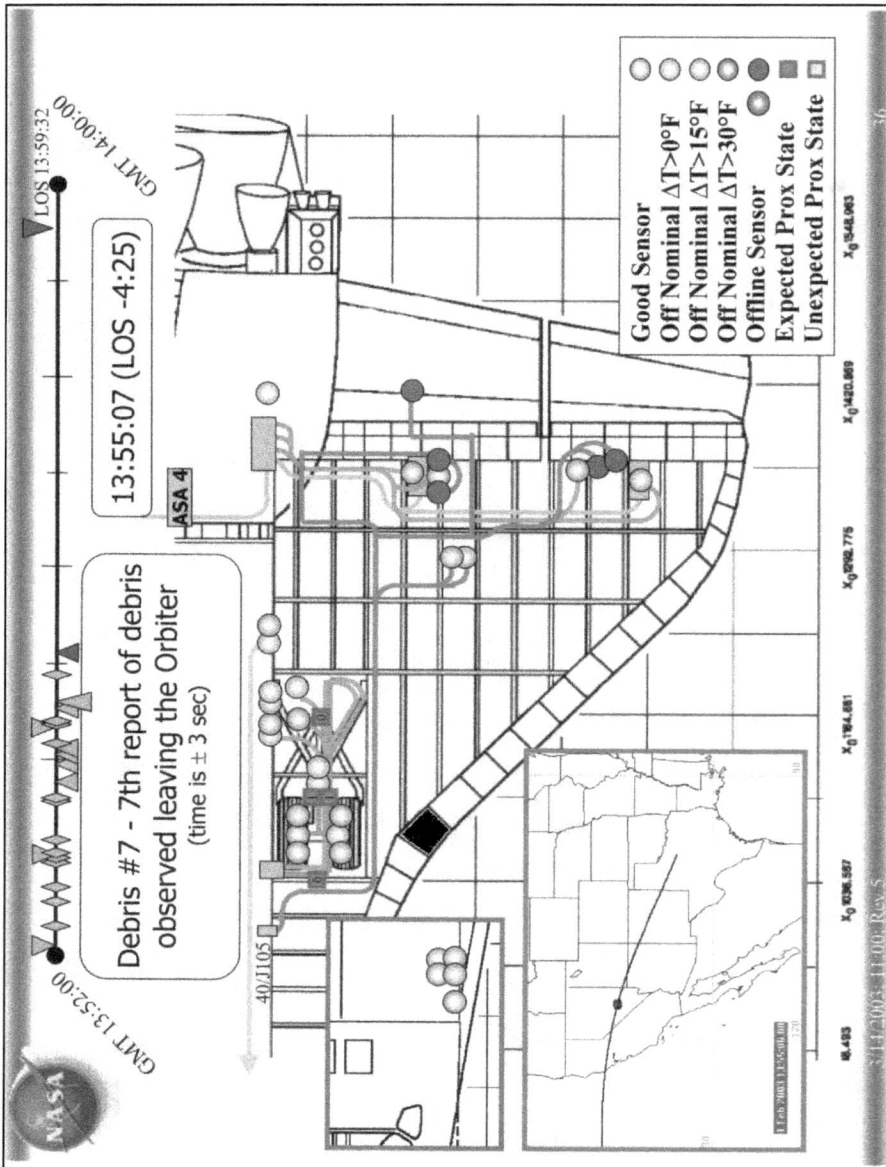

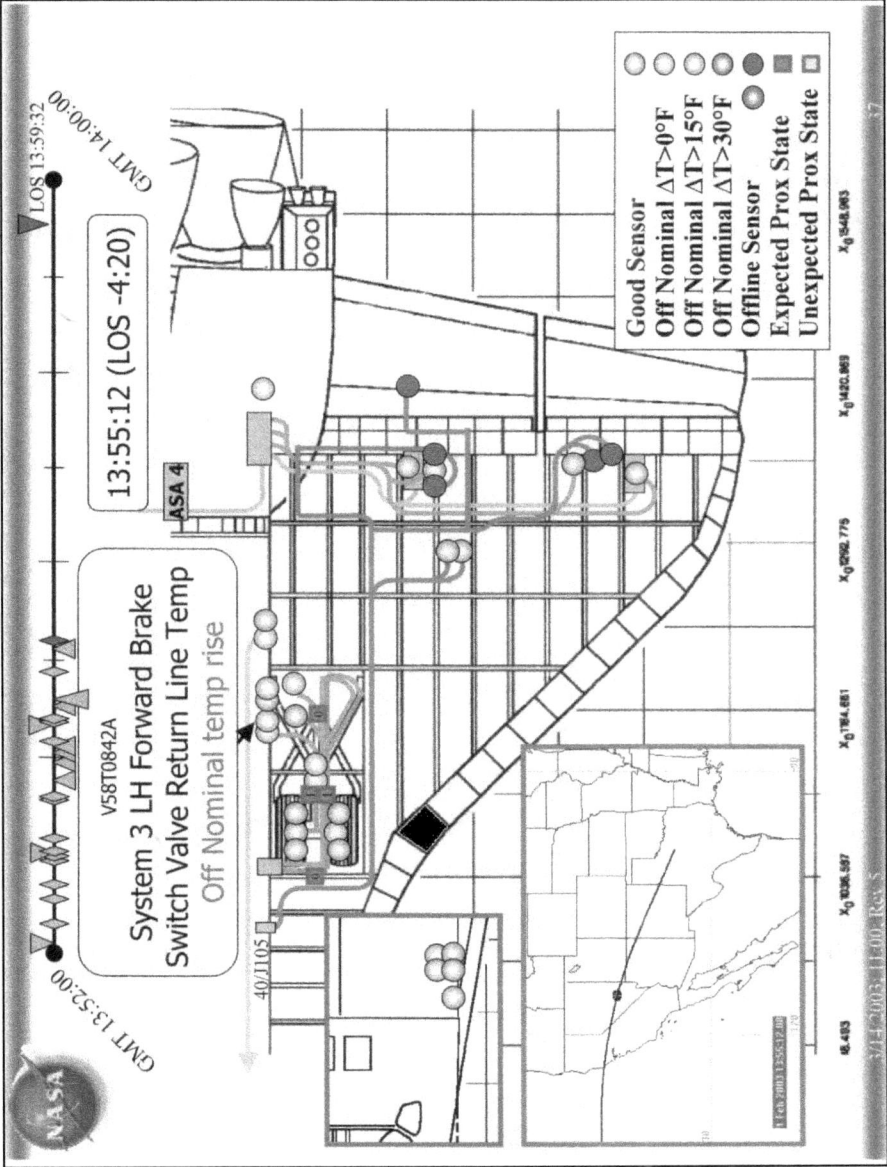

System 3 LH Forward Brake
Switch Valve Return Line Temp
Off Nominal temp rise

V58T0842A

13:55:12 (LOS -4:20)

ASA 4

40/1105

LOS 13:59:32
GMT 14:00:00
GMT 13:52:00

Good Sensor
Off Nominal ΔT>0°F
Off Nominal ΔT>15°F
Off Nominal ΔT>30°F
Offline Sensor
Expected Prox State
Unexpected Prox State

$X_0$548.983
$X_0$1420.863
$X_0$1292.775
$X_0$1164.681
$X_0$1036.597
48.483

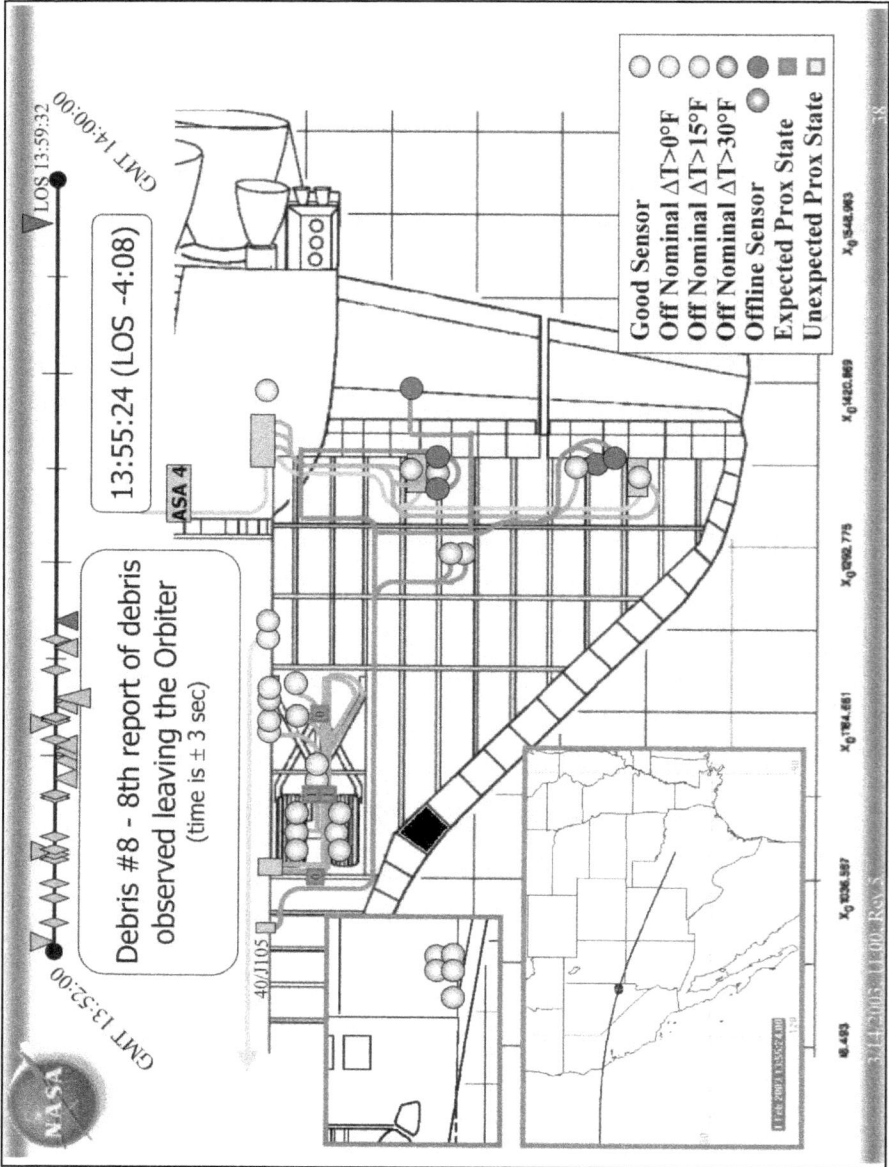

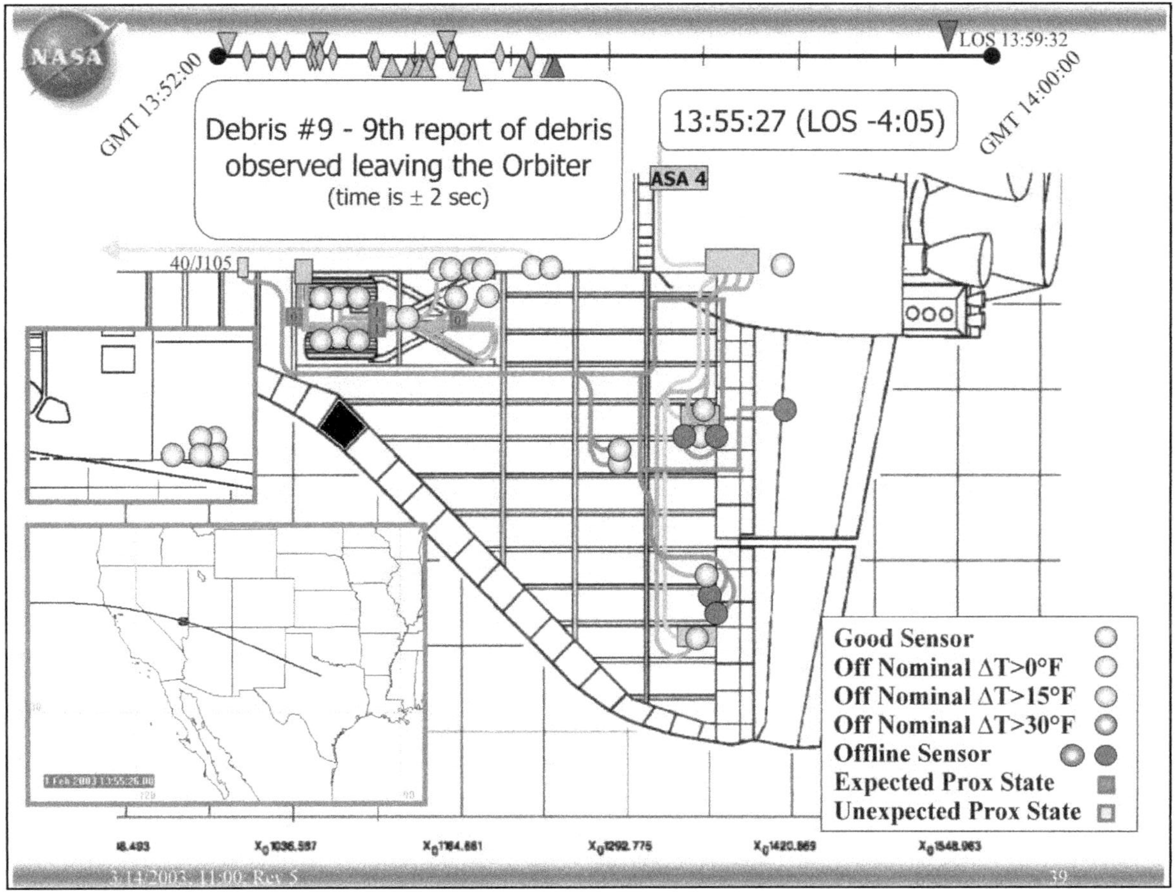

Debris #9 - 9th report of debris observed leaving the Orbiter
(time is ± 2 sec)

13:55:27 (LOS -4:05)

GMT 14:00:00
LOS 13:59:32

GMT 13:52:00

Good Sensor
Off Nominal ΔT>0°F
Off Nominal ΔT>15°F
Off Nominal ΔT>30°F
Offline Sensor
Expected Prox State
Unexpected Prox State

ASA 4

40/1105

NASA

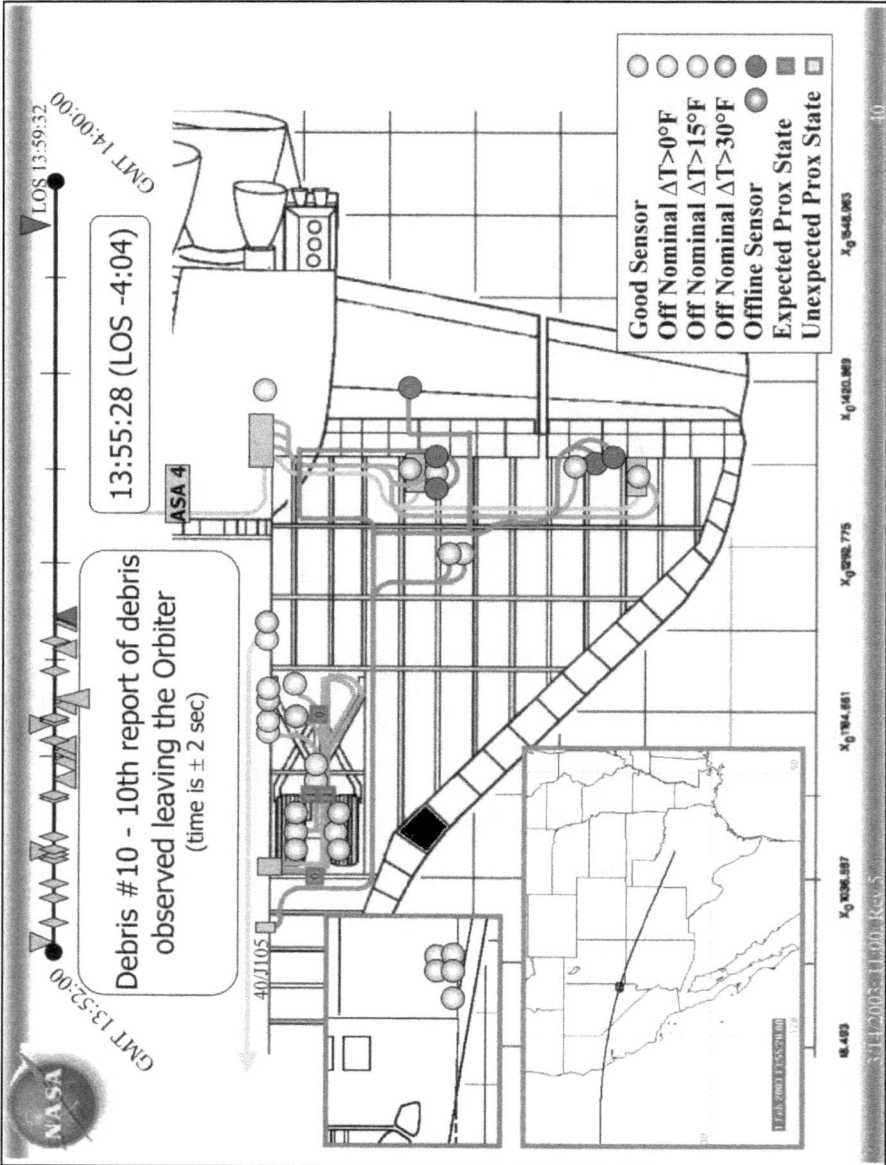

94

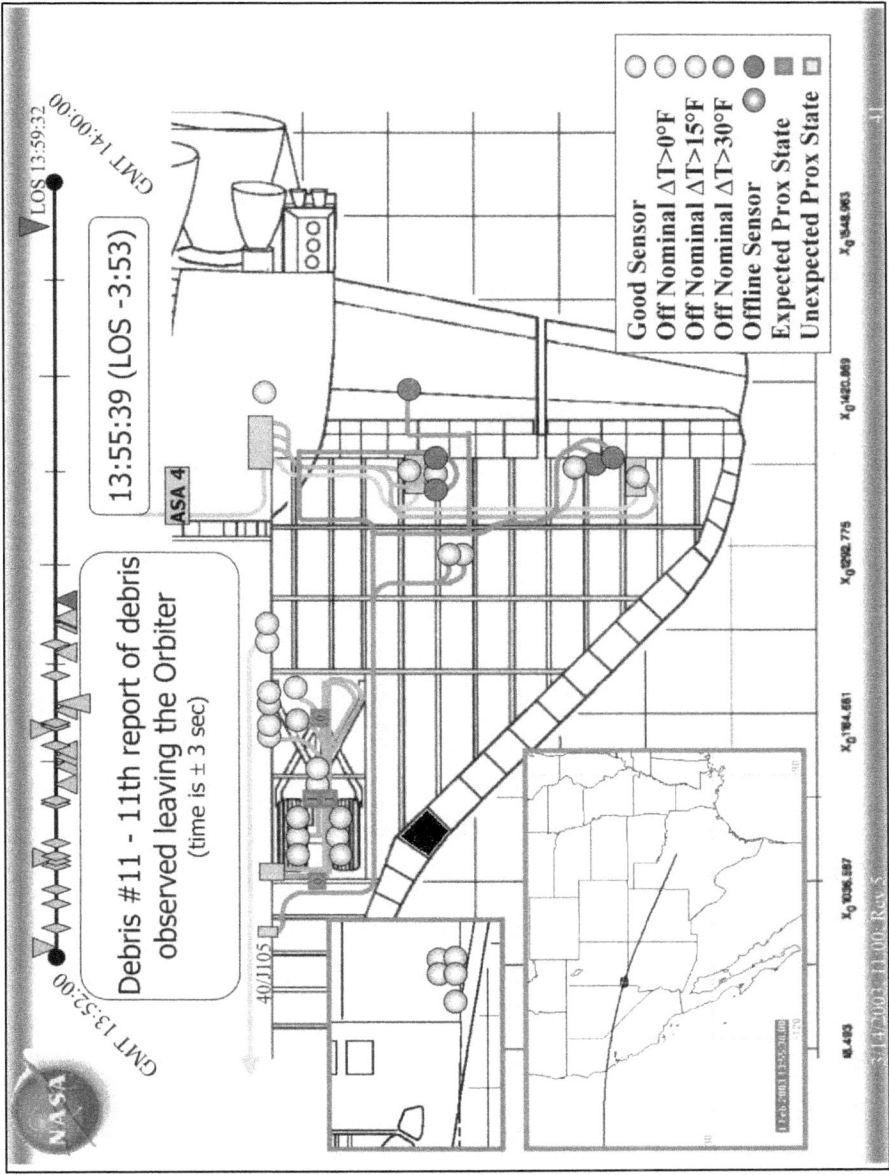

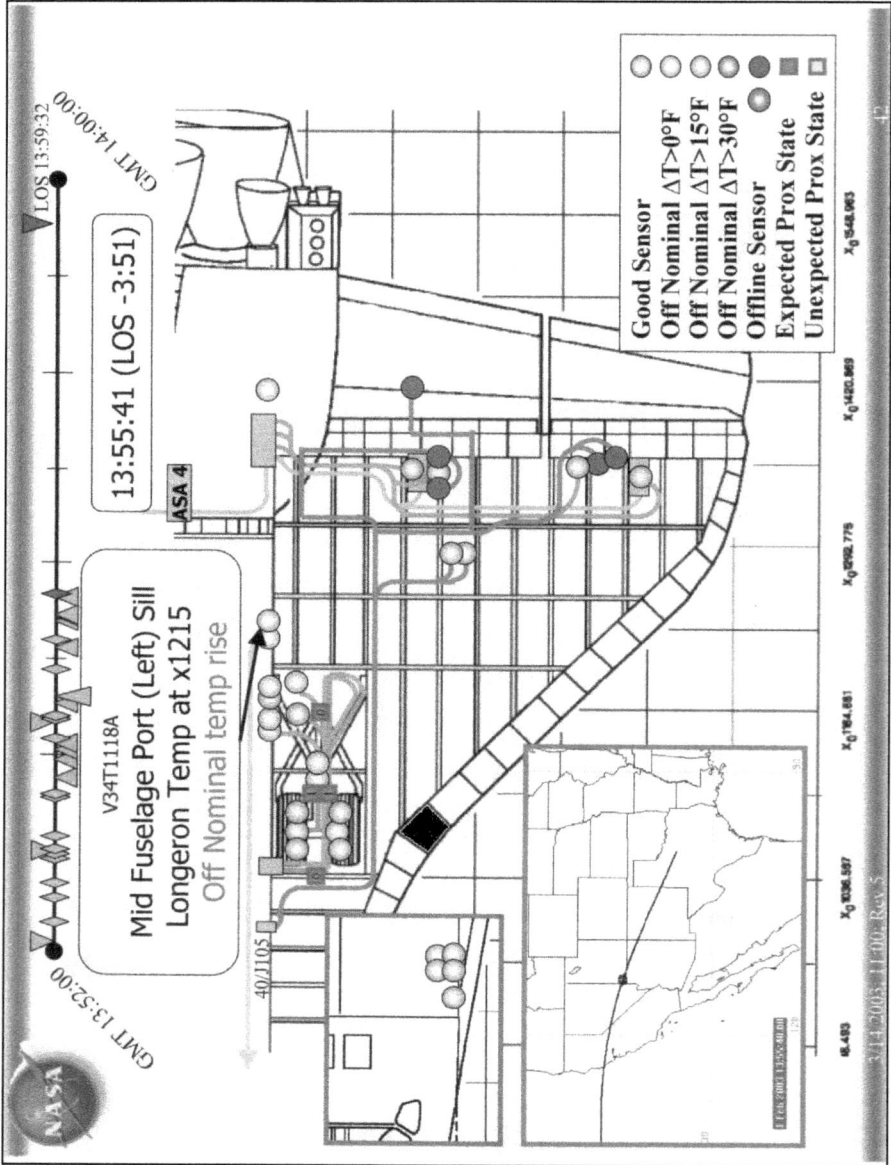

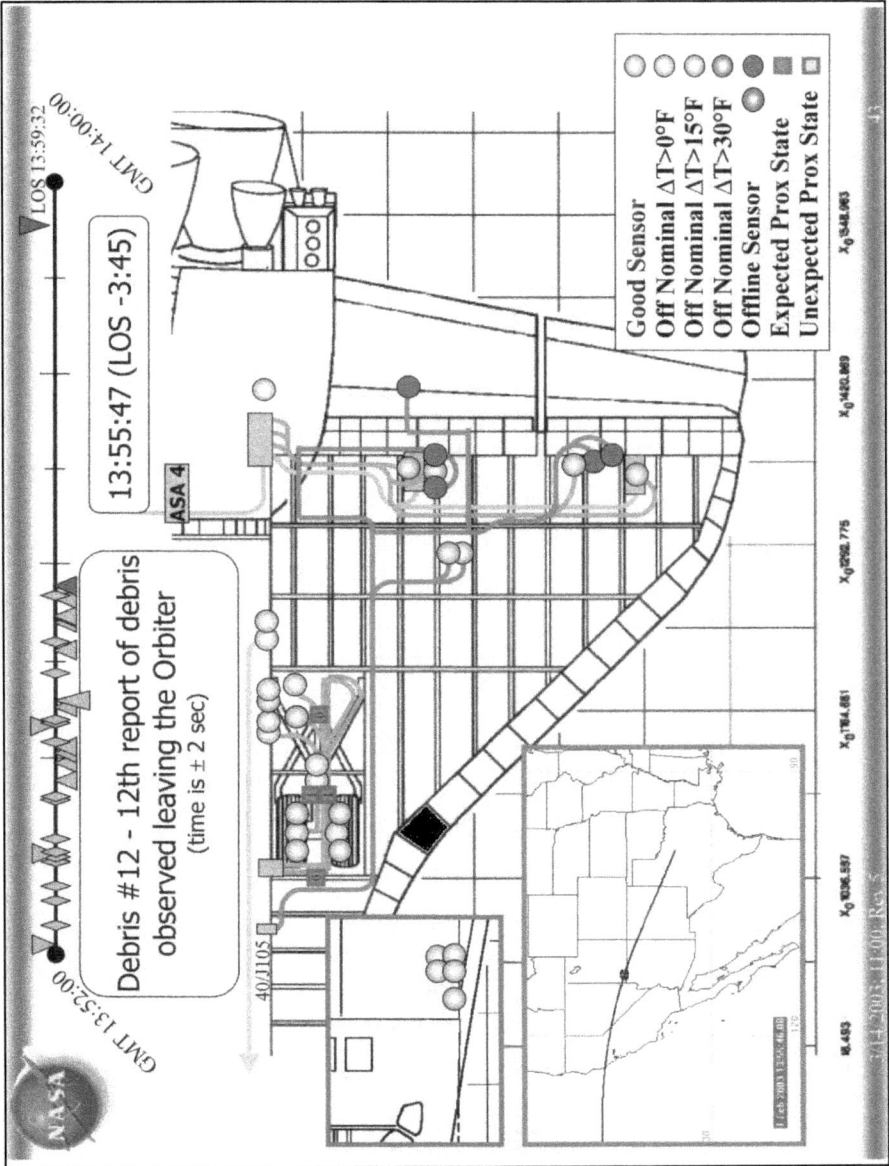

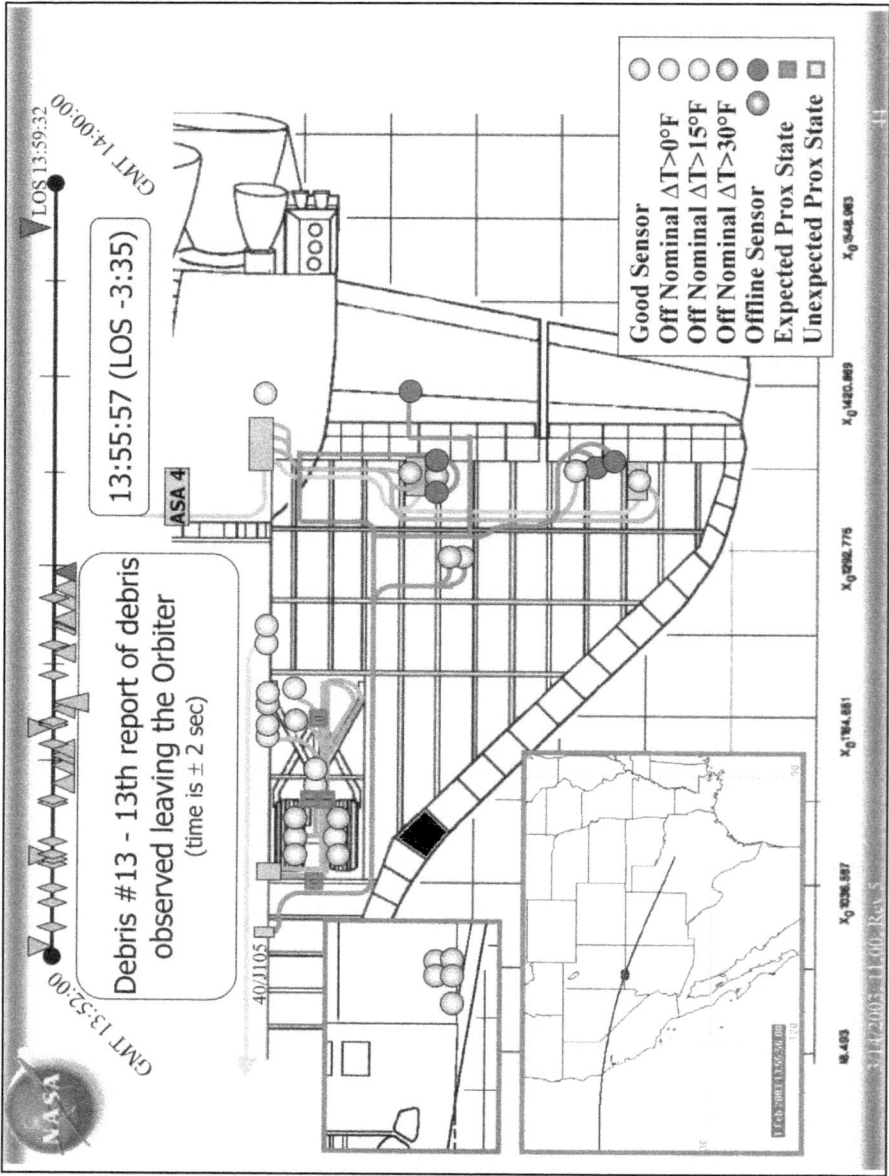

Debris #13 - 13th report of debris observed leaving the Orbiter
(time is ± 2 sec)

13:55:57 (LOS -3:35)

ASA 4

LOS 13:59:32

GMT 14:00:00

GMT 13:52:00

Good Sensor
Off Nominal ΔT>0°F
Off Nominal ΔT>15°F
Off Nominal ΔT>30°F
Offline Sensor
Expected Prox State
Unexpected Prox State

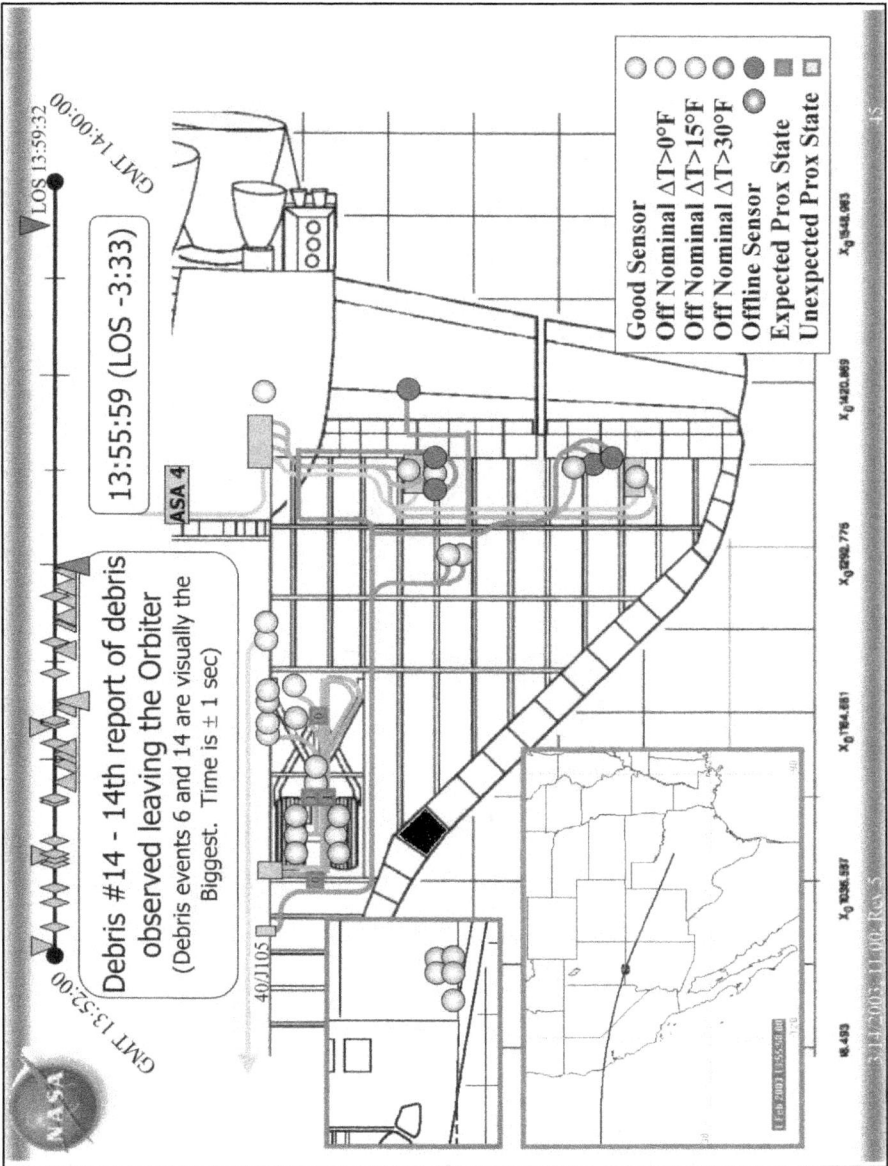

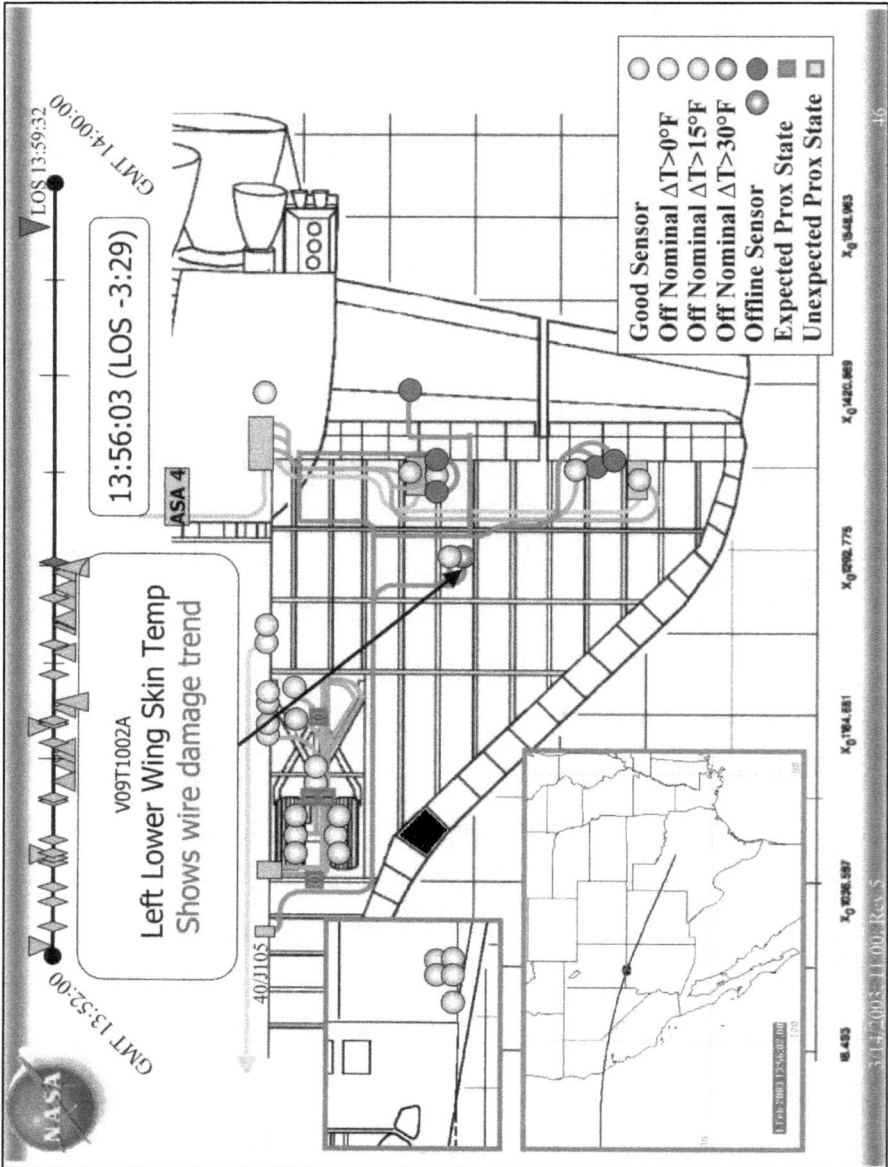

Left Lower Wing Skin Temp
Shows wire damage trend
V09T1002A

13:56:03 (LOS -3:29)

ASA 4

40/J1105

GMT 13:52:00
GMT 14:00:00
LOS 13:59:32

Good Sensor
Off Nominal ΔT>0°F
Off Nominal ΔT>15°F
Off Nominal ΔT>30°F
Offline Sensor
Expected Prox State
Unexpected Prox State

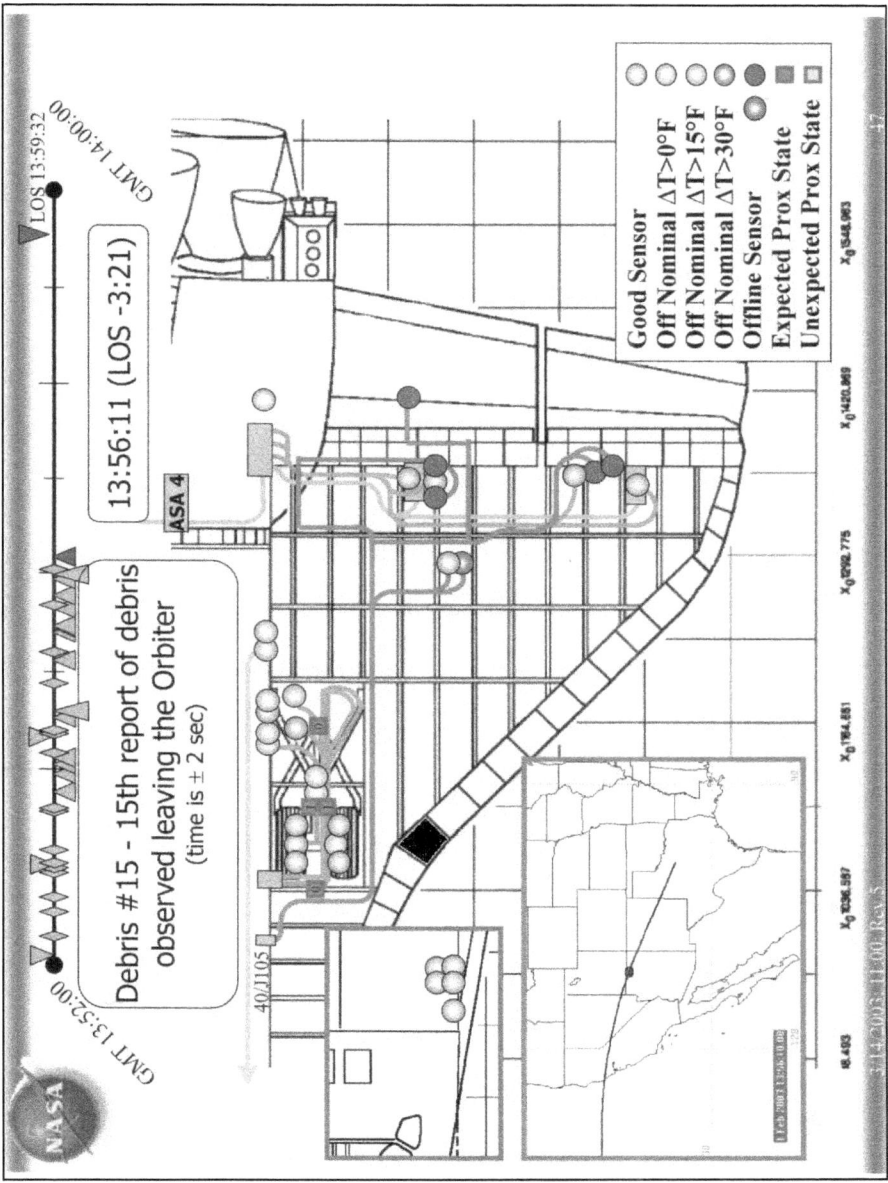

Debris #15 - 15th report of debris observed leaving the Orbiter
(time is ± 2 sec)

13:56:11 (LOS -3:21)

ASA 4

40/J105

Good Sensor
Off Nominal ΔT>0°F
Off Nominal ΔT>15°F
Off Nominal ΔT>30°F
Offline Sensor
Expected Prox State
Unexpected Prox State

LOS 13:59:32

GMT 14:00:00

GMT 13:52:00

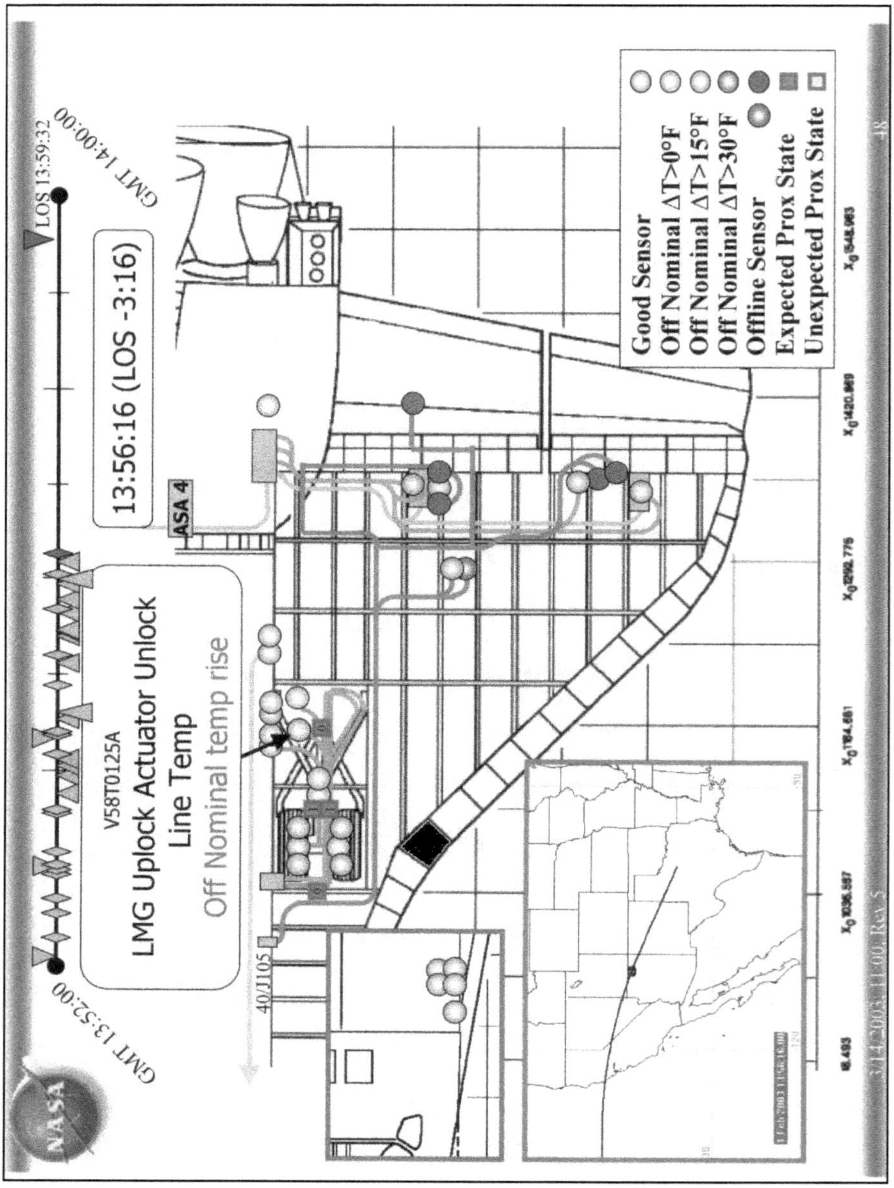
GMT 13:52:00
GMT 14:00:00
LOS 13:59:32
13:56:16 (LOS -3:16)
V58T0125A
LMG Uplock Actuator Unlock
Line Temp
Off Nominal temp rise
ASA 4
40/J105
Good Sensor
Off Nominal ΔT>0°F
Off Nominal ΔT>15°F
Off Nominal ΔT>30°F
Offline Sensor
Expected Prox State
Unexpected Prox State
3/14/2003, 11:00, Rev 5
48

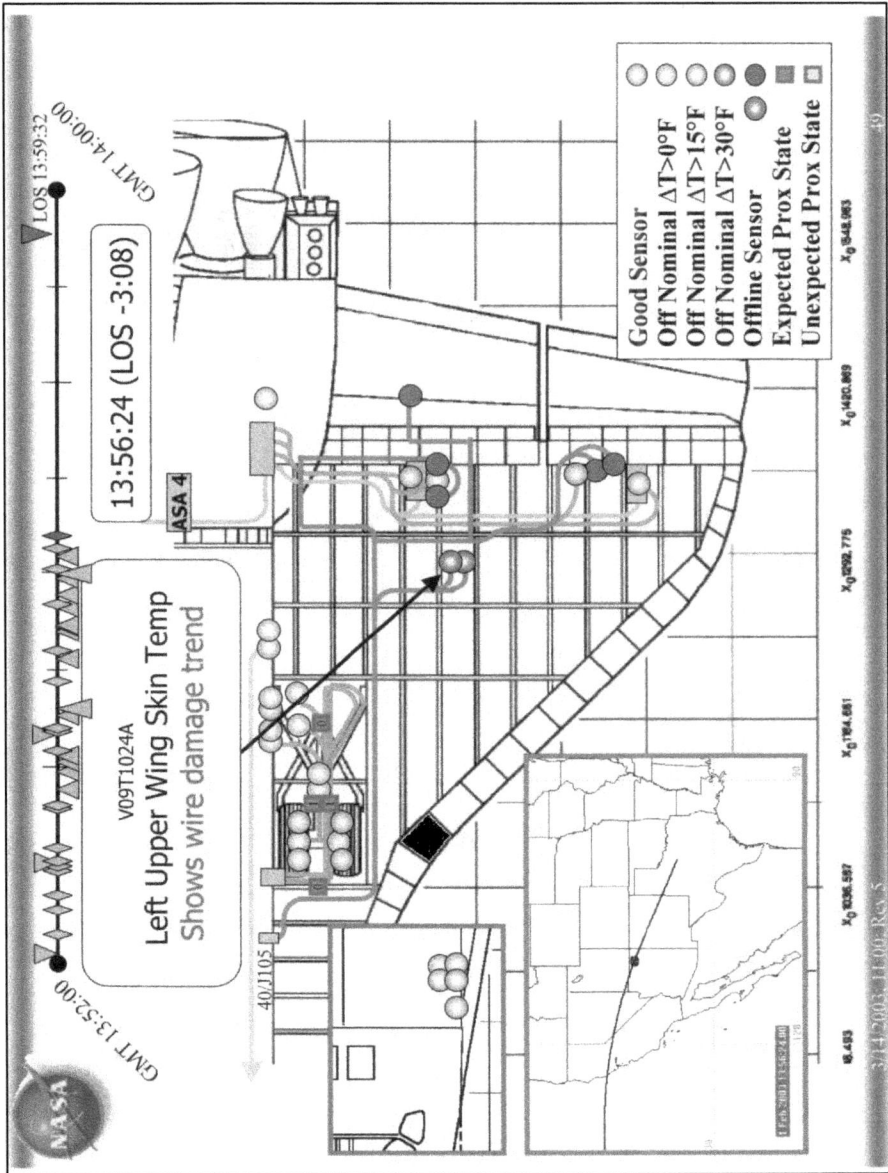

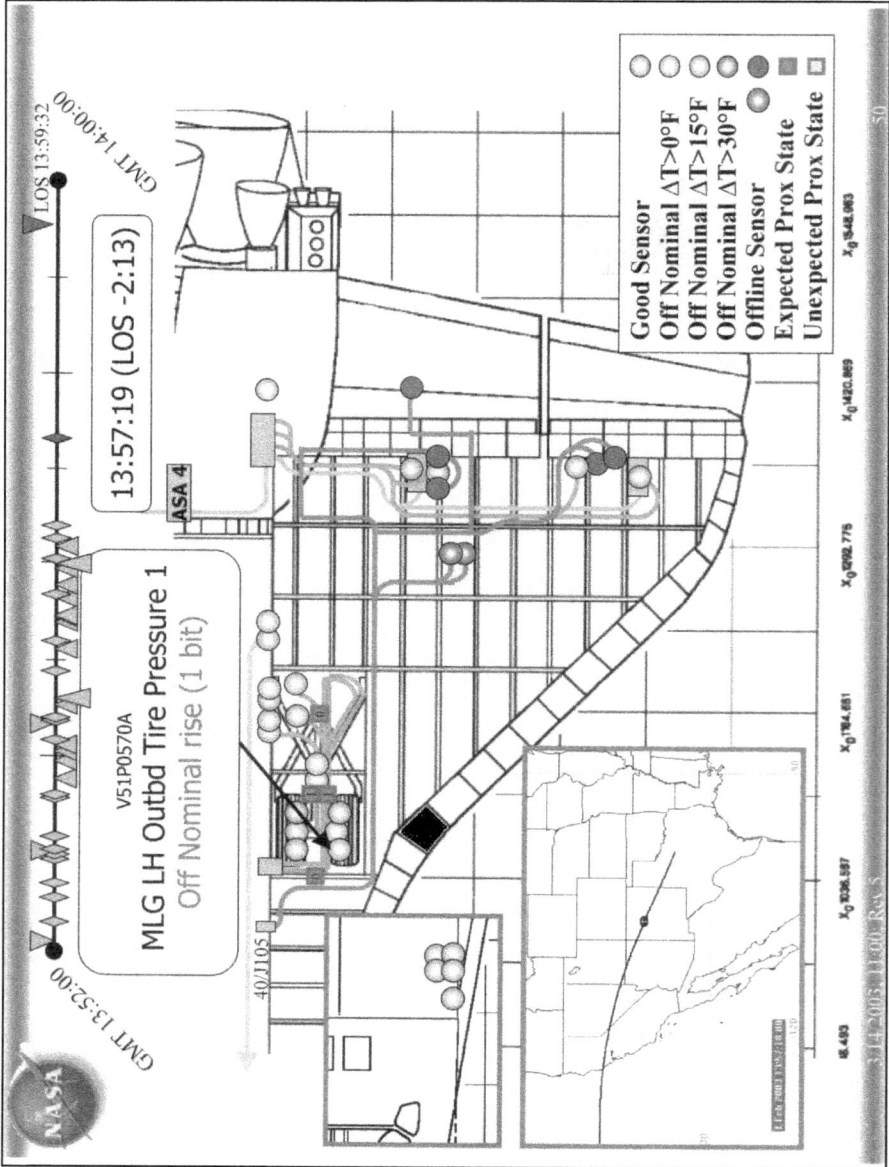

104

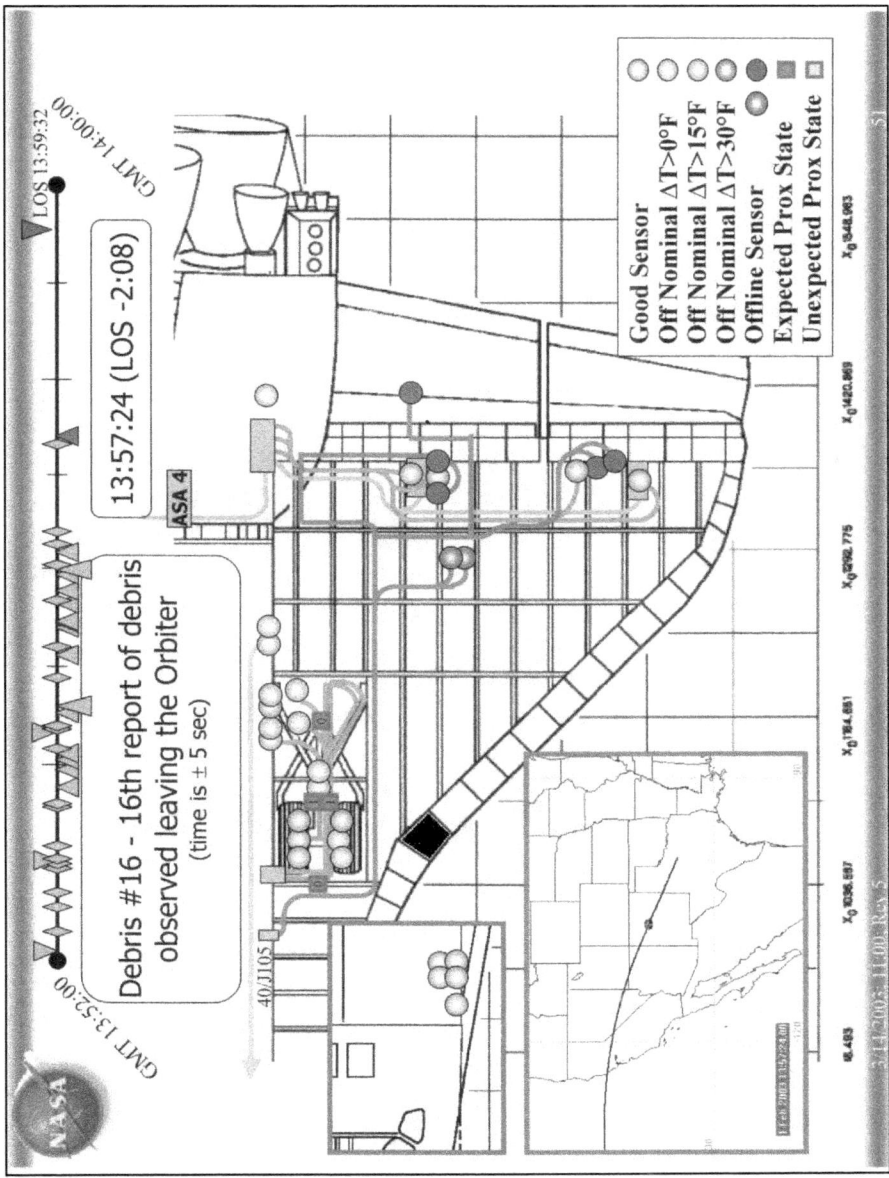

Debris #16 - 16th report of debris observed leaving the Orbiter
(time is ± 5 sec)

13:57:24 (LOS -2:08)

LOS 13:59:32

GMT 14:00:00

GMT 13:52:00

ASA 4

40/J1105

Good Sensor
Off Nominal ΔT>0°F
Off Nominal ΔT>15°F
Off Nominal ΔT>30°F
Offline Sensor
Expected Prox State
Unexpected Prox State

$X_0 848.003$
$X_0 1420.969$
$X_0 1292.775$
$X_0 1764.681$
$X_0 1036.597$
0.403

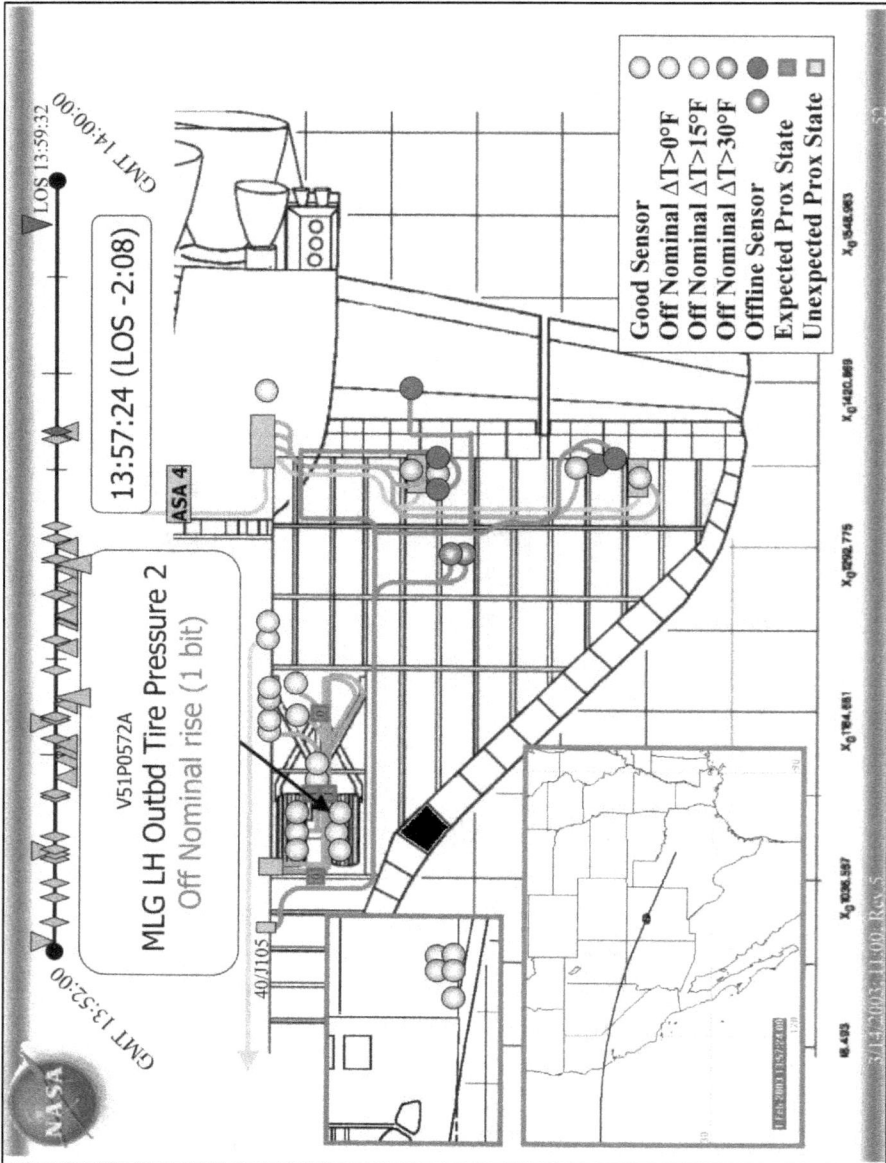

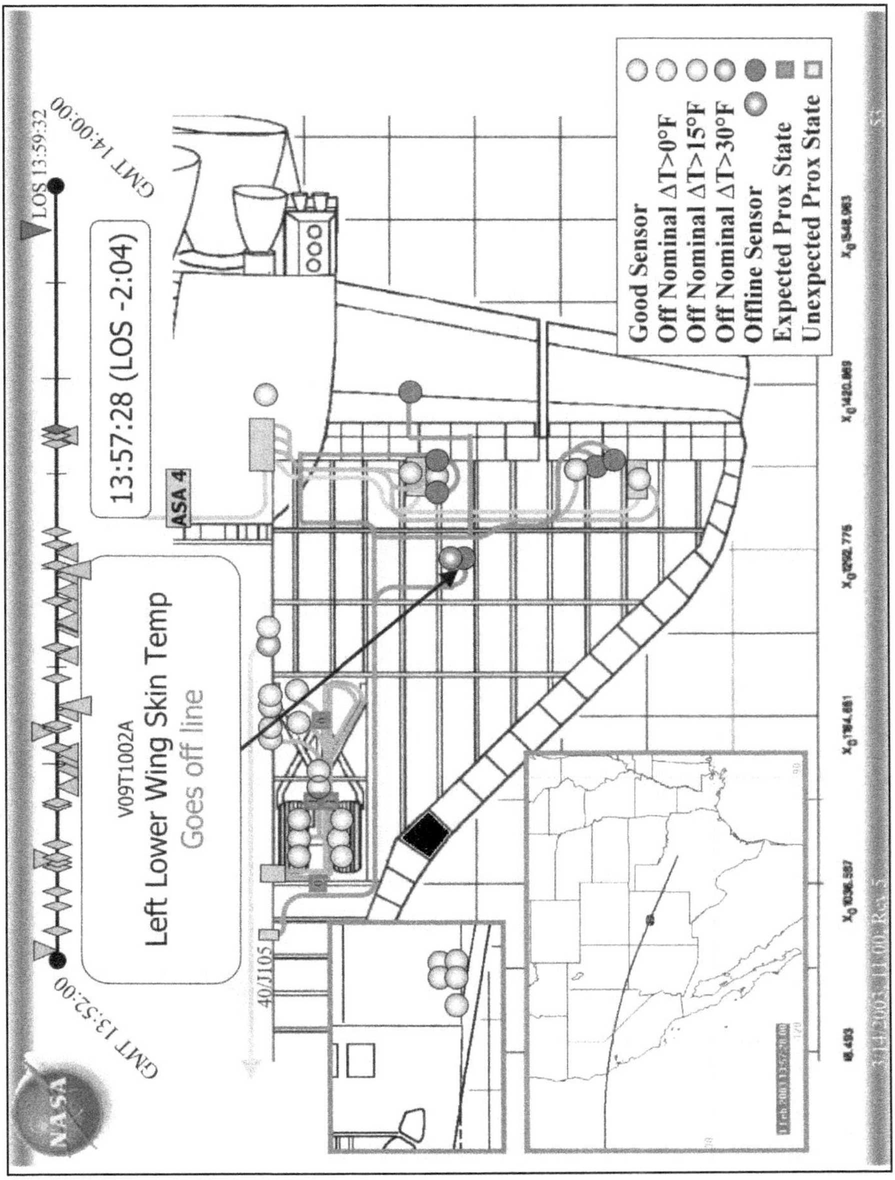

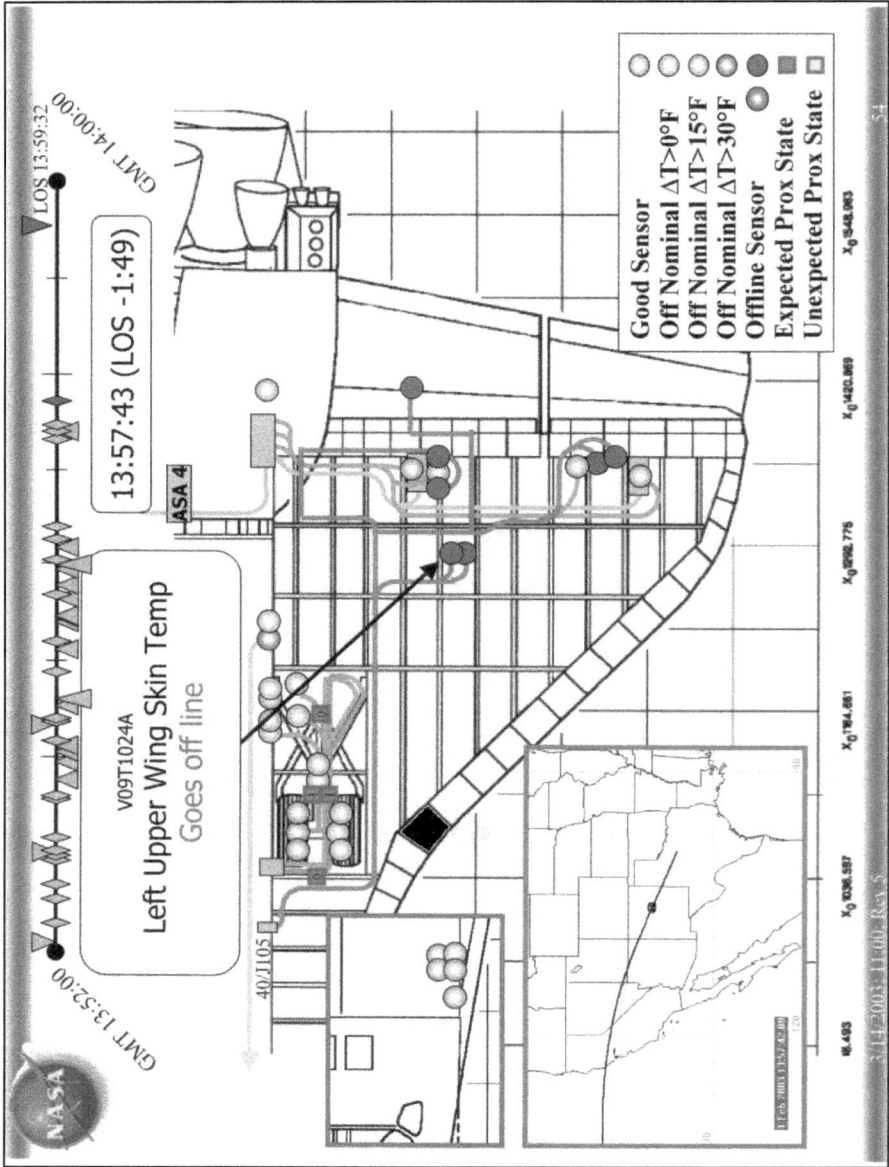

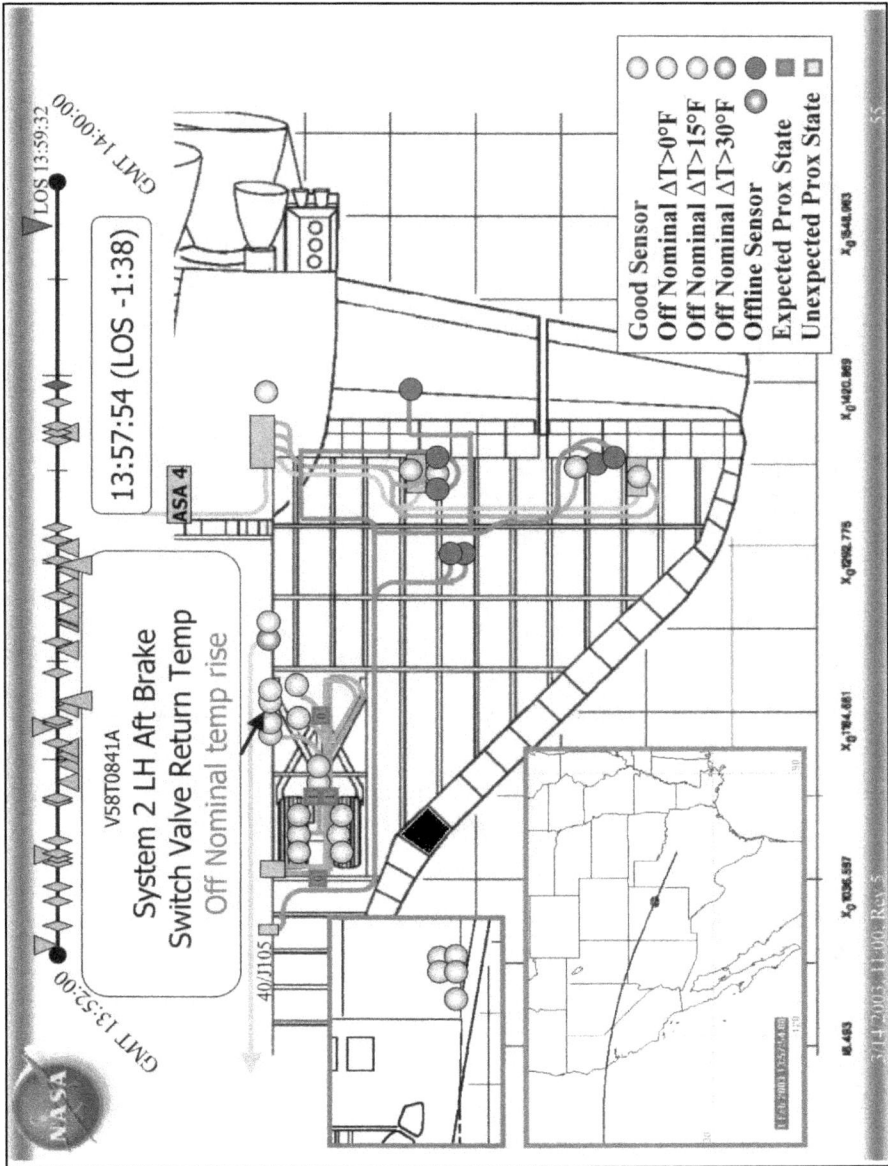

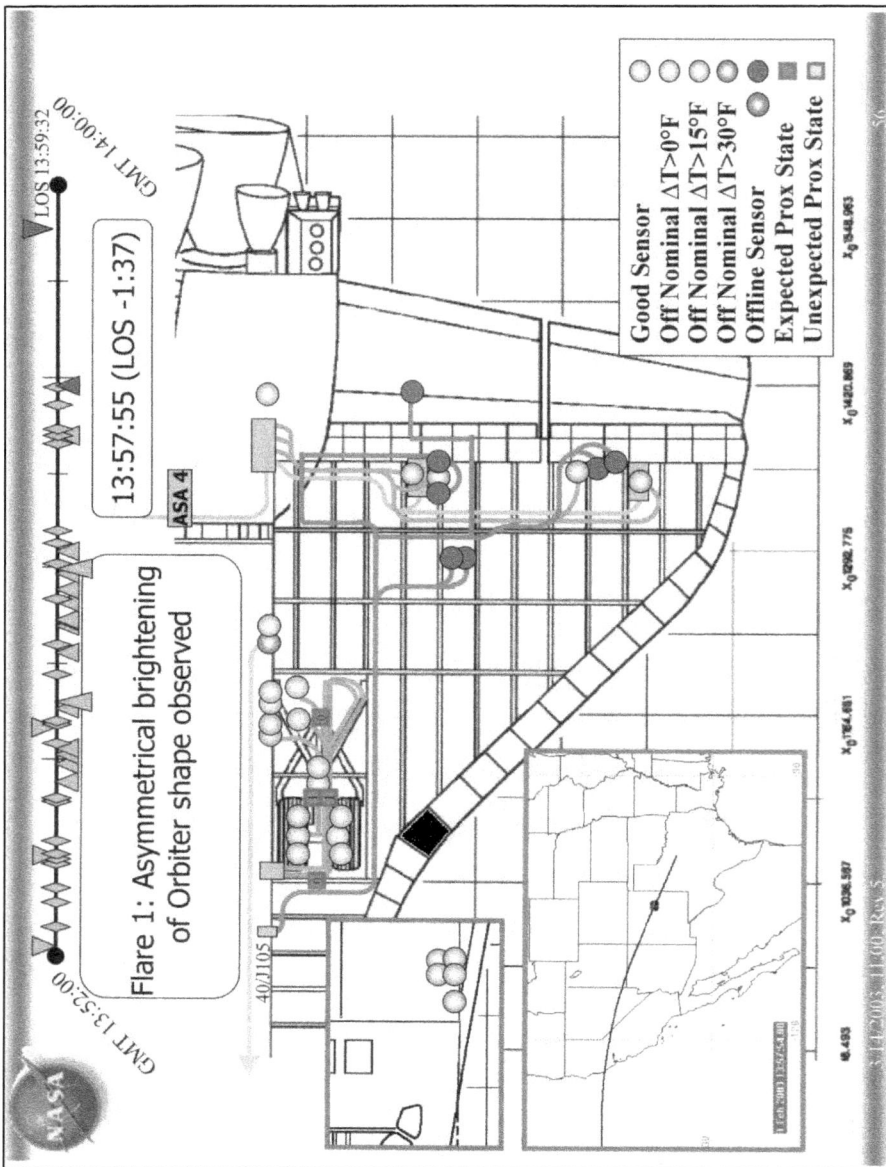

Flare 1: Asymmetrical brightening of Orbiter shape observed

13:57:55 (LOS -1:37)

Good Sensor
Off Nominal ΔT>0°F
Off Nominal ΔT>15°F
Off Nominal ΔT>30°F
Offline Sensor
Expected Prox State
Unexpected Prox State

GMT 13:52:00
GMT 14:00:00
LOS 13:59:32

110

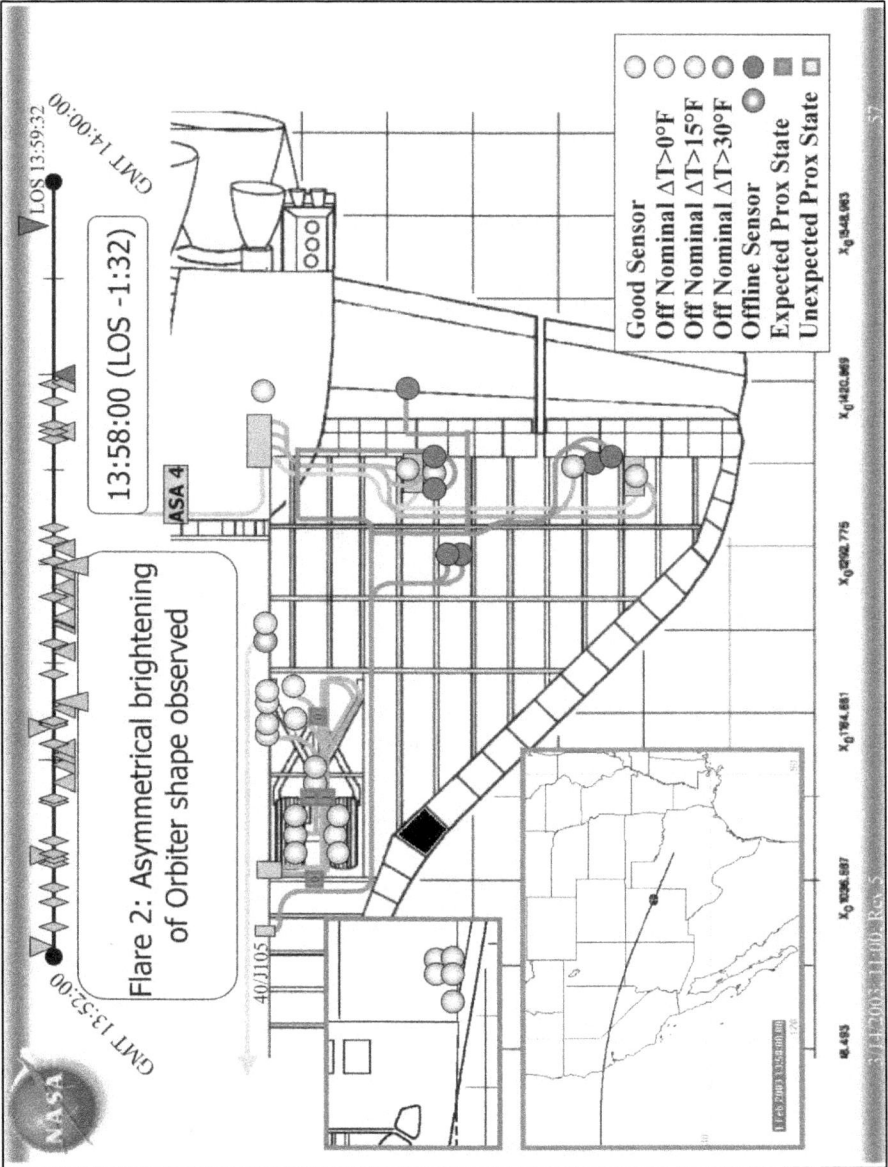

Flare 2: Asymmetrical brightening of Orbiter shape observed

13:58:00 (LOS -1:32)

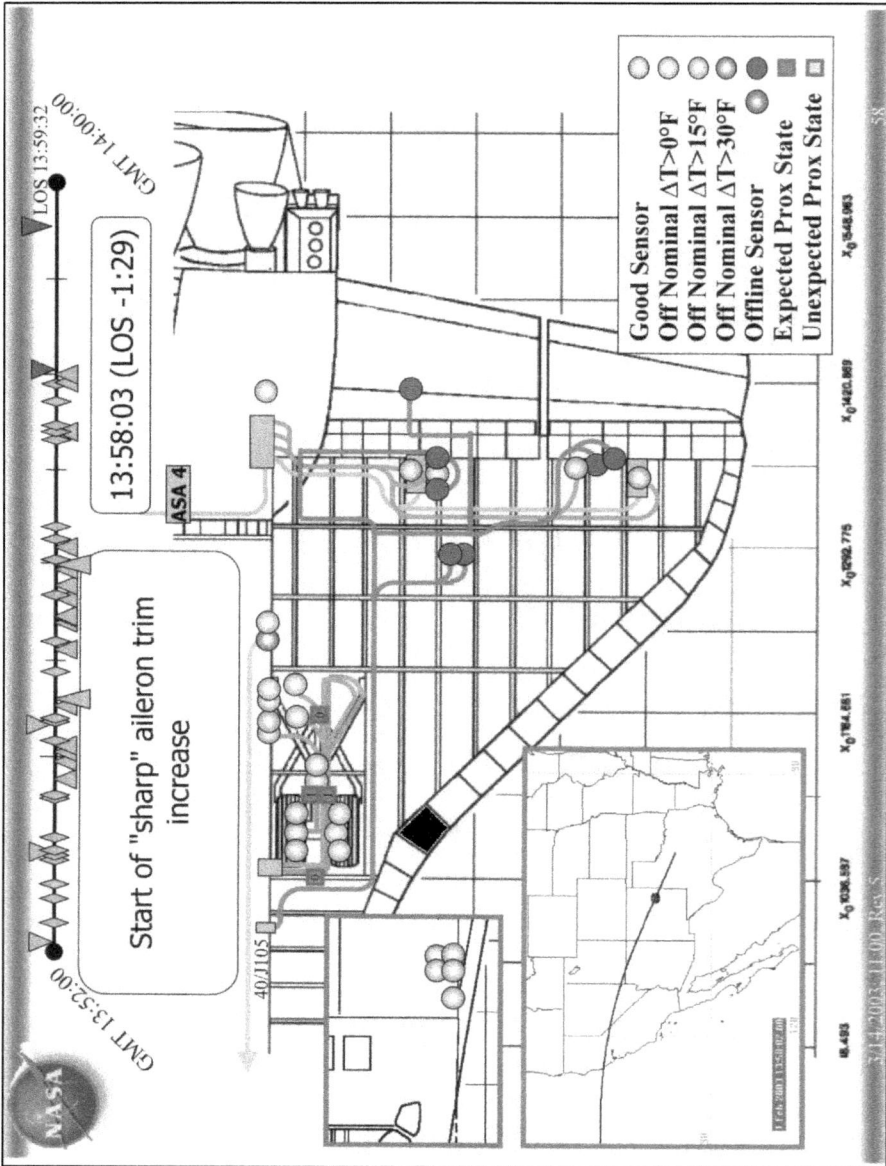

Start of "sharp" aileron trim increase

13:58:03 (LOS -1:29)

ASA 4

40/J105

GMT 13:52:00

LOS 13:59:32

GMT 14:00:00

Good Sensor
Off Nominal ΔT>0°F
Off Nominal ΔT>15°F
Off Nominal ΔT>30°F
Offline Sensor
Expected Prox State
Unexpected Prox State

NASA

$X_0$348.963
$X_0$420.969
$X_0$292.775
$X_0$164.681
$X_0$036.587
68.493

113

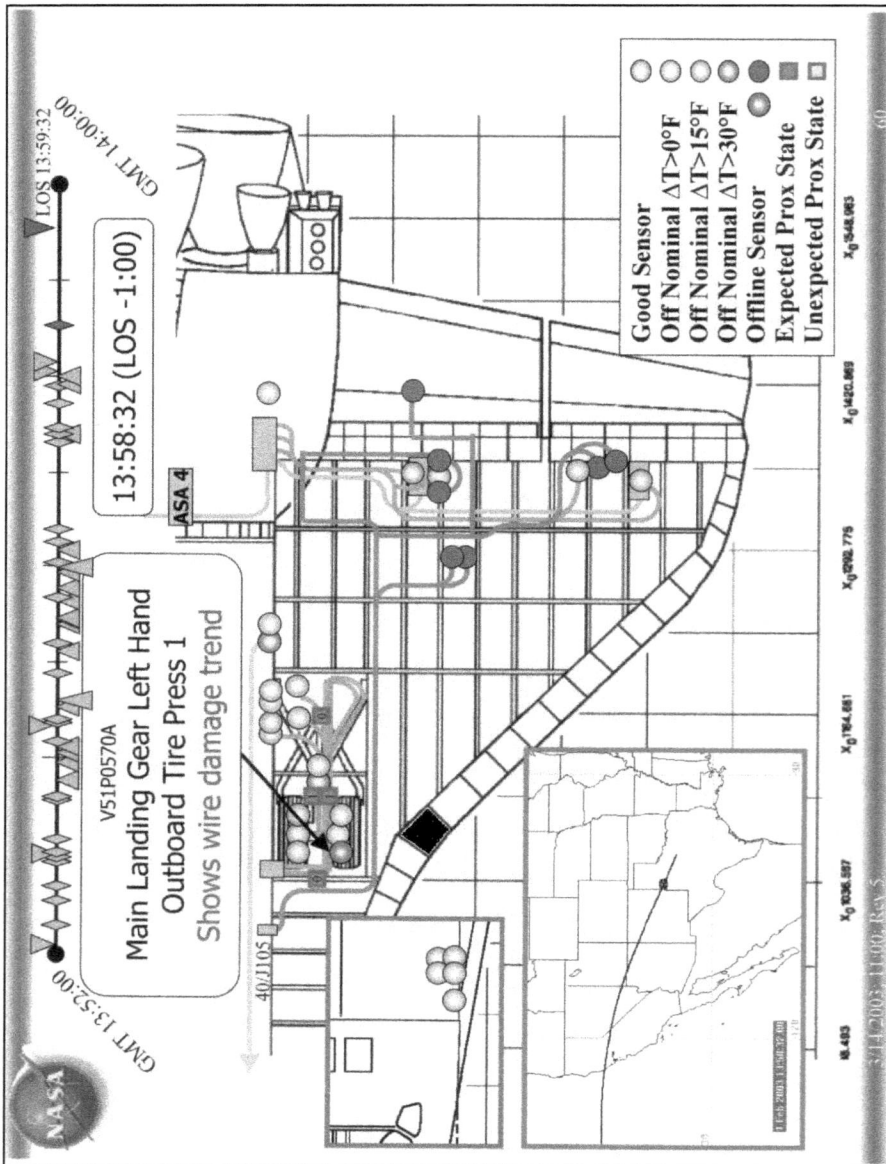

Main Landing Gear Left Hand
Outboard Tire Press 1
Shows wire damage trend

V51P0570A

13:58:32 (LOS -1:00)

ASA 4

LOS 13:59:32
GMT 14:00:00

GMT 13:52:00

Good Sensor
Off Nominal ΔT>0°F
Off Nominal ΔT>15°F
Off Nominal ΔT>30°F
Offline Sensor
Expected Prox State
Unexpected Prox State

114

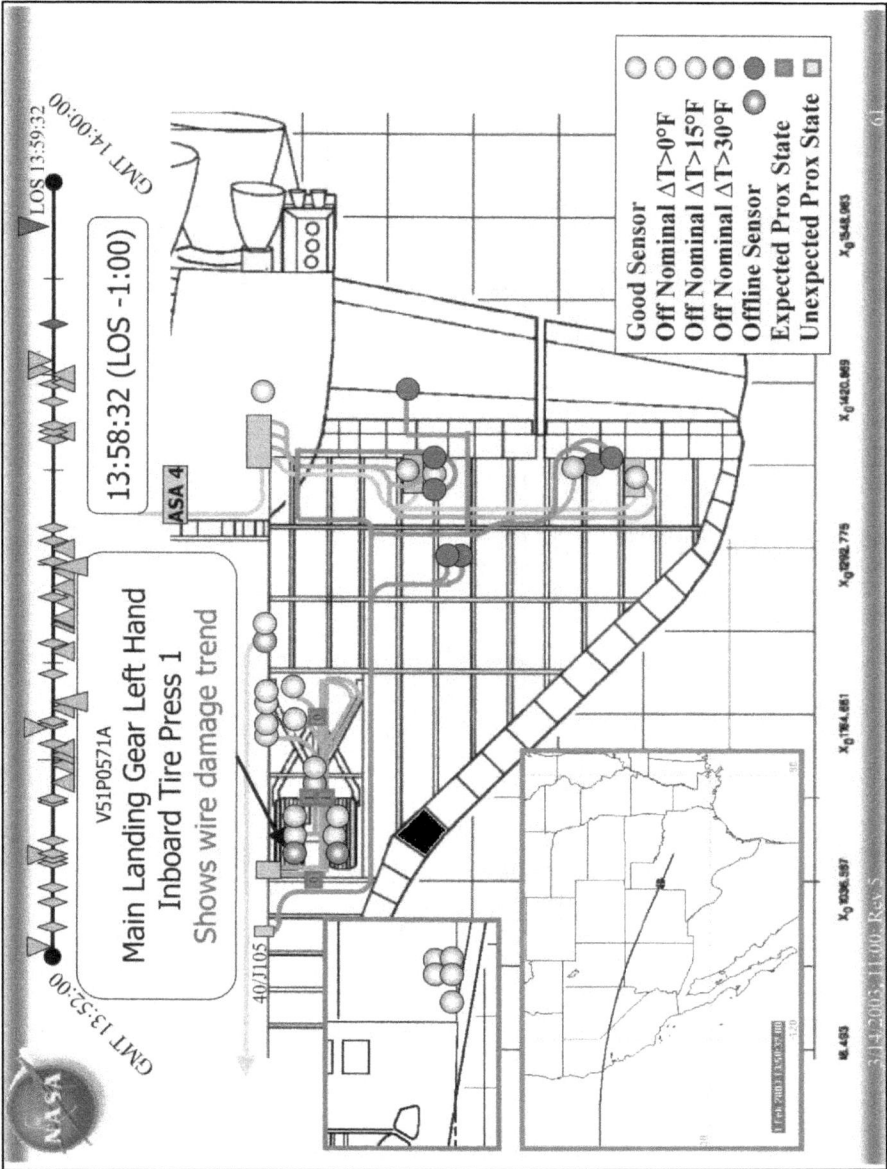

Legend:
- Good Sensor
- Off Nominal ΔT>0°F
- Off Nominal ΔT>15°F
- Off Nominal ΔT>30°F
- Offline Sensor
- Expected Prox State
- Unexpected Prox State

V51P0571A
Main Landing Gear Left Hand
Inboard Tire Press 1
Shows wire damage trend

13:58:32 (LOS -1:00)

ASA 4

40/J105

LOS 13:59:32
GMT 14:00:00

GMT 13:52:00

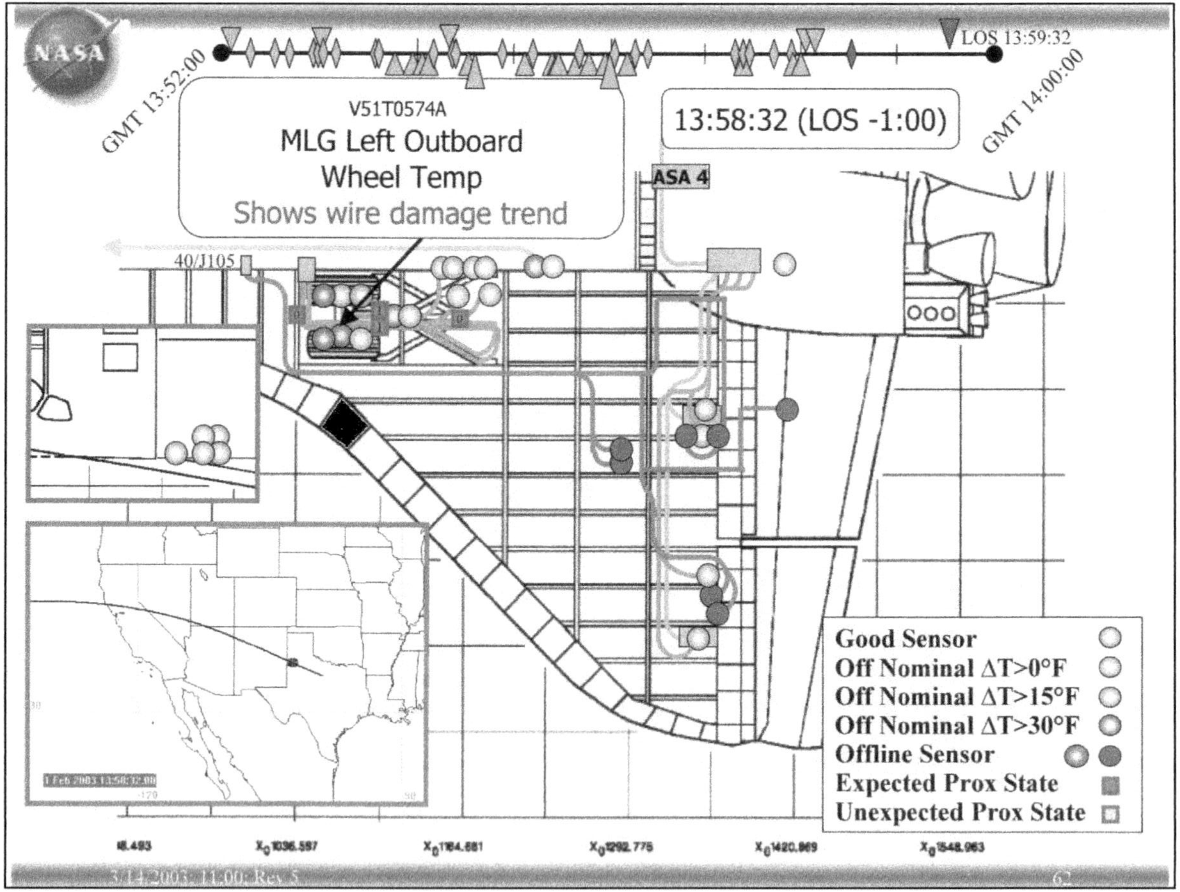

LOS 13:59:32
GMT 13:52:00
GMT 14:00:00
V51T0574A
MLG Left Outboard
Wheel Temp
Shows wire damage trend
13:58:32 (LOS -1:00)
ASA 4
40/J105
Good Sensor
Off Nominal ΔT>0°F
Off Nominal ΔT>15°F
Off Nominal ΔT>30°F
Offline Sensor
Expected Prox State
Unexpected Prox State

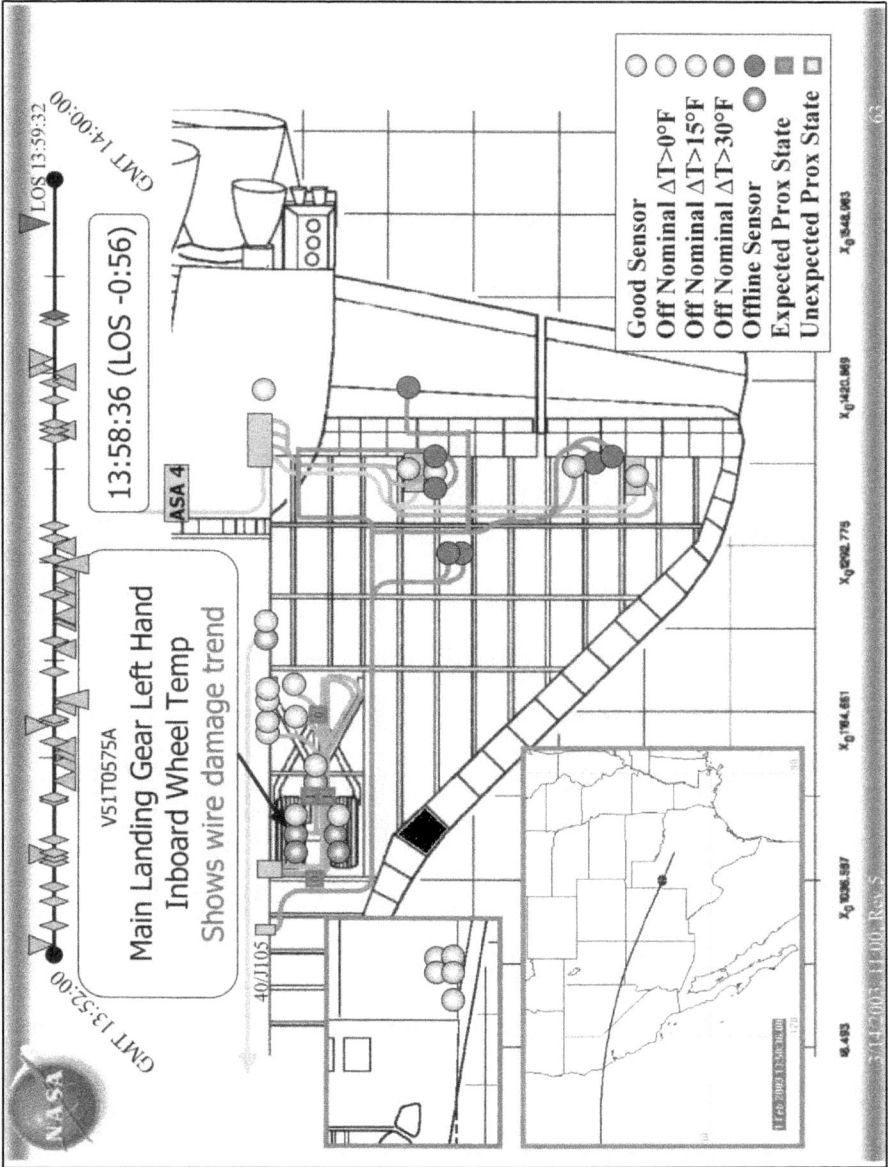

Main Landing Gear Left Hand Inboard Wheel Temp

Shows wire damage trend

V51T0575A

13:58:36 (LOS -0:56)

ASA 4

Good Sensor
Off Nominal ΔT>0°F
Off Nominal ΔT>15°F
Off Nominal ΔT>30°F
Offline Sensor
Expected Prox State
Unexpected Prox State

LOS 13:59:32

GMT 14:00:00

GMT 13:52:00

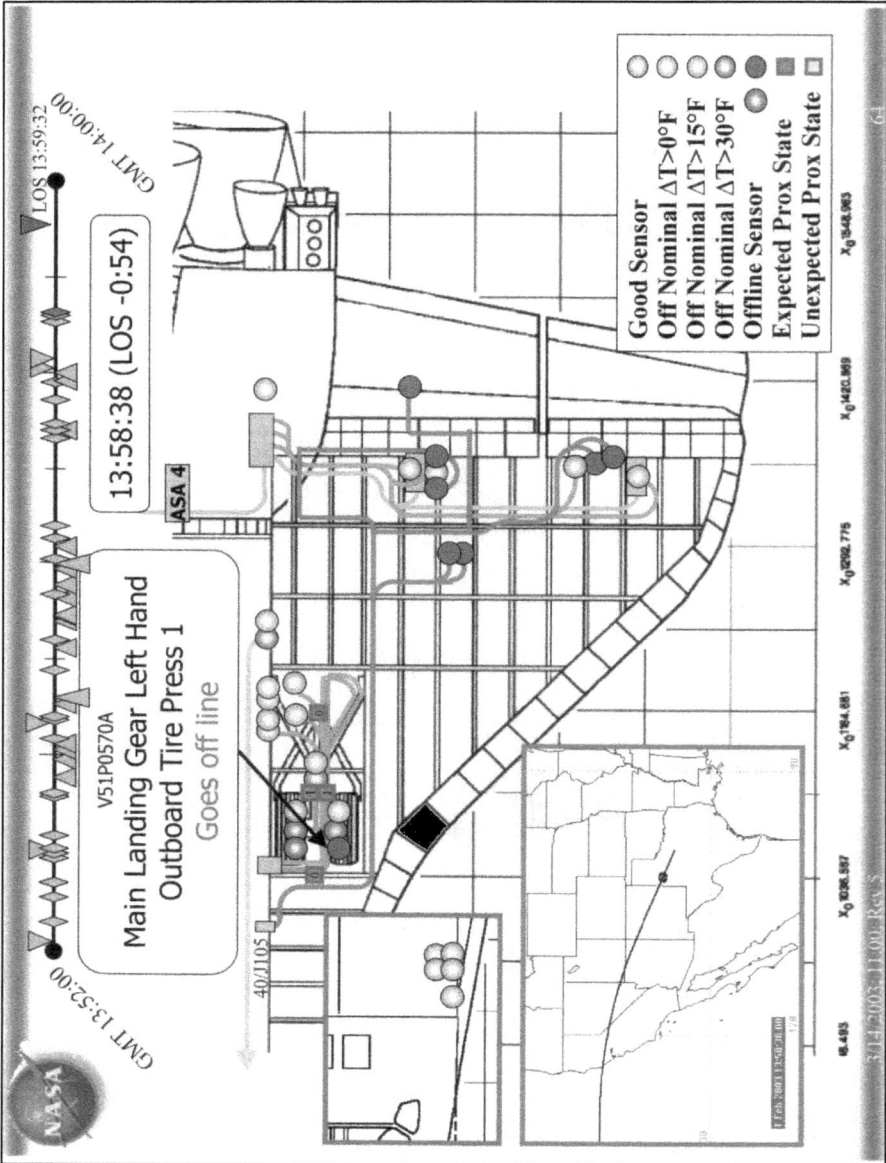

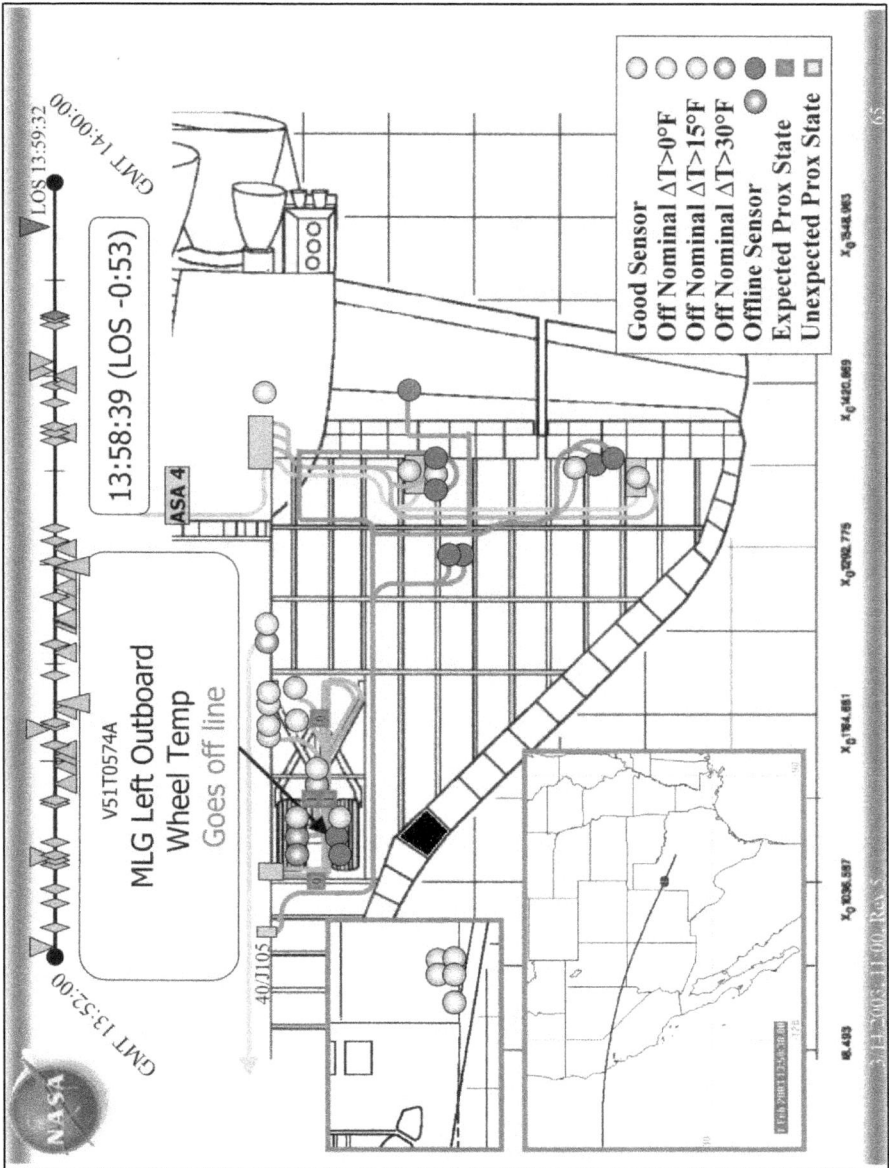

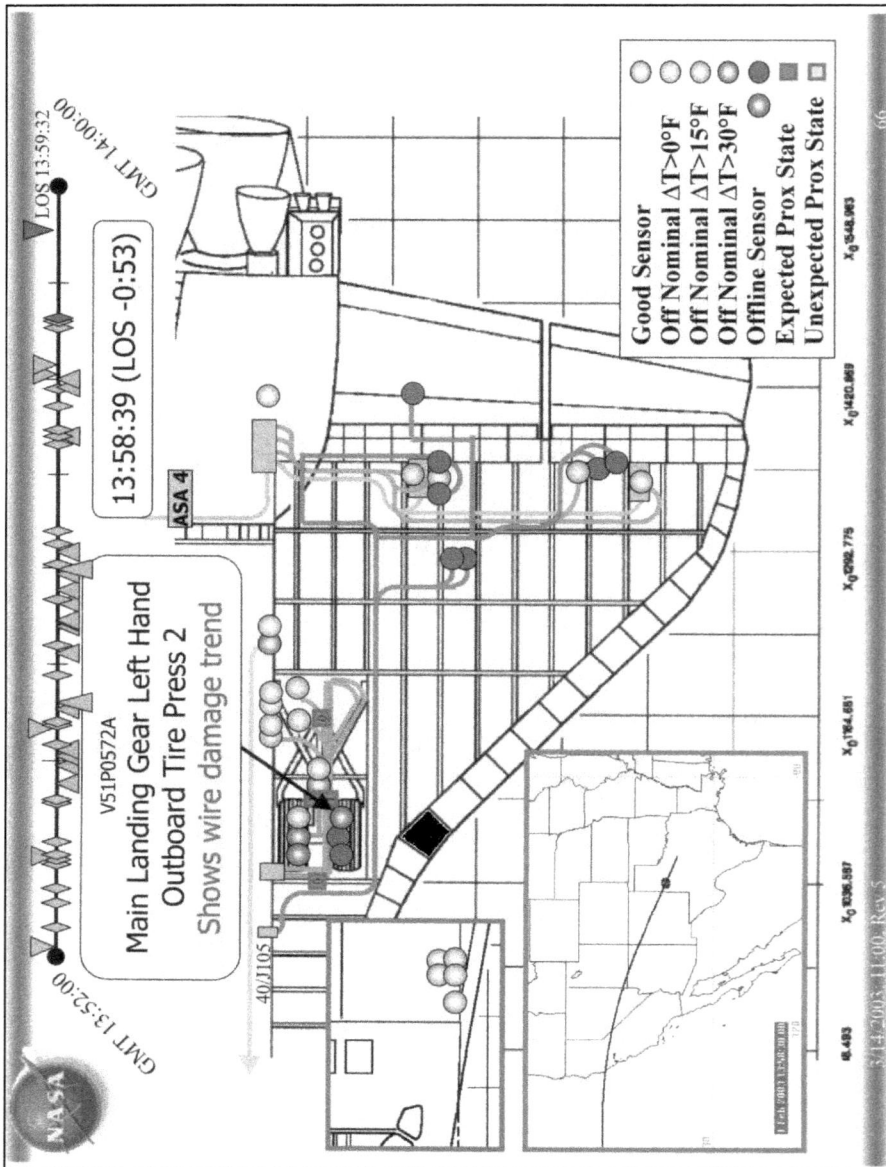

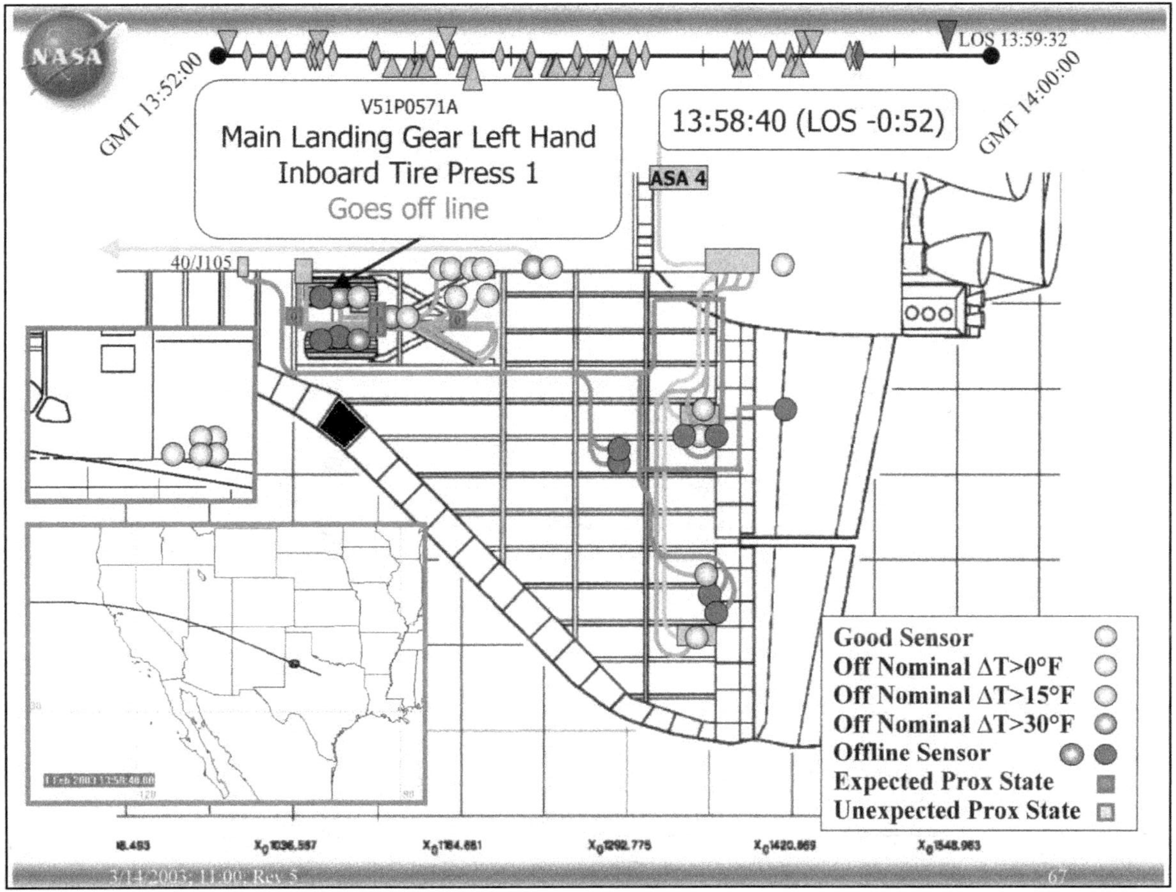

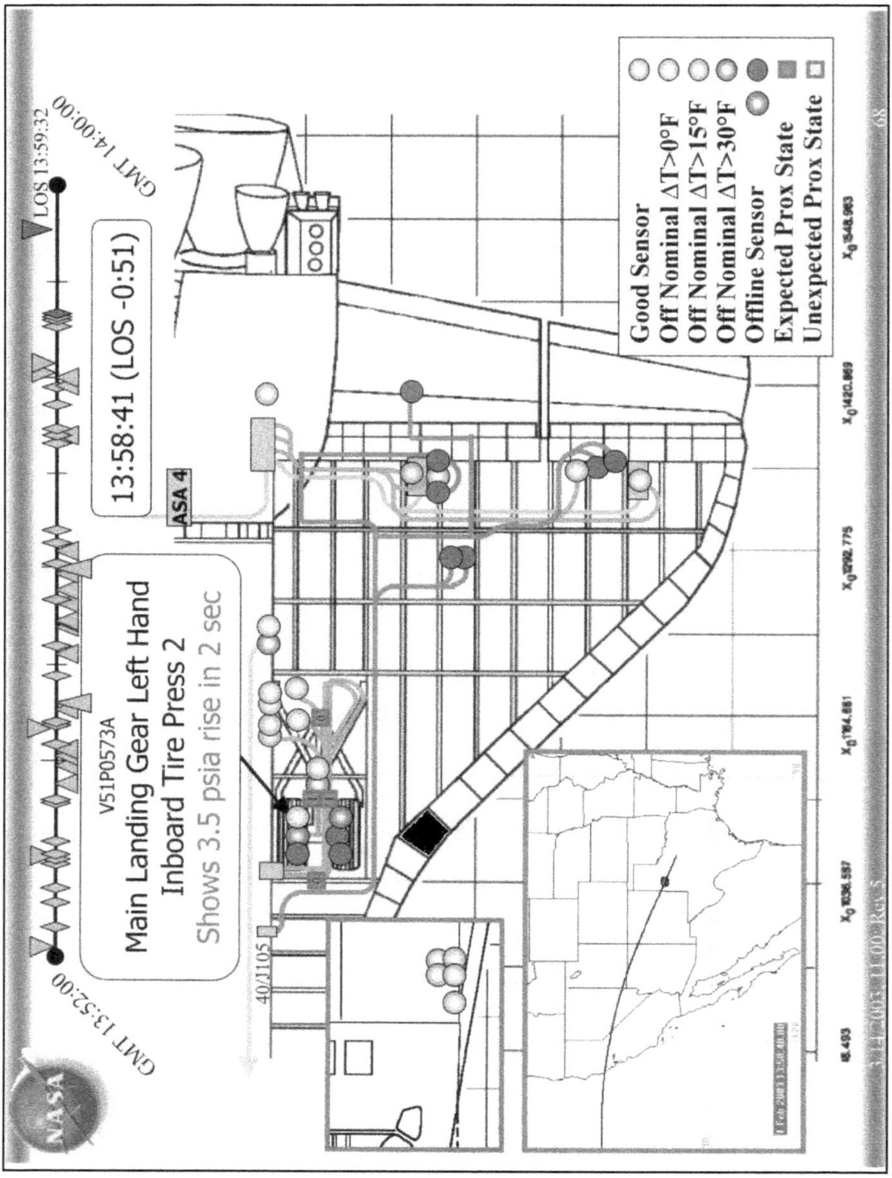

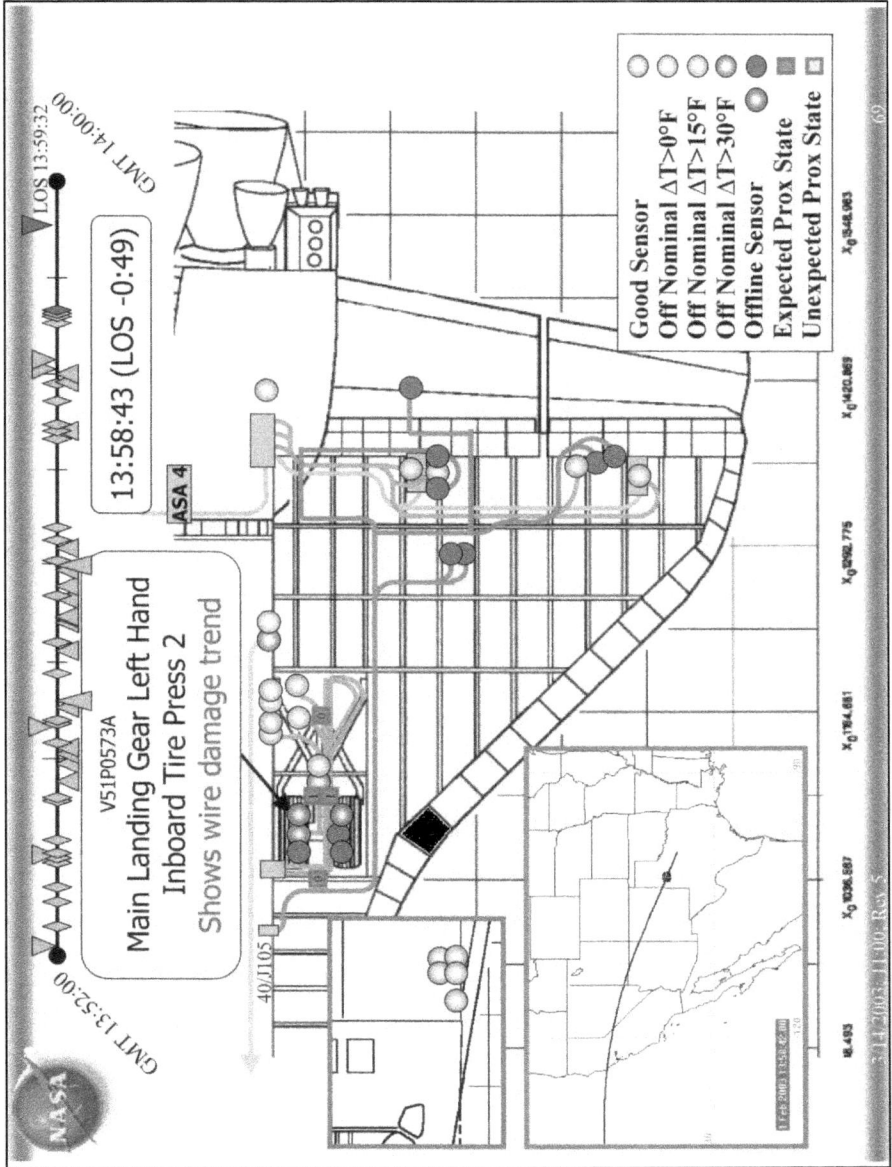

Good Sensor
Off Nominal ΔT>0°F
Off Nominal ΔT>15°F
Off Nominal ΔT>30°F
Offline Sensor
Expected Prox State
Unexpected Prox State

13:58:43 (LOS -0:49)

V51P0573A
Main Landing Gear Left Hand
Inboard Tire Press 2
Shows wire damage trend

ASA 4

LOS 13:59:32
GMT 14:00:00

GMT 13:52:00

NASA

123

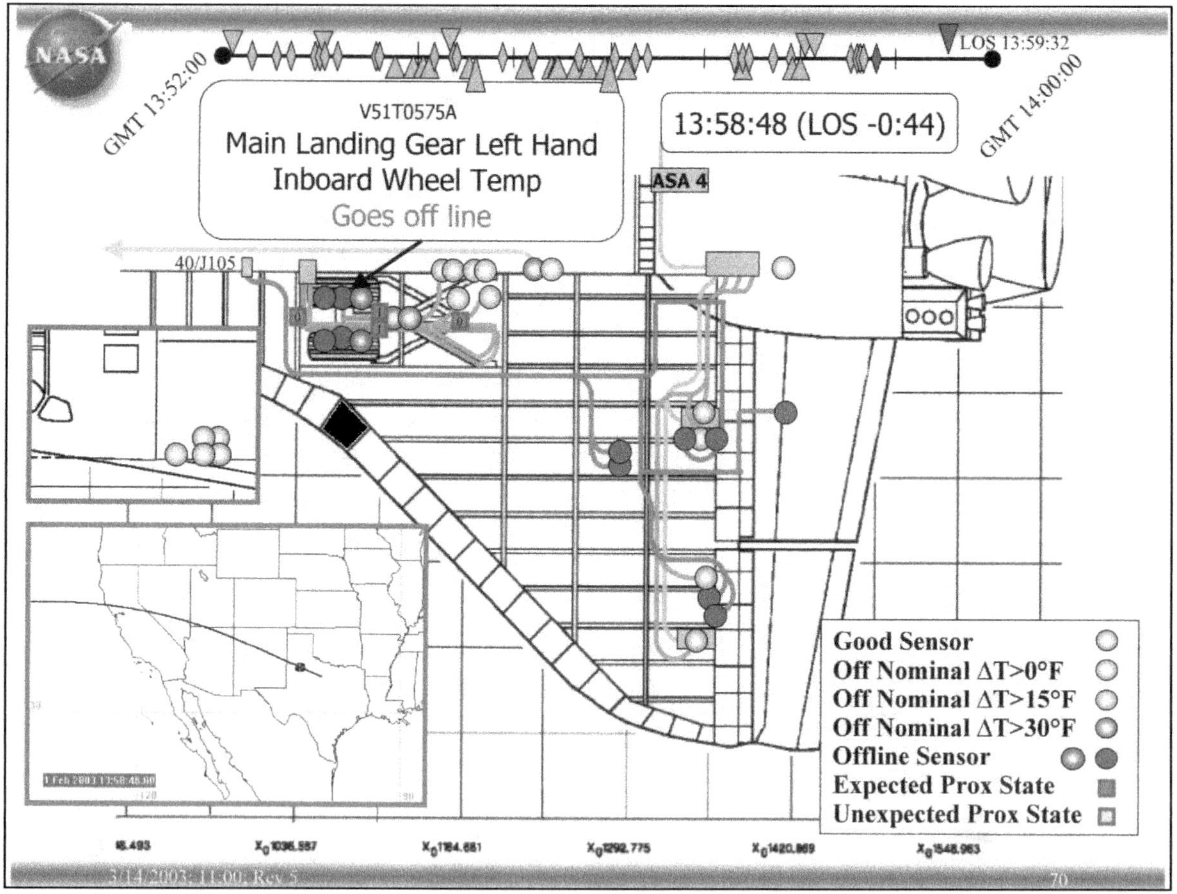

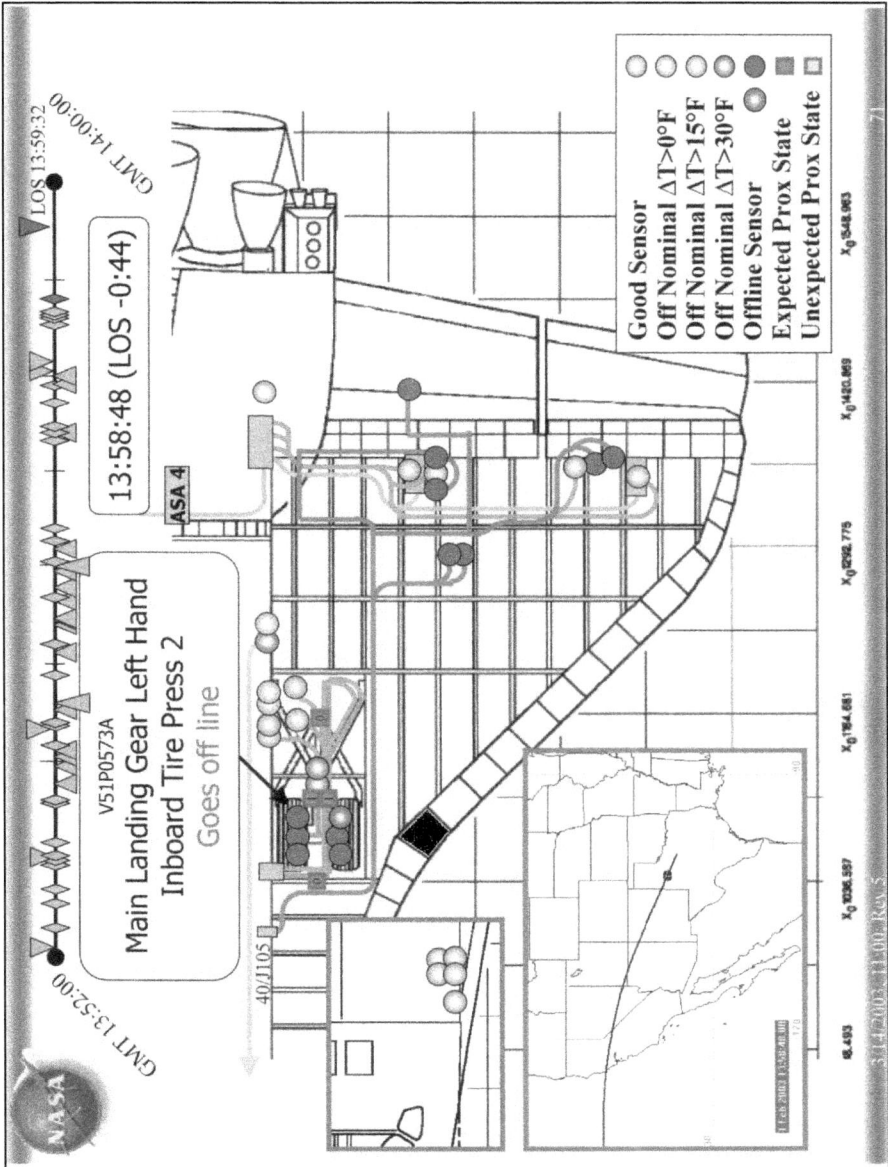

Main Landing Gear Left Hand
Inboard Tire Press 2
Goes off line

V51P0573A

13:58:48 (LOS -0:44)

ASA 4

40/J105

GMT 13:52:00

LOS 13:59:32

GMT 14:00:00

Good Sensor
Off Nominal ΔT>0°F
Off Nominal ΔT>15°F
Off Nominal ΔT>30°F
Offline Sensor
Expected Prox State
Unexpected Prox State

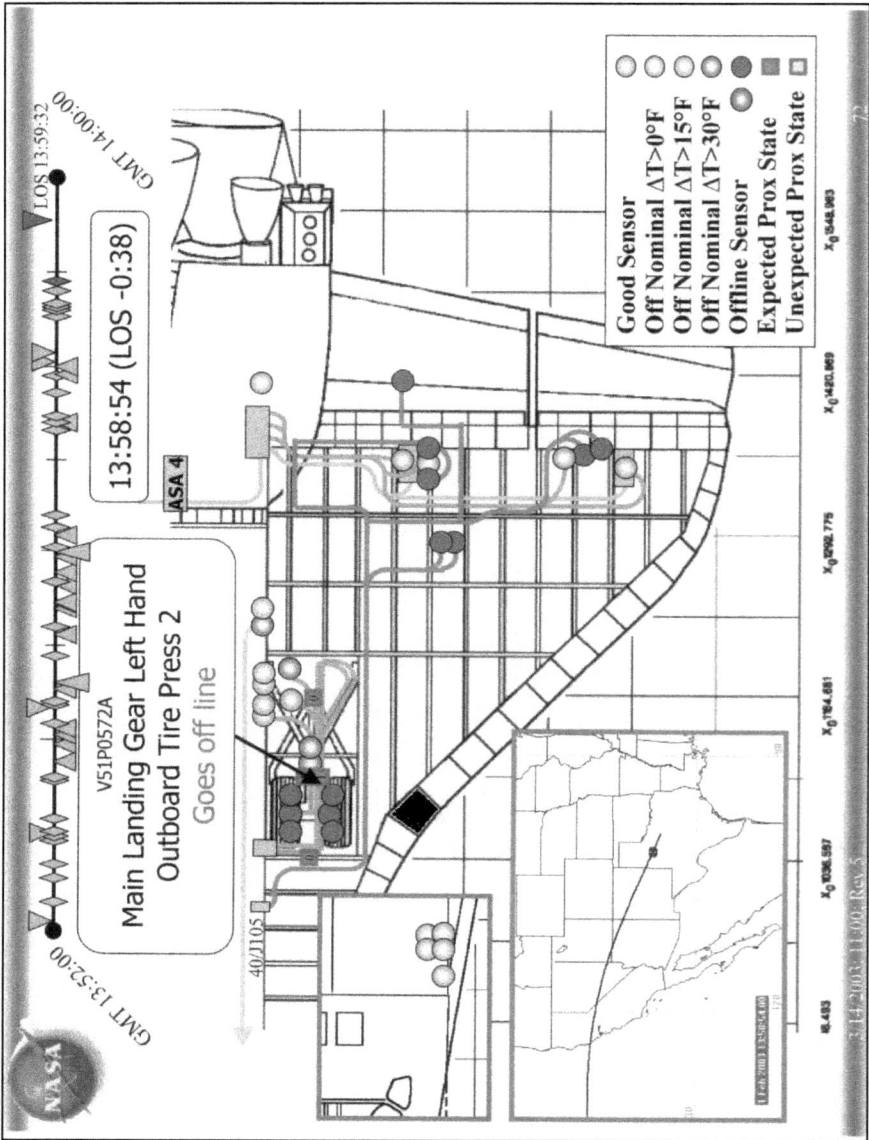

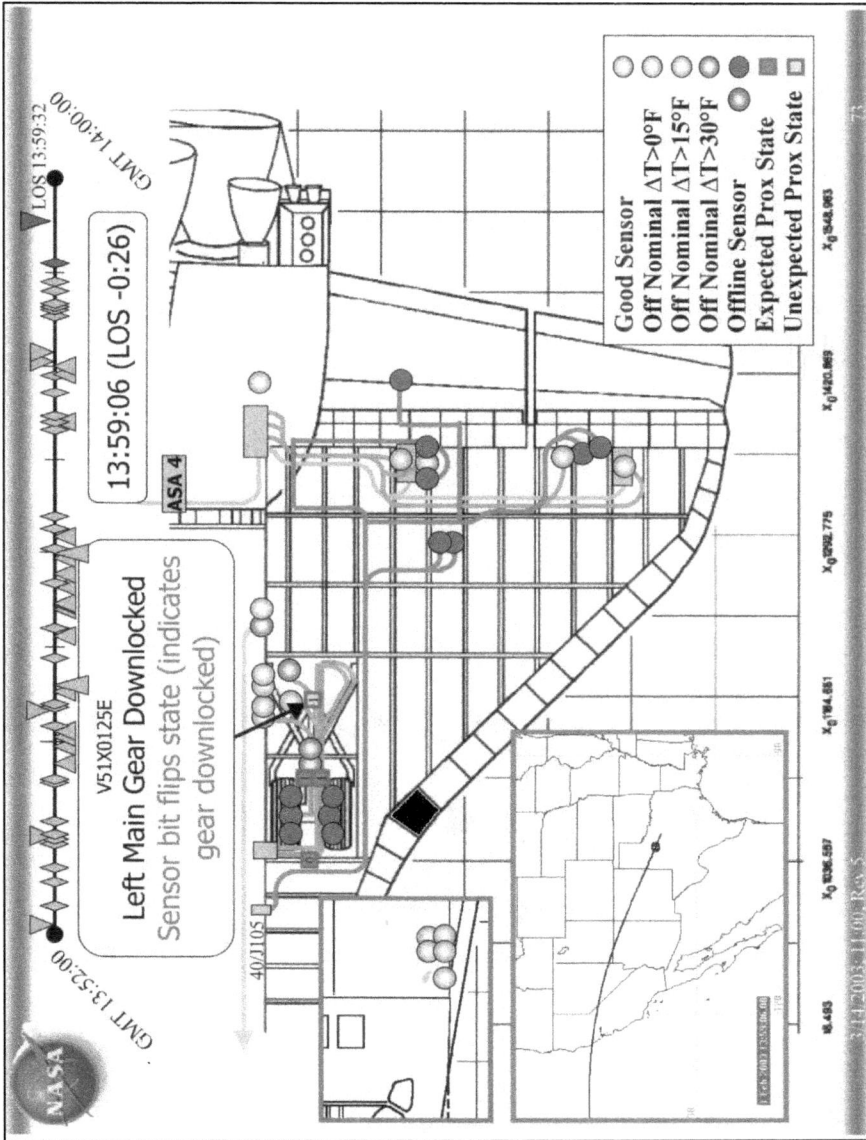

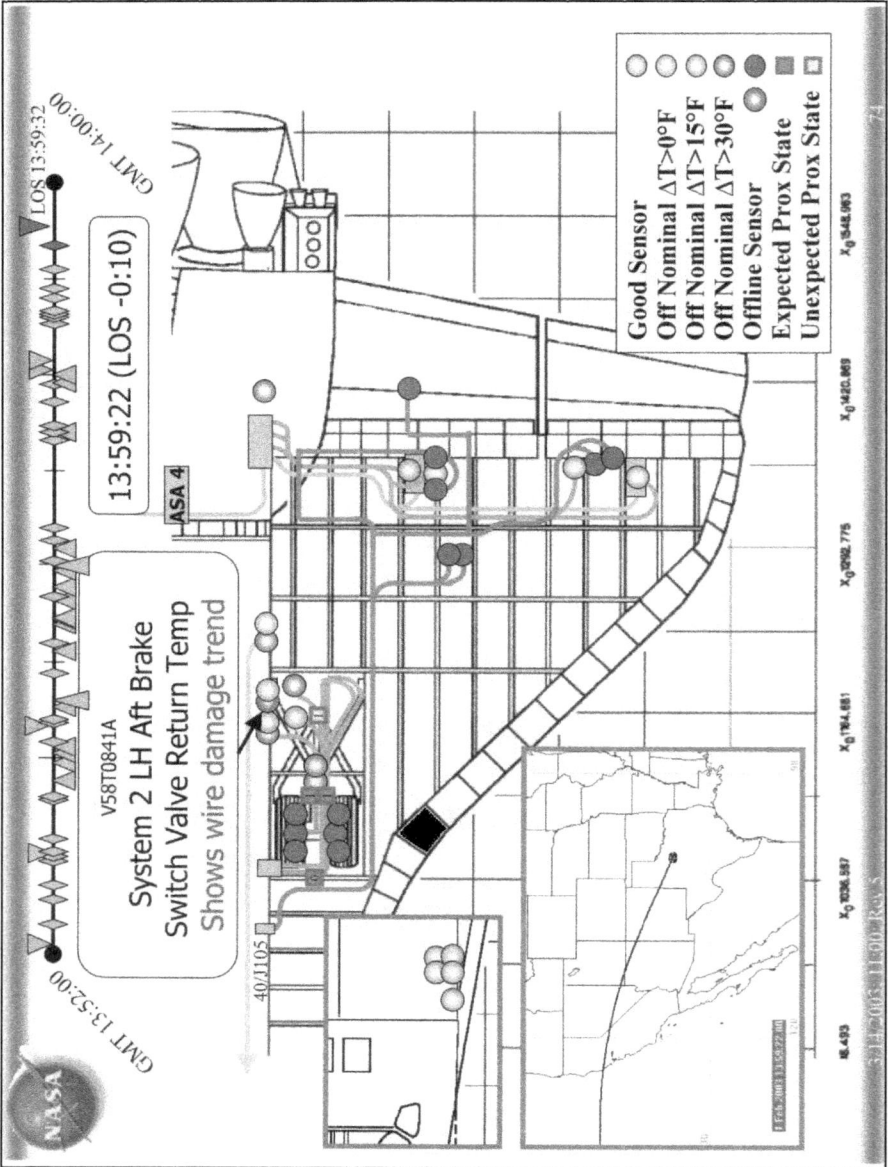

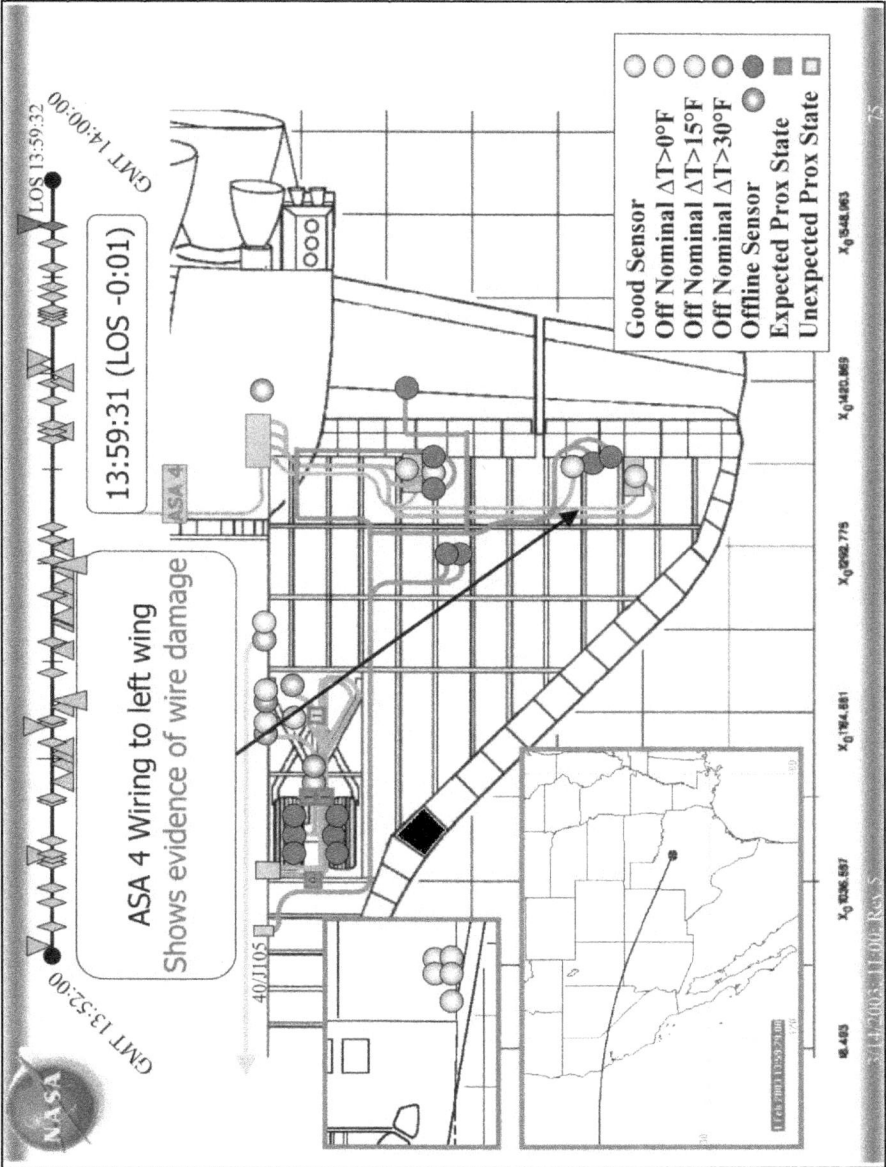

ASA 4 Wiring to left wing
Shows evidence of wire damage

13:59:31 (LOS -0:01)

Good Sensor
Off Nominal ΔT>0°F
Off Nominal ΔT>15°F
Off Nominal ΔT>30°F
Offline Sensor
Expected Prox State
Unexpected Prox State

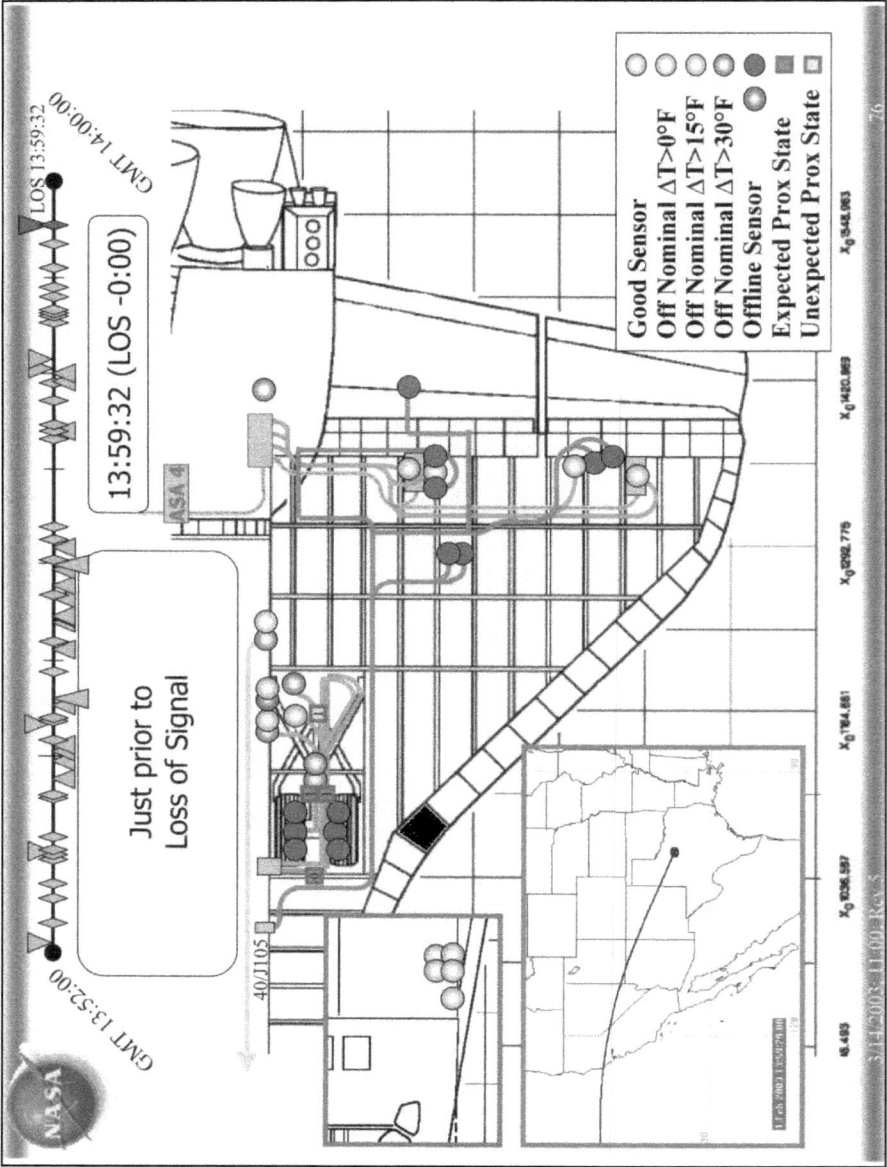

Sensor Names and MSIDs (I)

No.	Measurement Nomenclature	MSID	No.	Measurement Nomenclature	MSID
1	LMG Brake Line Temp D	V58T1703A	20	MLG LH Inbd Wheel Temp	V51T0575A
2	LMG Brake Line Temp A	V58T1700A	21	MLG LH Inbd Tire Press 2	V51P0573A
3	LMG Brake Line Temp C	V58T1702A	22	MLG LH Outbd Tire Press 2	V51P0572A
4	LH Inbd Elev LWR Skin Temp	V09T1006A	23	Hyd Sys 3 LH Inbd Elvn Rtn Ln Temp	V58T0833A
5	Hyd Sys 3 LOE Rtn Ln T	V58T0394A	24	Hyd Sys 2 LH Otbd Elvn Rtn Ln Temp	V58T0883A
6	Hyd 1 LH Inbd Elvn Actr Rtn Ln T	V58T0157A	25	Hydr Sys LH Inbd Elvn Actr Temp	V58T0830A
7	Hyd Sys 1 LOE Rtn Ln T	V58T0193A	26	Hydr Sys LH Outbd Elvn Actr Temp	V58T0880A
8	Hyd 2 LH Inbd Elvn Actr Rtn Ln T	V58T0257A	27	Mid Fuselage Port (Left) Sill Longeron Temp at x1215	V34T1118A
9	LMG Brake Line Temp B	V58T1701A	28	LH Aft Fuselage Sidewall Temp at x1410	V09T1724A
10	M-Fus Lt BL Temp at 1215	V34T1106A	29	Left Main Gear Up	V51X0100X
11	L Main Gear Strut Actuator Temp	V58T0405A	30	Left Main Gear Door Up	V51X0116X
12	Hyd Sys 1 LMG Uplk Actr Unlk Ln T	V58T0125A	31	Left Main Gear Down	V51X0125E
13	Hyd 3 LH Fwd Brake Sw Vlv Rtn Ln T	V58T0842A	32	Left Main Gear No WOW	V51X0130X
14	LH UPR Wing Skin Temp	V09T1024A	33	Supply H2O dump Nozzle temps A	V62T0440A
15	LH LWR Wing Skin Temp	V09T1002A	34	Supply H2O dump Nozzle temps B	V62T0439A
16	Hyd 2 LH Aft Brake Sw Vlv Rtn Ln T	V58T0841A	35	Waste H2O dump Nozzle temps A	V62T0520A
17	MLG LH Outbd Tire Press 1	V51P0570A	36	Waste H2O dump Nozzle temps B	V62T0519A
18	MLG LH Outbd Wheel Temp	V51T0574A	37	Vacuum vent	V62T0551A
19	MLG LH Inbd Tire Press 1	V51P0571A			

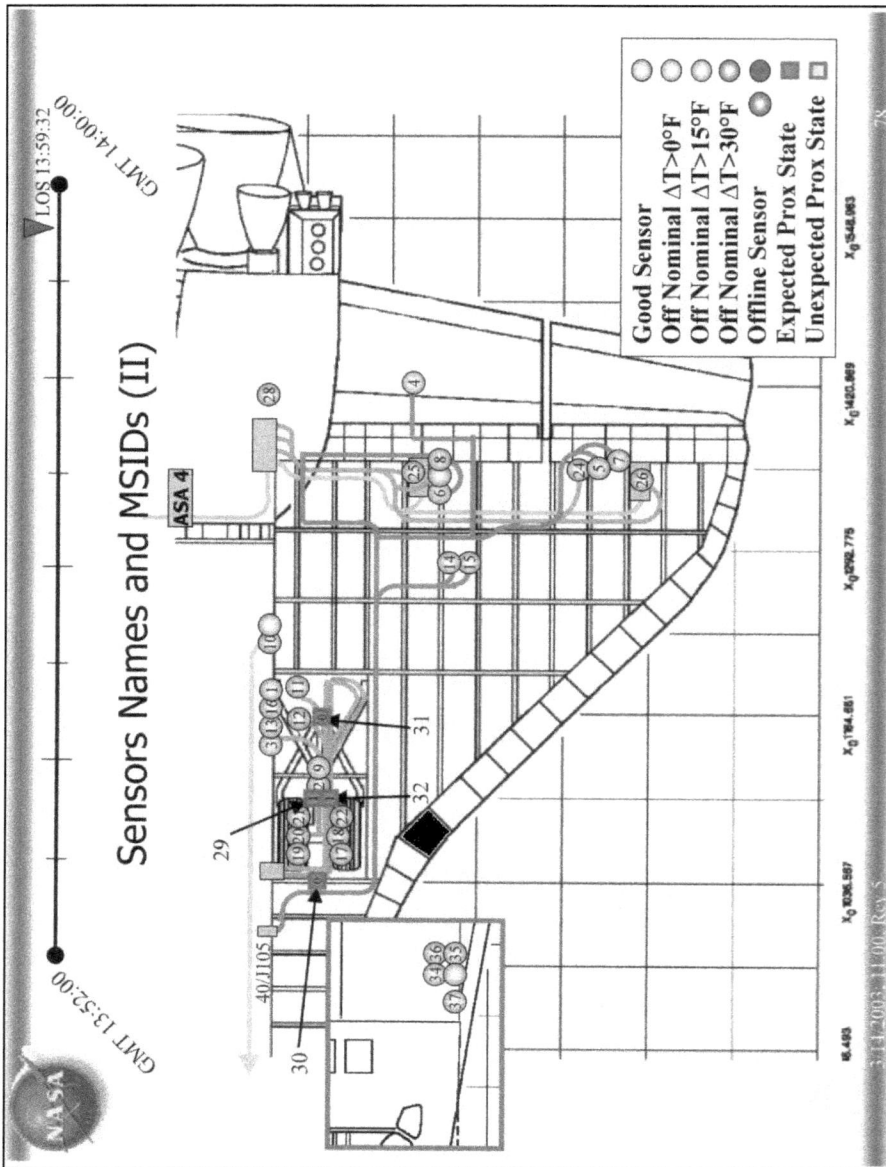

Sensors Names and MSIDs (II)

132

The following table emphasizes the correlation between sensor and cable locations relative to Panel 8...

Table Heading	Abbreviations
Seq # - Sequence number	WW – Wheel Well
LOS – Time to Loss of Signal	WTE – Wing Trailing Edge
LE – Time lapse from last event in Seconds (mm:ss)	F – Fuselage
Event – Event that occurred onboard the shuttle	CB – Cargo Bay
Loc – Location of the Event onboard the shuttle	OL – Off Line
Sensor (Ch) – Type of sensor and channel	WD – Wire Damage
Δ – Type of changes that occurred with the sensor	Nom – Nominal (Normal)
Near Panel 8 – Was sensor near the leading edge of the wing (panel 8)	Ind – Indication
WR – Wire Routing near Wheel Well	

Seq #	LOS	LE	Event	Loc	Sensor (Ch)	Δ	Near Panel 8	WR	Comments
1	-7:32	-	All Systems			Nom			
2	-7:27	0:05	First indication of off-nominal aero increments						
3	-7:15	0:12	Left Main Gear Brake Line	W W	Temp (D)	Rise	N	Y	
4	-7:00	0:15	Supply Water Dump Nozzle	CB	Temp (A/B)	Rise	N	Y	Nozzle Open
5	-7:00		Vacuum Vent	CB	Temp	Rise	N	Y	Vent Open
6	-6:51	0:09	Left Main Gear Brake Line	W W	Temp (A)	Rise	N	Y	
7	-6:51		Left Main Gear Brake Line	W W	Temp (C)	Rise	N	Y	
8	-6:36	0:15	Left Inboard Elevon Lower Skin	WTE	Temp	WD	N	Y	
9	-6:33	0:03	Left Inboard Elevon Lower Skin	WTE	Temp	OL	N	Y	

133

Seq #	LOS	LE	Event	Loc	Sensor (Ch)	Δ	Near Panel 8	WR	Comments
10	-6:31	0:02	First indication of off-nominal rolling moment increments						
11	-6:30	0:01	Hydraulic System 1 – Left Inboard Elevon Actuator Return Line	WTE	Temp	WD	N	Y	
12	-6:30		Hydraulic System 3 – Left Outboard Elevon Actuator Return Line	WTE	Temp	WD	N	Y	
13	-6:22	0:08	Hydraulic System 3 – Left Outboard Elevon Actuator Return Line	WTE	Temp	OL	N	Y	
14	-6:21	0:01	Hydraulic System 1 – Left Inboard Elevon Actuator Return Line	WTE	Temp	OL	N	Y	
15	-5:58	0:23	Hydraulic System 1 – Left Outboard Elevon Actuator Return Line	WTE	Temp	OL	N	Y	
16	-5:58		Hydraulic System 2 – Left Inboard Elevon Actuator Return Line	WTE	Temp	WD	N	Y	
17	-5:57	0:01	Supply Water Dump Nozzle	CB	Temp (A/B)	Nom	N	Y	Nozzle Closed
18	-5:57		Vacuum Vent	CB	Temp	Nom	N	Y	Vent Closed
19	-5:56	0:01	Hydraulic System 2 – Left Inboard Elevon Actuator Return Line	WTE	Temp	OL	N	Y	
20	-5:46	0:10	Debris #1 – 1st report of debris observed leaving Orbiter						
21	-5:44	0:02	Debris #2 – 2nd report of debris observed leaving Orbiter						
22	-5:36	0:08	Debris #3 – 3rd report of debris observed leaving Orbiter						
23	-5:30	0:06	Debris #4 – 4th report of debris observed leaving Orbiter						
24	-5:23	0:07	Debris #5 – 5th report of debris observed leaving Orbiter						
25	-5:22	0:01	Left Main Gear Brake Line	W W	Temp (B)	Rise	N	Y	
26	-5:12	0:10	Start of slow aileron trim change Reversal of growth trend of derived roll moment coefficient						

134

Seq #	LOS	LE	Event	Loc	Sensor (Ch)	Δ	Near Panel 8	WR	Comments
27	-5:10	0:02	Mid Fuselage Body Line	F	Temp	Rise	N	Y	Wing Root
28	-5:10		LH Aft Fuselage Sidewall	F	Temp	Rise	N	Y	Tail Section
29	-5:08	0:02	Left Main Gear Strut Actuator	W W	Temp	Rise	N	Y	
30	-4:59	0:09	Flash #1 – Orbiter envelope suddenly brightened (0.3 sec)						
31	-4:56	0:03	Debris #6 – 6th report of debris observed leaving Orbiter						
32	-4:39	0:17	Left Main Landing Gear Outboard Wheel	W W	Temp	Rise	N	Y	
33	-4:25	0:14	Debris #7 – 7th report of debris observed leaving Orbiter						
34	-4:20	0:05	System 3 LH Forward Brake Switch Valve Return Line	W W	Temp	Rise	N	Y	
35	-4:08	0:12	Debris #8 – 8th report of debris observed leaving Orbiter						
36	-4:05	0:03	Debris #9 – 9th report of debris observed leaving Orbiter						
37	-4:04	0:01	Debris #10 – 10th report of debris observed leaving Orbiter						
38	-3:53	0:11	Debris #11 – 11th report of debris observed leaving Orbiter						
39	-3:51	0:02	Mid Fuselage Port (Left) Sill Longeron	F	Temp	Rise	N	Y	Wing Root
40	-3:45	0:06	Debris #12 – 12th report of debris observed leaving Orbiter						
41	-3:35	0:10	Debris #13 – 13th report of debris observed leaving Orbiter						
42	-3:33	0:02	Debris #14 – 14th report of debris observed leaving Orbiter						

135

Seq #	LOS	LE	Event	Loc	Sensor (Ch)	Δ	Near Panel 8	WR	Comments
43	-3:29	0:04	Left Lower Wing Skin	Wing	Temp	WD	N	Y	
44	-3:21	0:08	Debris #15 – 15th report of debris observed leaving Orbiter						
45	-3:16	0:05	Left Main Gear Up-lock Actuator Unlock Line	W W	Temp	Rise	N	Y	
46	-3:08	0:08	Left Upper Wing Skin	Wing	Temp	WD	N	Y	
47	-2:13	0:55	Left Main Landing Gear Outboard Tire Pressure 1	W W	Press	Rise	N	Y	
48	-2:08	0:05	Debris #16 – 16th report of debris observed leaving Orbiter						
49	-2:08		Left Main Landing Gear Outboard Tire Pressure 2	W W	Temp	Rise	N	Y	
50	-2:04	0:04	Left Lower Wing Skin	Wing	Temp	OL	N	Y	
51	-1:49	0:15	Left Upper Wing Skin	Wing	Temp	OL	N	Y	
52	-1:38	0:11	System 2 Left Hand Aft Brake Switch Valve Return	F	Temp	Rise	N	Y	Wing Root
53	-1:37	0:01	Flare 1: Asymmetrical brightening of Orbiter shape observed						
54	-1:32	0:05	Flare 2: Asymmetrical brightening of Orbiter shape observed						
55	-1:29	0:03	Start of "sharp" aileron trim increase						
56	-1:23	0:06	Increase in derived rolling and yawing moment increments						
57	-1:00	0:23	Left Main Landing Gear Outboard Tire 1	W W	Press	WD	N	Y	
58	-1:00		Left Main Landing Gear Inboard Tire 1	W W	Press	WD	N	Y	
59	-1:00		Left Main Landing Gear Outboard Wheel	W W	Temp	WD	N	Y	

Seq #	LOS	LE	Event	Loc	Sensor (Ch)	Δ	Near Panel 8	WR	Comments
60	-0:56	0:04	Left Main Landing Gear Inboard Wheel	W W	Temp	WD	N	Y	
61	-0:54	0:02	Left Main Landing Gear Outboard Tire 1	W W	Press	OL	N	Y	
62	-0:53	0:01	Left Main Landing Gear Outboard Wheel	W W	Temp	OL	N	Y	
63	-0:53		Left Main Landing Gear Outboard Tire 2	W W	Press	WD	N	Y	
64	-0:52	0:01	Left Main Landing Gear Inboard Tire 1	W W	Press	OL	N	Y	
65	-0:51	0:01	Left Main Landing Gear Inboard Tire 2	W W	Press	Rise	N	Y	
66	-0:49	0:02	Left Main Landing Gear Inboard Tire 2	W W	Press	WD	N	Y	
67	-0:44	0:05	Left Main Landing Gear Inboard Wheel	W W	Temp	OL	N	Y	
68	-0:44		Left Main Landing Gear Inboard Tire 2	W W	Press	OL	N	Y	
69	*-0:38*	*0:06*	*Left Main Landing Gear Outboard Tire 2*	*W W*	*Press*	*OL*	*N*	*Y*	
70	*-0:26*	*0:12*	*Left Main Gear Down and locked*	*W W*	*Ind*		*N*	*Y*	
71	-0:10	0:16	System 2 Left Hand Aft Brake Switch Valve Return	F	Temp	WD	N	Y	Wing Root
72	-0:01	0:15	ASA 4 Wiring to Left Wing	Wing		WD	N	Y	
73	0:00	0:01	Loss of Signal						

137

The Investigation

At first, NASA officials were very cautious to not jump to any conclusions. Much to the media's dismay, NASA managers avoided suggesting that the foam insulation from the external tank caused a gaping hole in the leading edge of the shuttle left wing. Engineers do not make conclusions until every shred of evidence and every piece of information is put into proper perspective. No one can or will dispute that a significant sized object did collide with the shuttle. Everyone has seen the high-speed video of the object glancing off the wing. The significance of that collision is what is in question.

Only relying on human visual observation outside of the scientific community (i.e. the news media and the general public) to investigate an accident or situation is unreliable, and open to emotions and supposition. If you ask four people a question, normally you will get five different answers. Therefore, an investigation that is done by any type of committee, factual or not, the conclusion to what was observed becomes a compromise of opinions.

Ron Dittmore, former Shuttle program manager, went to great lengths immediately after the accident to be open and objective, yet concise with the initial information he had available to him while addressing the cause of the shuttle demise. He was clear during his initial briefings that the first sensors to show a temperature rise as the shuttle re-entered the atmosphere occurred inside the left main wheel well. Eventually, the sensors in the left wing began to indicate temperature rises for whatever reason. As I recall, he did not dismiss the possibility that a hole could have been present in the wing. He just did not want to jump to that conclusion so early in the investigation.

Four days after the accident, apparently against NASA's and popular opinion, Ron Dittmore insisted that the foam was not to blame for the accident. Apparently, he knew something that could not be openly divulged at the time. Ron Dittmore is not your run of the mill manager. He is a very articulate engineer. I doubt he would have made that statement unless he was 100% sure of what he was saying was credible. He is an engineer's engineer. So why would Sean O'Keefe, chief NASA administrator, be so outraged by Ron's remarks? The answer really is quite simple, but we will get to that later.

The following day the Columbia Accident Investigation Board (CAIB) convened in Houston. During the initial meetings, Ron Dittmore stated (or was coerced to acknowledge, I'm not sure) he was wrong to rule out anything so early in the investigation.

Shortly after the accident, the press cornered one member of the astronaut corps and asked if he thought the foam could have been the cause of the accident. His reply was "…the foam striking the shuttle is no different than a foam cooler falling off a truck in front of you on the interstate. No, the foam could not have caused enough damage to bring the shuttle down…"

What he was trying to say was that the mass and porosity of the foam flying near the same speed of the shuttle at the time of departure from the external tank could not have caused the kind of damage necessary to produce a hole significant enough for burn through of the ceramic tiles. All we are talking about is the basic science you learned in elementary school.

The fact of the matter is that in the few thousandths of a second that elapsed from the time the foam separated from the external tank until striking the shuttle, the difference of velocity of the foam and the shuttle was nowhere near the shuttle speed of 430 Nautical miles per hour (510 Statute MPH) at the point of impact. The piece of foam did not come to an immediate and complete stop after shaking loose from the external tank. For something like that to happen would defy the laws of Physics. The Orbiter and the debris were going in the same direction. The difference in speed was probably less than 60 miles per hour. Therefore, we can conclude with a high degree of certainty that the foam could not have caused the extensive damage to the leading edge of the wing that the media wants us to believe. Every competent engineer, scientist and physicist who can run the numbers knows that to be true.

To appease the media and general public that the foam had caused a gaping hole in the wing, the investigative board eventually went to great lengths several months later and spent nearly three million dollars to validate that the foam COULD HAVE CAUSED the damage everyone in the media and general public wanted to believe. The board commissioned a team of engineers to show that a two-and-a-half pound piece of foam the size of a briefcase, precisely aimed and fired at a full mock-up replica of the shuttles leading edge of the wing could damage the tiles.

There were at least two firings that day. The first test fire was made at a relative velocity of 60 feet per second, approximately the difference in velocity between the orbiter and the piece of foam that departed the external fuel tank. The result was that the foam skimmed the surface of the wing, causing a barely noticeable scuff mark on the surface of the wing replica. I am sure there were probably some microscopic cracks in the thermal tile that was struck, but there was nothing that resembled a hole in the wing.

To make sure the experiment produced the desired outcome, a second test was executed firing another piece of foam at a velocity of 750 feet per second, approximately the velocity of the orbiter at the time of impact. Sure enough, there was a 16-inch diameter hole in the tiles. The sigh of relief from the media was deafening, as if to say, "See, I told you so!"

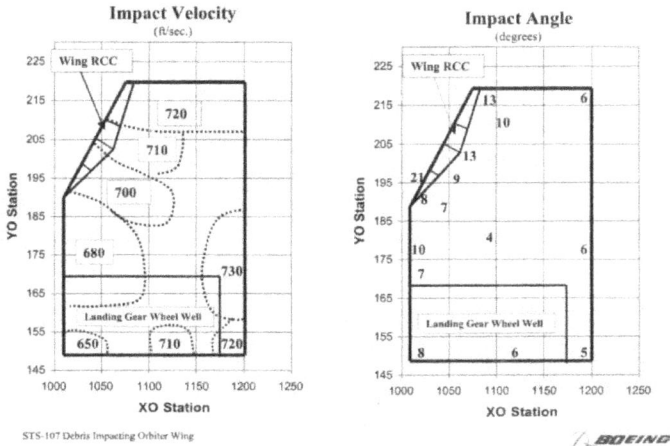

Velocity and Impact Angle Distribution Inside Impact Area
(Debris Size = 20" x 10" x 6", Density = 2.4 lb/ft3)

STS-107 Debris Impacting Orbiter Wing

BOEING

On this slide we can see numbers that represent the relative velocity and impact angles of the debris that was supposed to have struck the lower surface of the Orbiter. The image on the left raises all kinds of questions. Those numbers represent the velocity of the debris in question. At the moment of impact the velocity of the Orbiter was near 750 ft./sec. ($\approx$ 430 Nmph), and accelerating. The smallest difference of velocity between the Orbiter and the debris is 30 ft./sec ($\approx$ 17.9 Nmph). The largest difference of velocity is 100 ft./sec ($\approx$ 59.7 Nmph). Now that we can clearly see these numbers before us, why would the Columbia Accident Investigation Board setup an experiment to fire a piece of foam at the shuttle mockup at 750 ft./sec, when the relative velocity differences are between 30 ft./sec and 100 ft./sec? At 750 ft./sec, of course the impact of the foam is going to create a hole that everyone, especially the media, wants to believe brought down Columbia.

On the other hand, I see an investigating board acquiescing to the media; spending a tremendous amount of money and effort to show the media what they want to believe could be true. For Scott Hubbard, a

Physicist and at the time Director of the NASA Ames Research Center, to come out in public and say "…Oh my God…" when he saw the 16 inch hole in the wing replica after that test was nothing less than pure deception.

To add insult to injury, NASA put astronaut Story Musgrave up as a front man for the investigation. At the time, Story Musgrave was one of the most experienced astronauts in the Shuttle Program. The media trusted every syllable Mr. Musgrave has to say on the subject of the Shuttle. The media played over-and-over the clip when Mr. Musgrave stated that "a piece of foam coming at you at 500 MPH will rip your head off." No kidding. In fact, any object coming at you at 500 MPH will rip your head off; or punch a hole in the leading edge of the Shuttle wing. In reality, the difference in velocity between the Shuttle and the foam was much closer to 60 MPH and could not have caused anything that looked like a hole.

I would like to see is another test set up just like the first, only this time use the correct velocity and impact angle numbers and see what happens. I can assure you that there will not be a 16-inch hole in a tile. I doubt there would be a hole at all.

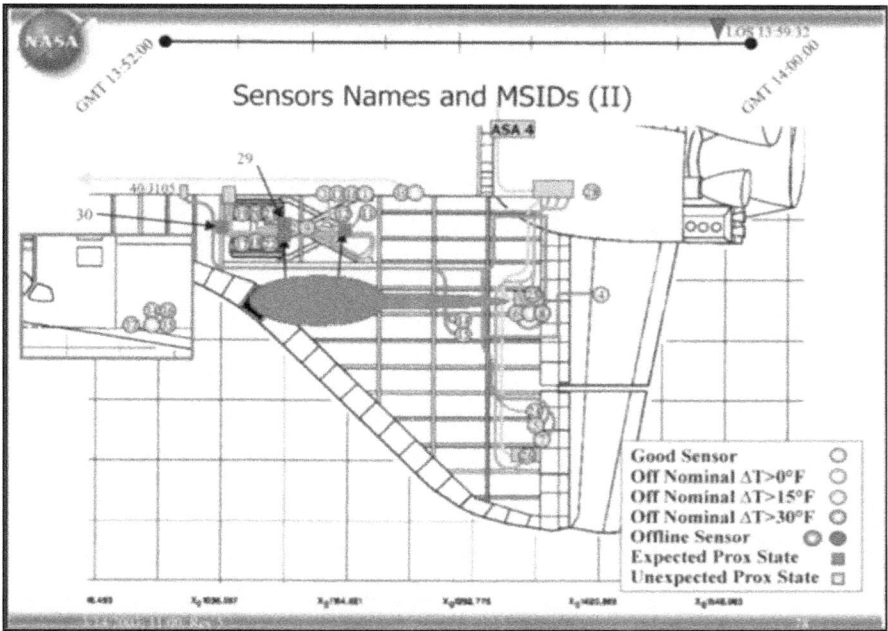

Sensors Names and MSIDs (II)

Good Sensor ○
Off Nominal ΔT>0°F ○
Off Nominal ΔT>15°F ○
Off Nominal ΔT>30°F ○
Offline Sensor ○ ●
Expected Prox State ▨
Unexpected Prox State ▢

From the illustration above we can see the order of sensor failure. Had there been a hole in the wing, the sequential order of sensor failure would have been something like this:

The temperature sensors in the wing would have given the first indication of a hole in the wing. From the intense heat flowing through the wing, the wire harness for sensors 14, 15, 4, 5, 7, 24 and 26 would have been damaged first. Once the heat had progressed through the wing, sensors 6, 8 and 25 would have been affected next.

If the wing was still attached by then, the Left Main Gear outside wheel temperature and tire pressure sensors (17, 18 and 22) would show signs that heat penetrating into the wheel well. As the heat built up across the wheel well, hydraulic line temperature and pressure sensors (2, 9, 11 and 12), Left Main Gear inside tire temperature and pressure sensors (19, 20 and 21) and hydraulic line sensors (1, 3, 13 and 16) would fall off line. Finally the fuselage sensor (10) would have indicated a problem. But, that is not what happened.

After the accident, there was a tremendous amount of correspondence within the NASA community. I find interesting that some of the concerns about debris striking the shuttle during the launch sequence have been known since the very first shuttle mission…

X-Sender: d.m.bushnell@express.larc.nasa.gov
Date: Wed, 5 Feb 2003 09:03:38 -0500
To: d.l.dwoyer@larc.nasa.gov, d.c.freeman@larc.nasa.gov,
    c.m.darden@larc.nasa.gov, c.e.harris@larc.nasa.gov,
    r.m.martin@larc.nasa.gov, a.kumar@larc.nasa.gov,
    m.p.saunders@larc.nasa.gov, j.m.mckenzie@larc.nasa.gov,
    m.j.shuart@larc.nasa.gov, g.r.taylor@larc.nasa.gov,
From: "Dennis m. Bushnell" <d.m.bushnell@larc.nasa.gov>
Subject: Shuttle Heating/TPS

Was on Travel – Just returned, reason this was not sent earlier…[called Doug on his Sunday around noon].Mayber "you all" already heard this…

1.Undersigned was on the Walt Williams/NASA Chief Engineer Shuttle First Flight Certification team in 1980/81 Responsible for Boundry LayerTransition/TPS/Re-entry Heating. The report we [John Bertin and I] sent in indicated the Following:

- Peak Heating is at some 218 Kft.IF the flow is turbulent at Peak heating the heat shield would/could burn through the wheel well doors [even with undamaged tiles].

- Transition data from previous flights [Prime,asset,etc.] indicated Transition Reynolds Numbers at Shuttle Hypersonic Conditions on admittedly rough surfaces well below a Million Reynolds Number but the data were all over the map. Taking the lower bound [with a rough surface] Turbulent flow at peak heating appeared possible…. We therefore specified tile-to-tile and tile gap smoothness criteria which were pretty severe.

- As I recall the observed shuttle transition is usually around 180Kft.

2.On the first flight there were thousands of dings/gouges in the tiles post flight which were almost all on the left wing and traced to ice impingement from launch vibrations dislodgement of the ice which builds up on the external tank dump line – WHICH IS LOCATED IN PROXIMITY OF THE LEFT

145

WING ON THE STACK [Dump line is attached to the tank but runs down the side of the tank near where the windward side of the left wing is positioned when mated to the tank in the launch stack]. Why this dump line was not repositioned to the other side of the tank away from the orbiter I do not understand....Over the years each flight has experienced a unique set of heat shield damage from the ice impingement and as a consequence shuttle transition varies mightily flight-to-flight. Several times this damage was quite severe.

3.All of this [1 above] is for undamaged [in the sense of thermal protection, not transition/roughness] tiles.More extensive tile damage, whether from external tank insulation or ice impingement, would obviously add insult to injury and compromise TPS integrity AS WELL AS ACT AS A BOUNDRY LAYER TRIP. IF the gouges were extensive enough then free shear layers form which have VERY LOW TRANSITION REYNOLDS NUMBERS [below a hundred thousand] AND large Impingement HEATING PEAKS.

We [the agency] should have done more analysis of this whole situation/taken it more seriously as well as repositioned that tank dump line to minimize ice impingement.... The ice buildup/fracture patterns/subsequent impact patterns/effects due to launch vibration/loads is not deterministic. Just the ice,sans tank insulation,could conceivably cause "Grievous Harm"...

Dennis Bushnell

The actual time of this email is not known. However, the contents does illustrate the extent that people within NASA were trying to understand what had happened to Columbia…

To: Cindy Lee <C.C.LEE@larc.nasa.gov>

Hi Cindy,

I would like to offer several observations regarding the theory that debris damaged Columbia's left wing during launch on January 16, 2003. I would like to be able to discuss these ideas during an appropriate Columbia accident investigation meeting here at LaRC.

1. The video footage (apparently provided by the KSC Ice & Debris Team) appears to show that the debris, assumed to be polyisocyanurate foam from theh external tank (ET), may not have originated from the ET. In the first few frames of the video sequence, the debris appears to come from a location obscured by the orbiter and ricochete off the ET. The origin of the debris still could be from the ET, or possibly the underside of the orbiter. After contacting the ET, the debris fragments into two visible pieces. The first, apprently smaller, debris fragmentproduces a small shower of particles that can be seen at the trailing edge of the left wing. The second, larger piece of debris appears to result in a much larger impact on the trailing edge of the left wing. The debris may have been made of ice or some other material(s) and could be much more massive than The calculated 1.211 kg (2.67 lb.). If the photgrammetric measurements accurately measured the debris to be 0.508 x 4.406 x 0.152 meters (20 x 16 x 6 inches), and it was made of solid ice, the mass could be approximately 28.7 kg (63.4 lb). The energy released from this impact could be almost 25 times greater than estimated. Other dense materials, such as aluminum, would make this impact even more damaging. I would like to suggest a re-examination of the debris impact video footage to determine if the fragment(s) could have originated from another location, possibly an ice buildup somewhere under the orbiter. As a reference, if the debris was 1.211 kg, and assuming a conservative relative impact velocity of 457.2 m/s (2 x 750 fps used in the JSC analysis), the kinetic energy would have equivalent to a 500 lb safe impacting at 75 mph. If the debris was 28.7 kg, that would be the equivalent of a 500 lb safe hitting the wing at 365 mph.

2. If the observation in #1 above can be proven incorrect, and it can be definitively determined that the debris was foam from the ET, there still appears to be an issue regarding its thickness. It has been estimated that the debris was 0.152 meters (6 inches) thick. Several sources that I have found indicate that the insulation is sprayed to a thickness of 1-2 inches. It is certainly possible that certain locations on the ET may have insulation that is 6 inches in depth, but how thick was the insulation at the point where it is believed to have generated? How accurately is this locationknown? I assume that the volume of ET insulation can be approximated by a thin walled cylindrical body with flat, circular plates on each end. I assumed that the ET was 46.8 meters (153.8 ft) in length, 8.412 meter (27.6 ft) in diameter. I used a density of 38.63 kg/m^3 (calculated from the mass and size of the foam debris assumed in #1 above).

Using a uniform thickness of 0.152 meters (6 inches), I estimated the total mass of the insulation to be 5080 kg (17,813 lb). This is 3.7 times greater than the 2187 kg (4823 lb) that is stated on the NASA Human Space Flight Shuttle Reference web page. A 0.0254 meter (1 inch) thickness results in a total mass of 1328 kg (2928 lb), and a 0.508 meter (2 inch) thickness results in a total mass of 2664 kg (5873 lb). These totals are not consistent with a thivckness of 1-2 inches. It I spossible that the numbers stated on the Space Flight web page are not very accurate, but I would not expect them to be that much off. I have not heard any discussion about the variations in the insulation thickness, and I would like to understand how certain we can be that the debris was entirely made of foam.

3. Even if the damage to the tiles was not obviously visible, could this type of impact carve out a significant channel in the protective tiles? This channel would then allow extreme heating to occur down the length of the wing. How many re-entries had the tiles in the area of the suspected damage been through?Is it possible that this area could have had "older" tiles that could be more easily loosened from the wing during impact, but only separated during re-entry or later during ascent? Could the impact result in a significant increase in the surface roughness of the tiles around the impact area, and could this result in a high turbulent heating that caused tiles to be shed during re-entry? Finally, it is reasonable that the impact could have multiple effects on the orbiter, such as damage to control surfaces.

Thanks very much for your attention to these observations. I hope that they are helpful to the investigation of this terrible loss for the astronauts and their families, NASA and our country.

Dan

--

Daniel D. Mazanek

Spacecraft and Sensors Branch, ASCAC
8 Langley Boulevard
NASA Langley Research Center   Phone: (757) 864-1739
Mail Stop 328   Fax: (757) 864-1975
Hampton, VA 23681-2199   E-mail: d.d.mazanek@larc.nasa.gov

The Conclusion is Obvious

A good number of the temperature and pressure sensors that were affected on the Columbia are located relatively the same distance from the nose of the shuttle, or ahead of the suspected hole. Common sense dictates that if there was a hole, the initial heat would have been felt past the suspected hole, not ahead of or some distance beside the hole.

The first sensors affected by the heat of re-entry are either inside of the wheel well, or on the fuselage side of the wheel well, (i.e. on the wrong side of the wheel well to be affected by the suspected hole in the wing). To conclude that a hole in the wing affected those sensors is literally ignoring all the data sent back to us by the Orbiter.

Another thought to consider, had there been a hole in the leading edge of the wing temperature sensors would have indicated some anomalies during the launch. The spacecraft was near Mach 2 during the collision with the piece of foam, and still had another 17,000 MPH to achieve orbital velocity. If these sensors indicated a problem during descent, does it not make sense that problems would have been noticed during ascent into orbit? We are talking about the same velocities and altitudes, just different directions. There were no problems noted during Columbia's ascent.

So clearly, what brought the shuttle down was not a hole in the wing, but a left main landing gear door that was damaged during launch or possibly not aligned properly prior to launch. Near the landing gear door hinge assembly, is a sensing switch. The switch is adjusted to indicate to the CC that the door is closed, locked and sealed. However, because the switch is adjustable, there is room for error during the adjustment process. In the case of the Columbia, the door could have appeared to be closed enough for the sensing switch to give an indication to the crew that the door was closed and locked, but the door may not have been completely sealed.

As you can see in the picture, the landing gear door is hinged on the outboard side of the door. The first sensors to indicate a temperature rise during re-entry are located inside the wheel well, just above the inboard edge of the door.

In reality, the landing gear door may not have been completely closed and therefore sealed, allowing hot gases near blow torch temperatures to enter the wheel well area. The same thing happens when you close a refrigerator door enough to turn out the light, but the door seal does not stick to the frame. The door is left open just enough to let outside air inside your refrigerator.

Sometime between T-0:38 and T-0:26 seconds before loss of signal one or both of the left main landing gear tires probably exploded, because of the extreme rise in tire pressure due to the heat of re-entry. The damage from this type of explosion is enough to cause significant and/or catastrophic damage to the wing structure of the Orbiter. If this theory did occur, the explosive energy could have been enough to force the main landing gear strut to extend to the down position, as indicated by the shuttle data approximately 26 seconds before Los of Signal. At twenty-three times the speed of sound, the aerodynamic drag on the airframe could have been enough to cause the left wing to tear away from the fuselage.

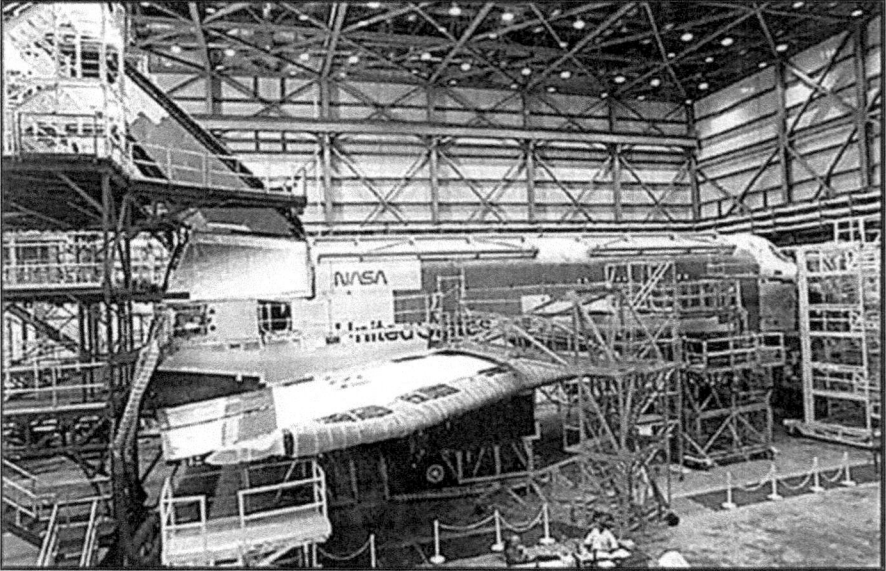

Aerospace engineers perform an overhaul of the space shuttle Columbia in a hangar at the Kennedy Space Center. Reusable space vehicles are carefully inspected before and after each flight, and they are periodically overhauled to ensure that all systems are operating at peak efficiency.

Then there is the routine maintenance. Every time some type of maintenance is performed to an aircraft the time, date, work performed and signatures of the mechanic or technician and inspecting official are logged in a maintenance log book; certifying the work had been done correctly. So, why has the Columbia maintenance log not been made public? Things that make you go, hmmm.

We may never know for certain what brought down the Columbia. However, from my experience, knowledge of high tech aircraft and expertise this is the only possible and logical explanation for the cause of Columbia's demise.

I sympathize with the engineers and managers of the shuttle program whose lives were affected by this accident, especially Ron Dittmore and Bob Daugherty. From the memo's he sent throughout the NASA community, apparently he was right on the money in his analysis of what would happen if the landing gear door seal was breached. To know what happened and be silenced or ignored by administrators and the CAIB who are trying to cover their behinds rather than tell the truth must be excruciating.

Appendix

STS-107 Mishap Investigation - Summary Time Line

-BASELINE-

02/27/2003 6 PM

Note: Rev 14 BASELINE corrects typo's, pinpoints last pt that MCC/MER received real-time data, adds new debris data & senior jet firings, adjusts GMTs for BPS entry messages and adds post-LOS data (including GNC). Rev 14 was approved by the OVE Working Group on 2/26/03.

Sum No.	GMT Day 32	Milestone	Entry Event	Remarks	MSID
1	13:10:39	TIG-5	APU 2 Start		
2	13:15:30	TIG	OMS TIG		
3	13:19:08		OMS End of Burn		
4	13:31:25	EI-15	APU 1 Start		
5	13:31:29		APU 3 Start		
6	13:44:09	EI	Entry Interface (400,000 ft)	Mach 24.57	
			------- 32:13:50:00 -------		
7	13:50:53	Start of Peak Heating		Determined by analysis	
			------- 32:13:51:00 -------		
7.3	13:51:19 / 13:52:49		Remote sensors indicate off-nominal external event	L2L, L3L, and R2R jet firings occurred near event	n/a
7.35	13:51:46		Inertial Beta goes and stays Negative until LOS		V90H2249C
			------- 32:13:52:00 -------		
7.4	13:52:05	Approx Vehicle Ground Location: 39.0 N / -129.2 W	First clear indication of off-nominal aero increments	Delta yawing moment coefficient only (as compared to nominal aero). Derived by analysis.	n/a
7.8	13:52:17		Altitude 236,800 ft / Mach 23.6 - Over the Pacific Ocean, approx 300 miles West of California Coastline	Approx vehicle position when first off-nominal data was seen. Data source: STS-107 GPS Trajectory Data	
8	13:52:17 / 52:41		LMG Brake Line Temps (D, A, C) (3) - start of off nominal trend	Unusual Temperature increase	V58T1703A V58T1700A V62T0440A V62T0551A
8.5	13:52:32/55		Supply H2O Dump Nozzle Temps (A, B) (2) and Vacuum Vent Temp (1) - transient (15 la and 23 seconds, respectively) increase in typical rise rates	GMT shown indicates initial rise duration. Supply H2O Dump Nozzle temps took additional 48 secs to return to nominal temp rise. vacuum vent temps took additional 40 secs to return to nominal rise	V58T1702A V62T0439A
9	deleted			Began trending down 3 secs earlier	
10	13:52:59		Left INBD Lower Skin Temp (1) - OSL		V09T1006A
			------- 32:13:53:00 -------		
10.5	13:53:01		First clear indication of off-nominal rolling moment increment	Start of steady (-) growth in roll moment. Derived by analysis.	n/a
11	13:53:10 / 36		Hydraulic System Left Outbd / Inbd Elevon Return Line Temps (4) - OSL	OSL was preceded by Nominal Temp rise.	V58T0944A V58T0157A
11.2	13:53:28	Approx Veh Grd Location: 36.7 N / -125.5 W	Altitude 231600 ft / Mach 23.0 - Crossing the California Coastline	Data source: STS-107 GPS Trajectory Data	
11.5	13:53:44 / 54 11		1st reported debris (5) observed leaving the Orbiter just aft of Orbiter envelope (Debris #1 thru 5)	EOC video # EOC2-4-0026. 0056. & 0094. No evidence of jet firings near events	n/a
			------- 32:13:54:00 -------		
12	deleted				
13	13:54:10 / 55:12		Left Main Gear Brake Line Temp B (1) / Strut Actuator Temp (1) / Sys 3 LMG Brake Sw	Unusual Temperature increase	V58T1701A V58T0405A V90H1500C
14	13:54:20		Vlv Ret Line Temp (FWD) (1) - start of off nominal trend. Start of slow aileron trim change. Reversal in trend of derived rolling moment coefficient.	GMT is approximate (+- 10 sec) for aileron. Observed roll moment changed from a negative to positive slope. Derived by analysis.	
15	13:54:22		Mid Fuselage LT BondLine Temp at x1215 (1) & LH Aft Fus Sidewall Temp at x1410 (1) - start of off nominal trend	Unusual increase in temperature rise rate	V34T1106A V09T1724A
15.3	13:54:33.3 / 37		Flash #1 - Orbiter envelope suddenly brightened (duration 0.3 sec), leaving noticeably luminescent signature in plasma trail, plus Debris # 6 - report of very bright debris observed leaving the Orbiter just aft of the Orbiter envelope	EOC video # EOC2-4-0026. 0034. & 0009B. R3R and R2R jet firings occurred near events. Debris events 6 & 14 are visually the biggest, brightest events & therefore may indicate the most significant changes to the Orbiter of the western debris events	V58T0842A
			------- 32:13:55:00 -------		
15.35	13:55:04 / 56:30		Debris # 7 thru 10 observed leaving the Orbiter just aft of Orbiter envelope. Debris #8 event was followed by momentary brightening of plasma trail. Debris #9 event was followed by multiple secondary plasma trails.	EOC video # EOC2-4-0005. 0017. 0021. 0028. and 0030. No evidence of jet firings near events.	n/a
15.4	13:55:30		Remote sensors indicate off-nominal external event	GMT is approximate. Preliminary match to debris shedding seen in video #10 (ivms. UT). No evidence of jet firings near event.	n/a

02/27/2003 6 PM

STS-107 Mishap Investigation - Summary Time Line
-BASELINE-

Integ Time Line Team - REV 14 BASELINE

Note: Rev 14 BASELINE corrects typo's, pinpoints last pt that MCC/MER received real-time data, adds crew debris data & assoc jet firings, adjusts GMT's for BFS entry messages and adds post LOS data (excluding GNC). Rev 14 was approved by the OVE Working Group on 2/26/03.

Sum No.	GMT Day 32	Milestone	Entry Event	Remarks	MSID
15.45	13:55:36 / 56:13		Debris # 11 thru 15 observed leaving the Orbiter envelope. Debris #12 event was preceded and followed by secondary plasma trails. Debris #13 event was followed by momentary brightening of plasma trail adjacent to debris. Debris #14 event consisted of very bright debris observed leaving the Orbiter.	EOC video # EOC2-4-0005, 0017, 0021, 0028, 0030, and 0050. No evidence of jet firings near events. (Nearest jet firings occur at 56:17.) Debris events 5 & 14 are visually the biggest, brightest events & therefore may indicate the most significant changes to the Orbiter of the western debris events.	n/a
15.5	13:55:41		Mid Fuselage Port (Left) Sill Longeron Temp at X1215 - start of off nominal trend	Unusual Temperature increase	V34T1118A
			32:13:56:00		
16	13:56:03 / 56:24		Left Lower/Upper Wing Skin Temp - Trending down (2)	Indication of potential measurement failures	V09T1002A / V09T1024A
16.5	13:56:16 / 56:53		Hyd Sys 1 LMG Uplock Actuator Unlock Line Temp; Sys 3 LMG Brake Sw V/v Ret Line Temp (FWD); LMG Brake Line Temp C; LMG Brake Line Temp B; Sys 3 Left Main Gear Strut Actuator Temp - all show a temp rise rate change	Significant increase in temp rise rate on all four lines	V58T0125A / V58T1701A, V58T0842A / V58T0405A, V58T1702A
			32:13:57:00		
16.7	13:57:19 / 24		MLG LH Outbd Tire Pressures 1 & 2 - start of small increase in pressures	Not seen in previous flights	V51P0570A / V51P0572A, V09T1002A / V09T1024A
17	13:57:28 / 43		Left Lower/Upper Wing Skin Temps (2) - OSL		
18	deleted				
19	13:57:54		Sys 2 LH Brake Sw V/v Return Temp (1)	Unusual Temperature increase	V58T0841A
			32:13:58:00		
20	13:58:03		Start of sharp aileron trim increase	GMT is approximate (+/- 10 sec)	V90H1500C
20.5	13:58:09		Increase in derived rolling and yawing moment increments	Substantial increase in observed growth rate of both roll and yaw moment increments. Derived by analysis.	n/a
21	deleted				
22	deleted				
22.5	13:58:16		LMG Brake Line Temp D - Temp rise rate change	Significant increase in temp rise rate	V58T1703A / V51P0573A, V51P0570A / V51P0571A, V51P0572A
23	13:58:32 / 54		MLG LH Inbd / Outbd Tire Pressures (4) - Decay to OSL		
24	deleted				
24.5	13:58:39 / 48		MLG LH Inbd/Outbd Wheel Temps (2) - OSL		V51T0574A / V51T0575A
25.5	13:58:40		BFS Fault Msg (4) - Tire Pressures - 1st Message		
26	13:58:56		BFS Fault Msg (4) - Tire Pressures - Last Message		
			32:13:59:00		
27	13:59:06		Left Main Gear Downlocked Indication - Transferred ON		V51X0125E
27.5	13:59:23		Loss of MCC real-time data to the workstations in the FCR and MER		
28	13:59:30.66 / 30.68		Start of two yaw jets firing (R2R and R3R)	Fired continuously until end of data at 13:59:37.4 Left: -8.11 deg (up) Right: -1.15 deg (up)	V79X2634X
29	13:59:31		Observed elevons deflection at LOS	ASAs responded appropriately. However, signature is indicative of failure of ASA.4	V79X2838X
29.3	13:59:31.4 / 34.5		Several events and PASS and BFS FSM messages during this time period all indicate the failure signature of ASA.4	-2.3 degrees	V57H0253A (5 Hz)
29.5	13:59:32		Observed aileron trim at LOS		
30	deleted				
31	deleted				
32	deleted				
32.5	13:59:32	Approx Veh Grd Location 32.9 N / 99.0 W LOS	Altitude ~200700 ft / Mach ~18.1 - Near Dallas TX	Approximate Vehicle Ground Location at Loss of Signal based on GMT. Data source: STS-107 GPS Trajectory Data	n/a
33	13:59:32.136		Last valid downlink frame accepted by ODRC - OI / BFS / PASS. Start of reconstructed data	Nominal loss of comm at this GMT (for ~15 sec max based on previous fit data)	V79X2838X
34	deleted				
35	13:59:35.36		Sideslip on vehicle changes sign.	The event occurred between the two times listed. Aerodynamic forces due to sideslip are now reinforcing aerodynamic asymmetry	V57H0253A n/a
36	13:59:38		Growth in Bank attitude error	Up until this time the flight control had been able to maintain the Bank error around 5 deg	

156

STS-107 Mishap Investigation - Summary Time Line
-BASELINE-

022772003 6 PM

Integ Time Line Team - REV 14 BASELINE

Note: Rev 14 BASELINE corrects typo's, plinpoints last pt that MCC/MER received real-time data, adds new debris data & assoc jet firings.
Adjusts GMTs for BFS entry messages and adds post-LOS data (including GNC). Rev 14 was approved by the DWE Working Group on 2/26/03.

Sum No.	GMT GMT Day 32	Milestone	Entry Event	Remarks	MSID
37	13:59:36.8		Aerojet DAP Requests Third Right Yaw RCS Jet (R4R)	This additional jet is required to counteract the increasing aerodynamic moments on the vehicle. Fired continuously until end of data at 13:59:37.4	
38	13:59:37.3		Aerojet DAP Requests Third Right Yaw RCS Jet (R1R)	This additional jet is required to counteract the increasing aerodynamic moments on the vehicle. Fired continuously until end of data at 13:59:37.4	
39	13:59:37.n		Last aileron data	The aileron position is now approx -5.2 deg with approx -2.5 deg of aileron trim. The rate of change of aileron trim had reached the maximum allowed by the flight control system	
40	13:59:37.396	End of 5-second period of reconstructed data	End of first 5-seconds of the 32-seconds period of post-LOS data. Start of approximately 25 seconds of no data available	GMT derived by MER data personnel	n/a
41	13:59:46.347 / 14:00:01.900*		PASS Fault Message annunciation - ROLL REF PASS Fault Message annunciation - L RCS LEAK BFS Fault Message annunciations - L RCS LEAK (2)	*Time info corrupted for 14:00:01.900 GMT event.	
			------- 32:14:00:00 -------		
42	14:00:02.06		Debris A observed leaving the Orbiter - Large debris seen falling away from the Orbiter envelope	EOC videos # EOC2-4-0024, EOC2-4-0018 & EOC2-4-0118	n/a
43	14:09:02.654	Beginning of 2-second period of reconstructed data	PASS Fault Message annunciation - L RCS LJET		
44	14:00:02.660		Start of last 2-seconds of the 32 second period of post-LOS data		
			During this final 2 second period of reconstructed data, the data indicates the following systems were nominal: APUs were running and WSB cooling was evident. MPS integrity was still evident. Fuel cells were generating power and the PRSD tanks/lines were intact. Comm and nav/aids systems in the forward fuselage were performing nominally. RSB, Body Flap, main engine, and right wing temps appeared active. ECLSS performance was nominal.		
			During this final 2 second period of reconstructed data, the data indicates the following systems were off-nominal: All three Hyd systems were lost. The left inbd/outbd elevon actuator temps were either OSL or no data exists. Majority of left OMS pod sensors were either OSH or OSL or no data exists. Elevated temps at bottom bondline centerline skin forward and aft of the wheel wells and at the port side structure over left wing were observed. EPDC shows general upward shift in Main Bus amps and downward shift in Main Bus volts. AC3 phase A inverter appeared disconnected from the AC Buss.		
			GNC data suggests vehicle was in an uncommanded attitude and was exhibiting uncontrolled rates. Yaw rate was at the sensor maximum of 20 deg/sec. The flight control mode was in AUTO. (Note that all Nav-derived parameters (e.g., alpha) are suspect due to high rates corrupting the IMU state.)		
45	14:00:03.470 / 14:00:03.637		BFS Fault Message annunciation - LOMS TK P BFS Fault Message annunciation - SM1 AC VOLTS PASS Fault Message annunciation - L RCS PVT		
46	14:00:03.637		PASS Fault Message annunciation - DAP DOWNMODE RHC	The s/w process which logs the PASS message runs every 1.92 seconds, so this event could have occurred as early as 14:00:01.717 GMT. However, during the 2 sec period, available vehicle data indicates RHC was in detent and DAP was in AUTO	n/a
47	14:00:04.826	End of 2-second period of reconstructed data	Last OI Downlink frame		
48	14:00:17 / 22		Debris B and C observed leaving the Orbiter	EOC videos # EOC2-4-0024 &-0118 (for both B and C)	n/a
49	14:00:21 / 25		Vehicle Main Body break-up	EOC videos # EOC2-4-0024, -0018 &-0118	n/a
50	14:00:53	End of Peak Heating		Determined by analysis	

* Nominal/Expected Event or Performance

157

The following is a detailed NASA briefing of the Orbiter flight path and every event leading up to the loss of signal. After the signal was lost, the remainder of information was calculated and inferred through the landing of all the Orbiter debris.

STS-107 Accident Investigation Ground Track, Events Summary, and Sighting Data Based on the Rev 15 Master Time Line

(Baselined, 03/10/03, 08:00 pm)

and Sighting Data Catalogued by the JSC Emergency Operations Center

March 17, 2003

Explanation of Ground Track & Events Summary

• GPS Ground Track Data Source: STS-107 GPS State Vector

• Event Time Line Source: STS-107 Accident Investigation Master Timeline (Baselined), Revision 15, dated 03/10/03 08:00 pm CST, from the Integrated Time Line Team.

• GPS-derived Latitudes and Longitudes are plotted on the map at 0.96 second time intervals, although there are numerous data dropouts. The symbol used for points from the trajectory data file is a red dot. Thirty-two seconds of down list data have been recovered from the post-Loss-of-Signal period, including some GPS data. The five data points from this period are indicated by turquoise dots.

• The time tags of events from the Master Time Line sometimes fall between trajectory data points, and in some cases they occur during GPS data dropouts. In these cases the location of the event is indicated by a blue dot.

• Explanation of the contents of Event Note Boxes:

   • Grey Header – Greenwich Mean Time (GMT) of the event and the Event Sequence Number from the Master Time Line (in parentheses)

   • Geodetic Latitude and W. Longitude of the event (red dots only) in decimal degrees.

   • Event description and remarks from the Master Time Line (augmented by text boxes as required)

   • Geodetic Altitude (H, ft) & Mach Number (Mach), interpolated when necessary

   • Some nominal events have been intentionally omitted.

Explanation of Ground Track & Events Summary (continued)

• For events that cover a range of times, or have a range of uncertainty greater than one second in the time tag, the time in the header is the center of the time span, followed by the comment "Center" in parentheses. For example, the time in the header for event 100 is shown as "14:00:04 GMT (Center)." The entire range of times is given in the note box text just before the event description. This is a change from previous versions of the ground track/time line maps, which put the earliest time in the note box header.

• Post Loss-Of-Signal Ground Track Data Source: The Descent Analysis Group (DM42) produced a ballistic trajectory for a hypothetical object with a Ballistic Number of 220.0 lb/ft^2. This trajectory was propagated from 13:59:37.00 GMT to ground impact at 14:03:34 GMT in Louisiana. One second time steps are shown. The symbol used for post-LOS trajectory data is a yellow dot. An update to the reference trajectory is pending.

The hypothetical post-LOS ground track is used here as a reference to locate post-LOS time line events and visual sighting data on the map background. It must be emphasized that the post-LOS ground track is provided as a reasonable visual reference only, and does not represent the actual trajectory of any known piece of the vehicle.

Explanation of Ground Observer Sighting Data

◁

• The location of a ground observer is indicated by a turquoise triangle.

• Sighting location note box headers contain the NASA sighting number and the observing site name.

• Sighting note boxes also contain the Latitude and Western Longitude of the observer, and Acquisition-Of-Sighting (AOS) and Loss-Of-Sighting (LOS) times (GMT). AOS and LOS times do not represent horizon break, but are the actual beginning and ending times of the observer's video coverage.

• For each sighting, the period of observation is indicated on the map by a colored region bounded by the lines-of-sight from the observer to the ground track at AOS and LOS.

• When colored regions overlap, one color overlays the other, but the AOS or LOS line-of-sight of the underlying region is indicated by a thick line of the underlying color.

• In selected cases AOS or LOS points associated with specific sightings are labeled using note boxes. This is done for clarity when needed, usually if the sighting location does not appear on the same map with its AOS or LOS point.

• The post-LOS maps show the locations of four sightings that occurred after Loss-Of-Signal with the vehicle, when no GPS ground track data were available. Sighting lines-of-sight are shown with respect to the hypothetical reference post-LOS ground track (yellow dots).

162

Entry Interface to Coastal Crossing

Based on Master Time Line Rev 15, 03/10/03

Approaching the Coast

Based on Master Time Line Rev 15, 03/10/03

Crossing the California Coast

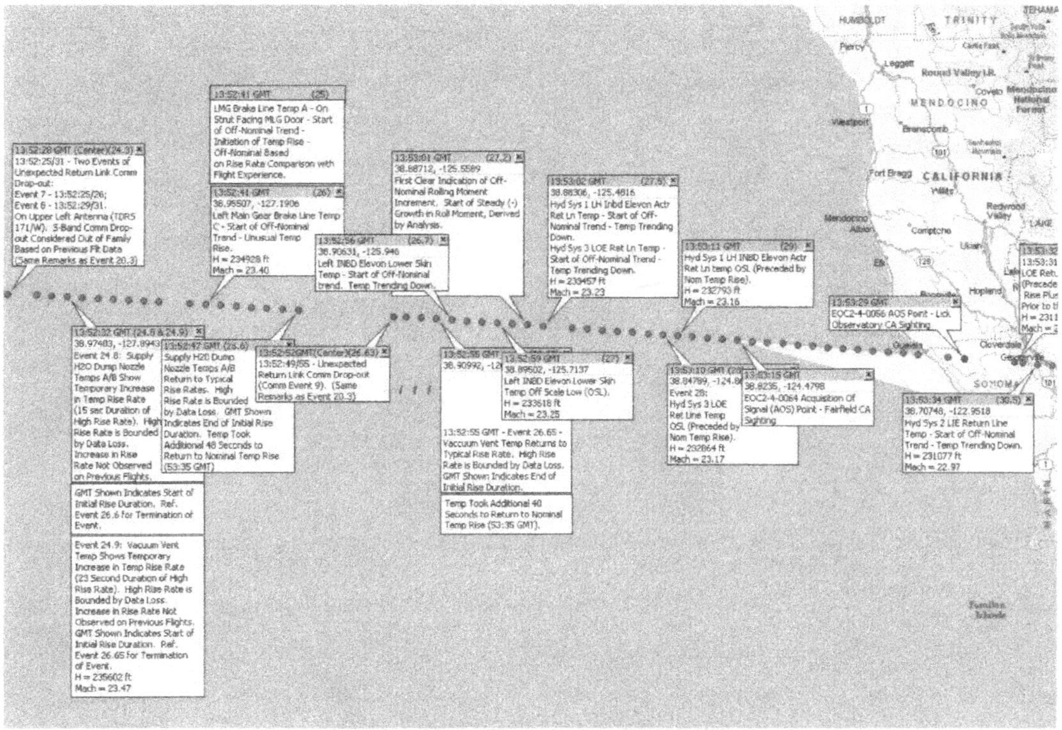

Based on Master Time Line Rev 15, 03/10/03

165

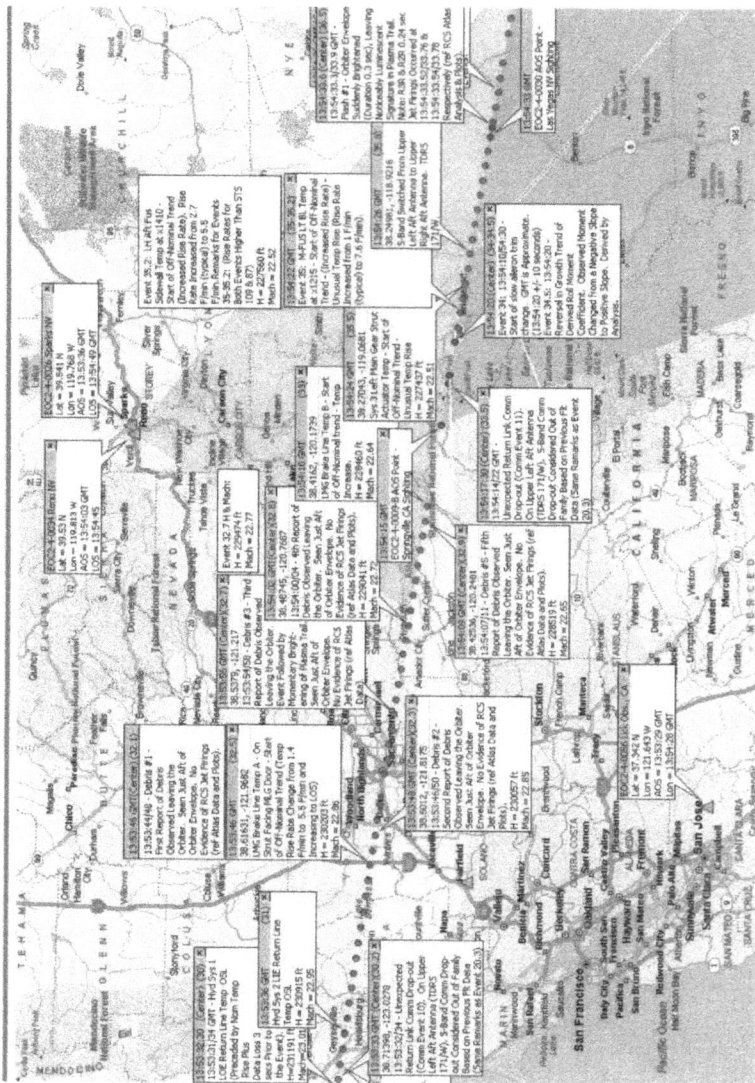

Based on Master Time Line Rev 15, 03/10/03

Crossing from California to Nevada

Based on Master Time Line Rev 15, 03/10/03

Crossing Nevada and Utah

Based on Master Time Line Rev 15, 03/10/03

168

Crossing Arizona

Based on Master Time Line Rev 15, 03/10/03

169

Based on Master Time Line Rev 15, 03/10/03

Crossing North Texas

Based on Master Time Line Rev 15, 03/10/03

Crossing Texas to Loss of Signal

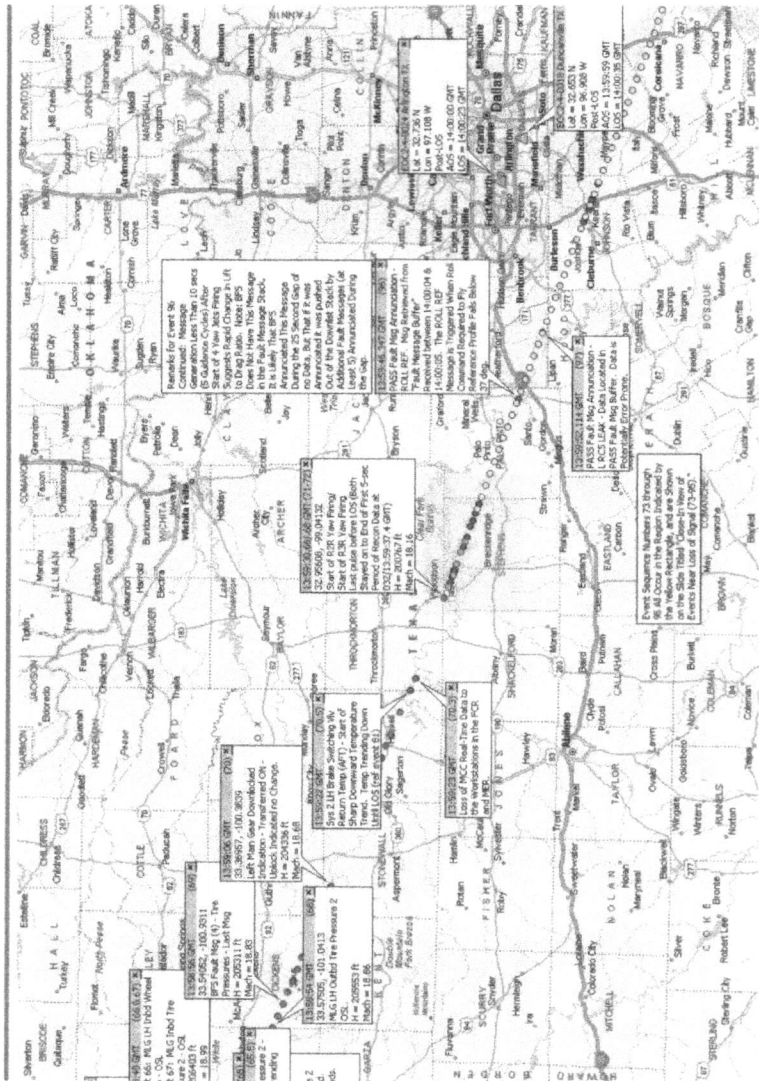

Based on Master Time Line Rev 15, 03/10/03

Close-In View of Post-LOS Events (98-107) – Reference Trajectory

Based on Master Time Line Rev 15, 03/10/03

Close-In View of Events Near Loss of Signal (73-95)

Event 73.3 Remarks:
Speedbrake Was Commanded to "Overdose" (-18 deg).
Position Measurements for Channels 1 thru 3 were 0.0 deg. Secondary Delta Pressure on Ch 4 Went to Zero, which Indicates That the Channel was Bypassed. This is Real Data and the ASAs Were Responding Appropriately.

13:59:31.7 GMT
Speedbrake Channel 4 of Position Measurement Indicated Successively 19 deg, 20 deg, 24 deg Over Last Three Samples Prior to LOS (Should be Closed/0.0 deg).

Event 94 13:59:32.0 1/95 - ASA 4 RPC PRC Trip Indication ASA Logging Indicator of ASA Transducer Excitation Short Condition.

Event 82.5: 13:59:32.13 - RCS Ch 4 Fail Flag Raised (-1 Hz) on all Aerosurface Actuators. ASA Position Measurement Discrepancy.

Event 85.5: 13:59:32.59R GMT - Left Outboard Force Fight Begins, Resulting in a Force Fight Between Channels 1/2/3 and Channel 4 Begins. Indicates a Difference of up to 0.5 Degrees Observed Between the Left Outboard and Inboard Elevons. Indicates a Short in Bypass Valve Has Grown Sufficient to Drop Below Voltage Threshold of Valves; RPC B is Current Limiting.

Event 88 Remarks: Leading Indicator of RPC B Trip/ASA Power Down, i.e. Indicates Opening of All Bypass Valves (Due to RPC B Trip Removing Power) On ASA 4. Force Fight Goes Away Since Actuators are Already at the Last Commanded Position (So Channel 4 Has no Hyd Load for the Servo Asking for Position Change).

Event 89 Remarks: Indicates Opening of All Bypass Valves (Due to RPC B Trip Removing Power) On ASA 4. Since the Speedbrake is at Zero But is Being Commanded to "Overdose" Position (-16) This Results in a Force Fight Between Channels 1, 2, 3, and Channel 4.

(93):
Aerojet DAP Requests Thru 4 Right Yaw RCS Jet (R4R). This Additional Jet is Required to Counteract the Increasing Aerodynamic Moments on the Vehicle. The RCS Jet Fired as Expected and Stayed on to End of First 5-sec Period of Recon Data at 13:59:37.4 GMT.

13:59:37.3 - R4R GMT (93-94):
Aerojet DAP Requests Thru 4 Right Yaw RCS Jet (R4R). This Additional Jet is Required to Counteract the Increasing Aerodynamic Moments on the Vehicle. The RCS Jet Fired as Expected and Stayed on to End of First 5-sec Period of Recon Data at 13:59:37.4 GMT.

13:59:36 GMT
Growth in Bank Attitude Error Up Until The Time the Flight Control Has Been Able to Master the Bank Error Around Stag. Aerojet DAP Drops Left Wing to Compensate for Increasing Aerodynamic Moments, Creating a Bank Attitude Error.

Event 86: Left Outboard Force Fight Ends, Driver Currents Go to Zero (RPC B Trip Indication).

Event 89: Speedbrake Force Fight (Continues to LOS).

13:59:35.36 - GMT
13:59:35.36 - Sideslip on Vehicle Changes Sign - the Event Occurred Between the Two Times Listed. Just Prior to Initial LOS the Magnitude of the Negative Sideslip Started to Decrease and Between 59:34 & 59:37 Sideslip Grew From -0.6 to +0.8 deg. With This Change, the Normal Roll & Yaw Moments on the Vehicle Would Change Sign.

(80):
Force Due to Sideslip Are Now Reinforcing Aerodynamic Asymmetry.

Event 85.6: 13:59:33.68 - BPS Fault Msg Annunciation (1) - Indicates a Limit Indicating the Pressure Across Actuator Exceeds a Limit When Sensed Delta Hardware When Sensed Delta Pressure Across Actuator Exceeds a Limit. PCS Ch is no Longer Driving the Actuator. PCS Ch 4 Failure.

Event 85.7: 13:59:33.68 - BPS Fault Msg Annunciation (1) Following: LIB1OBBRB08 Elevon Actuator 4, Rudder Actuator 4, Speedbrake Actuator 4, SBME 1/2/3 F/Y Actuator (D), & UR SRB R/T

Event 86: 13:59.33.863 - PASS Fault Msg Annunciation (1) - PCS CH 4 - TDRS-E
Data.

Event 97: 13:59.33.976 - Master Alarm Noted. CRC Analysis is Continuing to Determine Cause of Alarm.

Event 73: 13:59/31.40 - PCS Channel 4 Aerosurface Position Measurements Start Trending Towards Their Null Values. Indicates Worsening Failure of Transducer Excitation Via a Wiring Short Condition.

Event 73.2: 13:59:31.47R - All PCS Channel 4 Bypass Valves Close (Indicating Bypassed), Leading Indicator of ASA Fail (High-Rate Data.)

13:59:31 GMT
Observed Elevon Deflection at
LOS:
Left:
-8.11 deg (leo),
Right:
-1.15 deg (up)

13:59:31.7 GMT
Observed Aileron Trim at LOS (-2.3 deg).
LOS for all of the Following:
Event 74: M-P-US LT B, Temp at x1315,
Event 74.5: LH AR Plus Sidewall Temp at x1410).
Event 75: LMG Brake Line Temp B (154.25),

Event 73.5: Observed Aileron Trim at LOS (-2.3 deg).

Event 76: LMG Brake Line Temp C (104.9F)
Event 78: LMG Brake Line Temp D (98.3F)
Event 79: LMG Strut Actuator
Event 80: Hyd Sys 1 LMG Uplk Actr Unls Ln Temp (52.2F)
Event 81: Sys 2 LH Brake Sw W/ return Line Temp (62.8F)
Event 82: Sys 3 LMG Brake Sw W/ return Line Temp (62.8F)

Event 83: 13:59:31.136 - Loss of Signal - Last Valid Downlink Frame Accepted by ODRC - OI/BFS/PASS (This Time has been Referred to as "LOS" Throughout the Investigation.) Start of Reconstructed Data.

Event 84: 13:59:37.0 - Last Aileron Data - The Aileron Position is now Approx -5.2 deg With Approx -2.5 deg of Aileron Trim. The Rate of Change of Aileron Trim Had Reached the Maximum Allowed by the Flight Control System.

Event 95: 13:59:37.396 - End of First 5-Second Period of Reconstructed Data. End of First 5-Second Period of 32-Second Period of Post-LOS Data. Start of Approximately 25 Seconds of no Data Available. GMT Derived by MER Data Personnel.

Event 93 Remarks: Upper Right (URA) Quad Antenna was Selected by BFS Antenna Management S/W to Communicate with TDRS-W. The Pointing Angle to TDRS-W was Off the Orb Tail at -46 Deg. and Trending Further Into Blockage. Previous Environmental Calcs Predict Probable Loss of Comm at Elevation Angles > -60 Deg. Loss of Comm at This GMT is Therefore Considered Nominal.

Based on Master Time Line Rev 15, 03/10/03

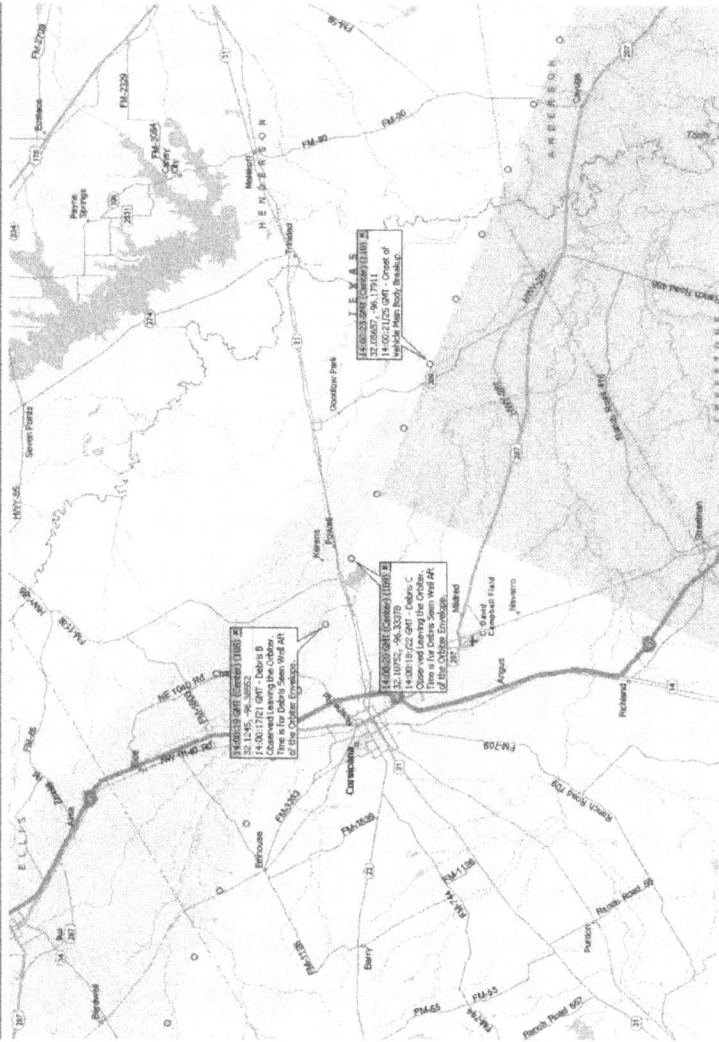

Close-In View of Post-LOS Events (108-110) - Reference Trajectory

Based on Master Time Line Rev 15, 03/10/03

175

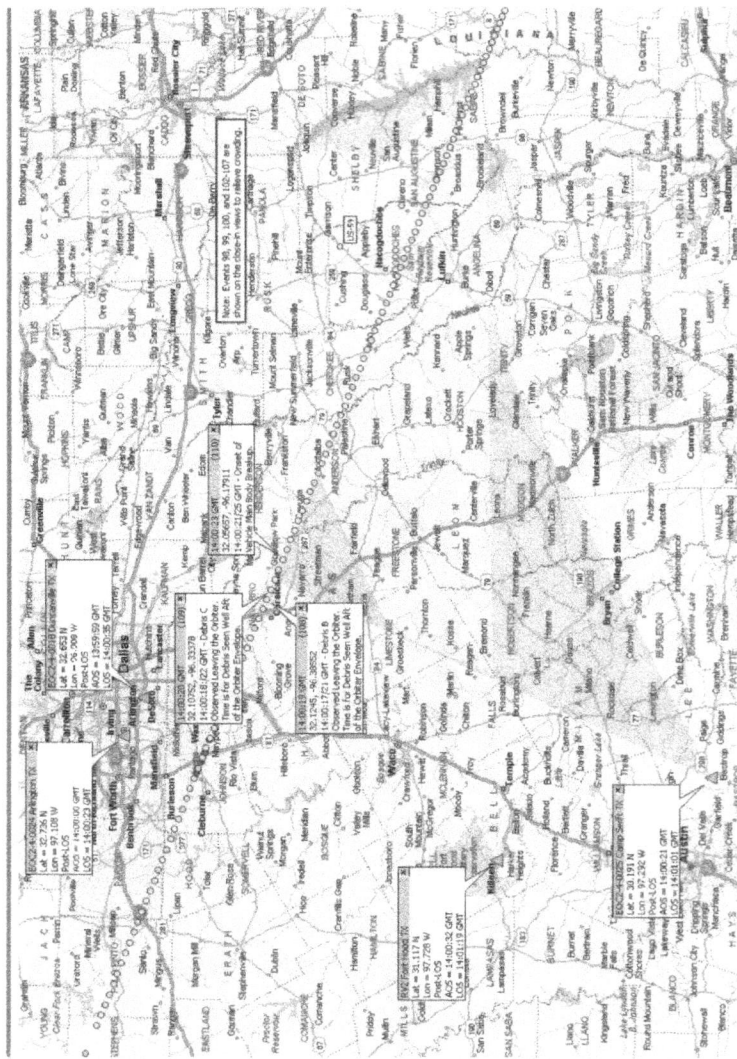

Post-Loss of Signal Sightings - Reference Trajectory

Based on Master Time Line Rev 15, 03/10/03

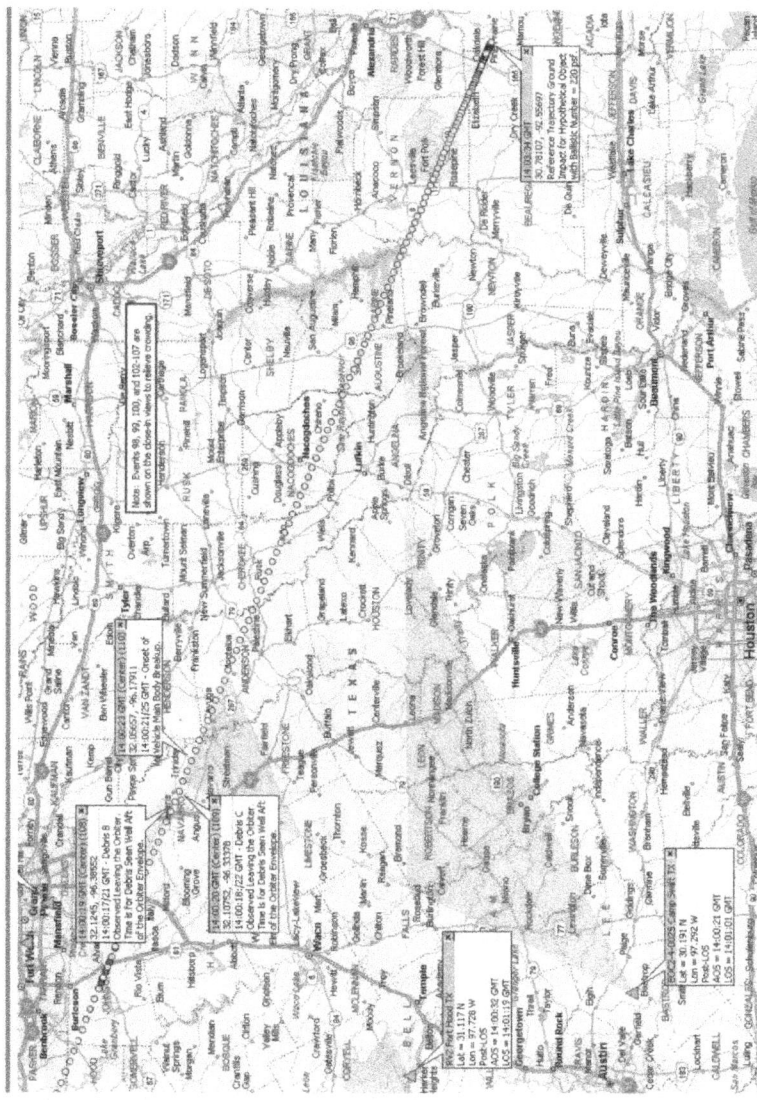

Reference Trajectory from Texas to Louisiana

Based on Master Time Line Rev 15, 03/10/03

Illustrations, briefings, pictures, memos and some tables retrieved from the NASA website: http:/www.nasa.gov

www.ingramcontent.com/pod-product-compliance
Lightning Source LLC
Chambersburg PA
CBHW071126280326
41935CB00010B/1126